PHILOSOPHY, RELIGION, AND CONTEMPORARY LIFE

BOSTON UNIVERSITY STUDIES IN
PHILOSOPHY AND RELIGION

General Editor: Leroy S. Rouner

Special Issue

Philosophy, Religion, and Contemporary Life

Essays on Perennial Problems

Edited by

Leroy S. Rouner
and
James Langford

UNIVERSITY OF NOTRE DAME PRESS
Notre Dame, Indiana

Library of Congress Cataloging-in-Publication Data

Philosophy, religion, and contemporary life : essays on perennial
  problems / edited by Leroy S. Rouner and James R. Langford.
    p. cm.
  ISBN 0-268-03807-4 (alk. paper)
    1. Religion—Philosophy.   2. Religion and sociology.
  I. Rouner, Leroy S.   II. Langford, James R.
  BL51.P546   1994
  100—dc20   94-26256
                                                                  CIP

∞ The paper used in this publication meets the minimum requirements
of the American National Standard for Information Sciences—Permanence of Paper
        for Printed Library Materials, ANSI Z39.49-1984

FOR RITA AND JILL

Contents

Preface

Boston University Studies in Philosophy and Religion is a joint project of the Boston University Institute for Philosophy and Religion and the University of Notre Dame Press. The essays in each annual volume are edited from the previous year's lecture program and invited papers of the Boston University Institute. The Director of the Institute, who is also the Editor of these Studies, chooses a theme and invites participants to lecture at Boston University in the course of the academic year. The Editor then selects and edits the essays to be included in the volume. Dr. Barbara Darling-Smith, Assistant Director of the Institute, regularly copy edits the essays and prepares the manuscript for the Press. We are currently working on Volume 17, *The Longing for Home*.

The Boston University Institute for Philosophy and Religion was begun informally in 1970 under the leadership of Professor Peter Bertocci of the Department of Philosophy, with the cooperation of Dean Walter Muelder of the School of Theology, Professor James Purvis, Chair of the Department of Religion, and Professor Marx Wartofsky, Chair of the Department of Philosophy. Professor Bertocci was concerned to institutionalize one of the most creative features of Boston Personalism, its interdisciplinary approach to fundamental issues of human life. When Professor Leroy S. Rouner became Director in 1975 the Institute became a Center of the Boston University Graduate School. Every effort was made to continue that vision of an ecumenical and interdisciplinary forum.

Within the University the Institute is committed to open interchange on fundamental issues in philosophy and religious study which transcend the narrow specializations of academic curricula. We seek to counter those trends in higher education which emphasize technical expertise in a "multi-versity," and gradually transform undergraduate liberal arts education into preprofessional training.

Our programs are open to the general public, and are regularly broadcast on WBUR-FM, Boston University's National Public Radio affiliate. Outside the University we seek to recover the public tradition of philosophical discourse which was a lively part of American intellectual life in the early years of this century before the professionalization of both philosophy and religious reflection made these two disciplines topics virtually unavailable even to an educated public. This commitment to a public tradition in American intellectual life has important stylistic implications. At a time when too much academic writing is incomprehensible, or irrelevant, or both, our goal is to present readable essays by acknowledged authorities on critical human issues.

Contributors

ROBERT N. BELLAH is Ford Professor of Sociology and Comparative Studies at the University of California at Berkeley. He studied at Harvard and received his Ph.D. in Sociology and Far Eastern Languages in 1955. In addition to numerous articles, his books include *Religion in America*; *Beyond Belief: Essays on Religion in a Post-Traditional World*; *The Broken Covenant: American Civil Religion in Time of Trial*; and, most recently, the three books *Habits of the Heart: Individualism and Commitment in American Life*; *Individualism and Commitment in American Life: Readings On the Themes of Habits of the Heart*; and *The Good Society*.

PETER BERGER, University Professor at Boston University and Director of the Institute for the Study of Economic Culture there, came to this country from Vienna in 1947. After beginning study for the Lutheran ministry, he became a sociologist and is well known for his many books on religion and society, including *The Precarious Vision*, *A Rumor of Angels*, *The Heretical Imperative*, and *The Sacred Canopy*.

SISSELA BOK received her Ph.D. in Philosophy from Harvard University and her A.B. and M.A. in Clinical Psychology from George Washington University. She is the author of *Lying: Moral Choice in Public and Private Life*, which received the George Orwell Award and the Melcher Book Award. She has also written a biography of Alva Myrdal, *A Strategy for Peace*, and *Secrets: On the Ethics of Concealment and Revelation*.

ELIOT DEUTSCH received his Ph.D. from Columbia University and is Professor of Philosophy at the University of Hawaii, where he is also Director of Graduate Studies in the Department of Philosophy. Formerly Editor of *Philosophy East and West*, he continues in an editorial capacity for a number of scholarly publications, including the *Journal of Chinese Philosophy* and the *Journal of Buddhist Philosophy*. His books include *Personhood, Creativity, and Freedom* and *Creative Being: The Crafting of Person and World*.

MANSOUR FARHANG is Professor of Politics at Bennington College and has written extensively on Iran, international relations, and United States foreign policy. He served as revolutionary Iran's first ambassador to the United Nations, resigning in protest when the Ayatollah Khomeini broke his promise to accept the United Nation's Commission of Inquiry's recommendation to release the American hostages in Tehran. He has written (with William A. Dorman) *The United States Press and Iran: Foreign Policy and the Journalism of Deference*.

CHARLES L. GRISWOLD is Professor of Philosophy at Boston University and chairs the Department of Philosophy there. He is the author of *Self-Knowledge in Plato's* Phaedrus; *Platonic Writings and Platonic Readings*; and the forthcoming *Liberalism, Virtue Ethics, and Moral Psychology: Adam Smith's Stoic Modernity*. He received his M.A. and Ph.D. from Pennsylvania State University.

JOHN E. MACK is Professor of Psychiatry at Harvard Medical School at Cambridge Hospital, where he teaches psychiatric residents and trainees. He did his residency training at Massachusetts Mental Health Center and is a graduate of the Boston Psychoanalytic Institute in child and adult psychoanalysis. He is also Founding Director of the Center for Psychological Studies in the Nuclear Age. Among his numerous writings are his book *A Prince of Our Disorder: The Life of T. E. Lawrence*, for which he won a Pulitzer Prize in biography.

ELIZABETH KAMARCK MINNICH is a philosopher who has taught at Barnard College, Scripps College, Hollins College, The New School College, and The Graduate School of the Union Institute, where she is presently Professor of Philosophy and Women's Studies. For over twenty years she has been writing, speaking, and consulting on the implications of feminist scholarship for the liberal arts curriculum. Her publications include the books *Transforming Knowledge*, winner of the Frederic W. Ness Prize, and *Reconstructing the Academy: Women's Education and Women's Studies*, edited with O'Barr and Rosenfeld.

LEROY S. ROUNER is Professor of Philosophy, Religion, and Philosophical Theology; Director of the Institute for Philosophy and Religion; and Director of Graduate Studies, Department of Philosophy at Boston University. He is General Editor of Boston University Studies in Philosophy and Religion and has also edited *Philosophy, Religion, and the Coming World Civilization*; *The Wisdom of Ernest Hocking* (with John Howie); and *Corporations and the Common Good* (with Robert Dickie). He is the author of *Within Human Experience*; *The Long Way Home* (a memoir); and *To Be At Home: Christianity, Civil Religion, and World Community*.

GEORGE RUPP is the author of numerous articles and several books, including *Commitment and Community*. President of Columbia University, he was previously president of Rice University, and prior to that he was John Lord O'Brian Professor of Divinity and Dean of the Divinity School at Harvard University. He has degrees from Princeton (A.B.), Yale (B.D.), and Harvard (Ph.D.) and has studied and done research at the Universities of Munich and Tübingen in Germany and Peradeniya in Sri Lanka.

HUSTON SMITH is Thomas J. Watson Professor of Religion and Distinguished Adjunct Professor of Philosophy Emeritus at Syracuse University. For the past three years he has served as Visiting Professor of Religious Studies at the University of California, Berkeley. His book *The World's Religions* (formerly *The Religions of Man*) has been for thirty years the most widely-used textbook for courses in world religions and has sold over 1.5 million copies. He is also the author of such books as *Beyond the Post-Modern Mind*, *Essays on World Religion*, *Forgotten Truth*, and (with David Griffin) *Primordial Truth and Postmodern Theology*.

MARX WARTOFSKY is City University of New York Distinguished Professor of Philosophy, Baruch College and the Graduate Center; and Editor of *The Philosophical Forum*. He has co-edited (with Robert S. Cohen) many volumes in *Boston Studies in the Philosophy of Science* and (with Carol Gould) *Women and Philosophy: Toward a Theory of Liberation*. He has also written a number of books, including *Conceptual Foundations of Scientific Thought*, which has been translated into a number of languages; *Feuerbach*; and *Models: Representation and the Scientific Understanding*. He received his B.A., M.A., and Ph.D. from Columbia University.

EDITH WYSCHOGROD received her A.B. from Hunter College and her Ph.D. from Columbia University. She is J. Newton Rayzor Professor of Philosophy and Religious Thought at Rice University and has also taught at Queens College of the City University of New York and at the State University of New York at Stony Brook. Her books include *Saints and Postmodernism: Revisioning Moral Philosophy*; *Spirit in Ashes: Hegel, Heidegger and Man-Made Mass Death*; and *Emmanuel Levinas: The Problem of Ethical Metaphysics*.

Introduction

LEROY S. ROUNER

After fifteen volumes of these Boston University Studies in Philosophy and Religion, it seemed appropriate to take stock of what we were doing by collecting essays which would highlight the philosophy of the series. They were selected not because they met some abstract criterion for the "best" papers we had published, but rather because they best illustrate our concern for perennial issues in philosophy and religious thought which have particular significance for contemporary life. This also gives us occasion to elaborate on those brief statements of purpose which have appeared in the Preface to each of our previous volumes.

In the period between the two world wars both philosophy and religious reflection became increasingly "professionalized" academic specializations. As a result, public interest declined, as philosophers and religious scholars tended to write increasingly technical pieces for other professionals. Earlier generations of writers in these fields, from Jonathan Edwards to Emerson, were often independent scholars or preachers who wrote for a larger public, out of their own personal philosophical and religious interests. Even as late as the early twentieth century, the golden age of American philosophy, men like John Dewey, William James, Josiah Royce, William Ernest Hocking, and Alfred North Whitehead, all of them highly skilled thinkers, came to philosophy and religious reflection because of their personal concern for fundamental issues of human experience. Today's generation of highly skilled professional philosophers and religious thinkers all have a general interest in "the field," to be sure. What they often lack, however, is concern for the "truth question" or belief in God. They have chosen the field because they got A's in their college courses and discovered that they were good at it. Since professional work in these fields is now almost exclusively confined to the academy and since

1

tenure decisions in academia are made on the recommendation of
other academic professionals, philosophy and religious reflection have
become academic "disciplines" in which young professionals are expected to become scholarly experts.

We have stood against this professionalization because we are
concerned with the relevance of religious philosophy to fundamental
issues in ordinary human experience. Professionalization, in emphasizing technical expertise at the expense of relevance to ordinary
human experience, has admittedly produced much intellectual bril-
liance, but has offered relatively little human wisdom. By way of
contrast, consider William James's *Varieties of Religious Experience*.
His "experts" were quite ordinary folk who had had some weird religious experiences. His categories of interpretation, which he made
up himself, included such loose, vague, and colloquial notions as
"healthy-mindedness" and "sick soul." We now revere the book as a
small classic. Were James a contemporary, however, he would have
great difficulty finding an academic publisher. And were he offering
the book in his dossier for tenure review at a major American research university, he would most surely soon be unemployed.

In saying this we note that virtually all of our authors are people
with impeccable professional qualifications who are committed to academic life, as we are. We mean only to remind our academic colleagues
that the philosophy of religion is a much wider venture than the work
of the academic departments which have isolated it as an academic discipline. And beyond the academy we offer readable, nontechnical
essays geared to a public renewal of philosophical reflection and religious study. Truth to tell, we also mean to chide many of our academic
colleagues for having made philosophy and religious study part of our
"culture of expertise." This expertise has taken two directions: one analytical, the other historical.

Analytical expertise focuses on methods of argumentation. It
asks, for example, what criteria a statement would have to meet in
order to be considered as possibly true. It does not necessarily address the truth question itself. This analytical exercise is a necessary
prolegomenon to the truth question, but it is serious work only insofar as it serves that question. The "culture of expertise" encourages
such absorption in the intricacies of analytic method as to lose sight
of the question which brought one to the analysis in the first place.

Historical exegetical expertise, which is what we usually mean by
"scholarship," also falls short of the ultimate issue. It focuses on the

thought structure of important historical figures, with increasingly subtle interpretations of often obscure texts. The regular result is dazzling scholarship and geniunely profound understanding of historical figures. In itself, however, historical expertise does not do the creative work which the historical figures themselves did and which made them interesting to us in the first place. Historical expertise does not present a point of view so much as it analyzes someone else's point of view.

For us, philosophy is the critical examination of belief and the theoretical construction of new views based on the critical evaluation of old beliefs. The importance of analytical and historical work to this project is obvious. And there is a natural relation between philosophy and religious reflection because the most important of our beliefs are our religious beliefs. Here we decide not only what we are to do, but what our lives ultimately mean. Humankind is, we believe, a religious animal. All of us have a metaphysical sense and feel for the infinite, a moral sense of what we ought to be, and a yearning in our heart of hearts for some inexpressible spiritual fulfillment.

Given these persuasions, the purpose of our volumes has not been to promote some orthodoxy in either philosophy or religion, but to initiate conversation from various points of view on critical issues. In reaching out to a wider public beyond the academy we are mindful that American life has lost that common ground of meaning and values which was once provided by Protestant Christianity. We regard the resulting pluralism as a precious bane. It is precious in that pluralism is the genius of the American Dream. It is a commitment to a national community in which all sorts and conditions of folk can flourish freely. It is a bane, however, insofar as pluralism pure and simple is cultural fragmentation. To be creative pluralism must be undergirded by some common ground. American public life makes it increasingly clear that common ground is rapidly disappearing. It is no longer possible to have debate on critical issues, because debate assumes some ground rules and common values, including civility and mutual respect for those with whom we disagree. The abortion "debate," for example, is no longer a debate. It is at best a shouting match and at worst a murderous confrontation. Our purpose is to promote a civil conversation in which a variety of voices may be heard, in the good hope that this process will help create a new common ground.

In focusing on philosophies of human experience, we are committed to a style of philosophical writing which is clear, concise, comprehensible to any intelligent and reasonably well-informed reader, and free of technical jargon. In our editing we eschew those interruptive subordinate clauses so beloved of thinkers in the Germanic tradition. We try to hold footnotes to a minimum, since these are not academic conference papers and too much detail tends to be distracting. And we insist that our writers be mercifully brief.

We have divided this collection into two general sections. The first, on "Public Philosophy and the Common Good," reflects our concern for a renewal of a civil, public conversation on critical issues in our common life. The second section, on "Religion and the Search for Values," is broader still, exploring the primal "religiousness" of the human spirit in the quest for a meaningful life.

We begin, then, with Robert Bellah's essay on "Public Philosophy and Public Theology in America Today." Robert Bellah's discussion of public philosophy and theology reviews the recent seminal literature on the topic, beginning with John Dewey, Walter Lippmann, and Reinhold Niebuhr, and making the issue current with comments on Richard Neuhaus, William Sullivan, and Bellah's own *Habits of the Heart*. Dewey, Niebuhr, and Lippmann were all fine practitioners of the jeremiad, a hallowed tradition in American public discourse, and they were agreed that Americans lack not only a common set of values but even a common conversation about the central issues of American public life. They differed, however, in prescribing the renewal of such a conversation. Dewey sought a new individualism which could escape the merely traditional, bound as it was by custom and inertia. Informed by the methods of natural science, he proposed a new collectivism in which individualism would be fulfilled through personal participation in the development of a shared culture. Walter Lippmann, on the other hand, equated public philosophy with the perennial philosophy of classical antiquity. It was precisely the recovery of tradition which, for Lippmann, would provide the content of common conversation in morals and politics. Lippmann's world of rational discourse presupposes a natural law which is close to neo-Thomism.

Bellah finds Reinhold Niebuhr refreshing in his concreteness after the abstract traditionalism of Lippmann and the equally abstract historicism of Dewey. Niebuhr knew that there will always be unresolved social and political conflicts and sought enough common ground within the community so that these could be at least partly resolved. An example was Niebuhr's opposition both to those secular universalisms that are empty of meaning and to religious triumphalisms which provide too much meaning for too few. His context for public discourse was religious toleration inspired by religious humility, recognizing the conditional character of all human enterprises. Bellah is appreciative of Niebuhr's influence on Richard Neuhaus but criticizes Neuhaus's suggestion that all Americans should agree that "on balance, and considering the alternatives, the influence of the United States is a force for good in the world." Bellah finds this virtually impossible to test as an empirical proposition and argues that even Neuhaus's "critical patriot" would be tied into "a kind of civil orthodoxy that would irreparably rupture the Niebuhrian dialectic." Neuhaus warns of the disintegration of our public life into warring religious and political factions. Bellah notes that our intellectual life joins technical reason and psychological individualism to its peril. Bellah warns that academic specialization has turned many social and religious thinkers away from public discourse to discussions with other experts.

He concludes with observations on his and his colleagues' intentions in their recent *Habits of the Heart*, which he presents expressly as a contribution to both public philosophy and public theology, and on the first draft of the Catholic Bishops' Pastoral Letter on Catholic Social Teaching and the U.S. Economy. In both he emphasizes the critique of American individualism and the imperiled status of our public philosophy and theology.

For Peter Berger, the question whether to be pro- or anti-capitalist is not a morally neutral question. He examines the five major charges against capitalism in terms of empirical evidence and finds each of them wanting. On the basis of this analysis, Berger repudiates Marxism as a philosophical system and socialism as a practical system on the ground that it has compounded rather than diminished the amount of human misery in the modern world.

In brief, Berger observes that the original Marxist theory held that capitalism would lead to increasing misery among the populace, with resulting revolution. When indeed the economic lot of the masses improved, antagonists of capitalism, forced to look elsewhere for a charge, accused capitalism of creating or exacerbating inequality. Empirically, however, Berger finds that the capitalist societies are less unequal in terms of income distribution than socialist societies. Accordingly, the antagonists invented a new theory to the effect that misery and inequality were exported as the misery of the Third World became the foundation of the wealth of capitalist societies. Yet, Berger observes, this charge trivializes the fact that the natural human state is not one of wealth but of an absence of physical resources and vulnerability to disease, poverty, early death, infant mortality, and degradation.

The conservatism which concerns Mansour Farhang is not the economic policy of Thatcher and Reagan but the religious policy of the Ayatollah Khomeini. His essay on "Fundamentalism and Civil Rights in Contemporary Middle Eastern Politics" focuses on the alliance between state coercion and Muslim fundamentalism. As Western ideas like civil rights penetrate Islamic cultures, and as Middle Eastern economies become increasingly integrated into world markets, the pressure increases toward the transformation of traditional Islam. Emulation and fascination vie with resentment and resistance in this struggle between modernity and tradition.

Farhang notes that Islamic doctrine on the rights of the person is theoretically in tune with the United Nations Universal Declaration on Human Rights but that Islamic governments have generally ruled with arbitrary power. Traditionally, individual rights have constituted obligations toward the divine with the state enforcing the *shari'a*, the laws derived from the Qur'an. He notes, however, that a separation between religion and the state has existed in the Muslim world for at least eleven of Islam's fourteen centuries. Fundamentalism is not a historical norm but results from the failure of modernists and secularists to create a viable synthesis between Islam and modernization. This failure became critical in the lives of the urban poor, whom Farhang takes to be the determinative social force in the disintegration of the Pahlavi state and the establishment of the Islamic Republic. Traditional resistance to cultural change, combined with economic and social deprivation under the Pahlavis, made modernization so disrupting for the urban poor that classical anomie stimulated anxiety, hostility, and fantasy. Fundamentalist preachers then readily drew the disaffected to the dream of a sacred utopia which had existed in the past and would now become the Islamic Republic of the future.

Farhang rejects the view that Islam is an overriding motivational force in the Middle East and regards the upheaval in Iran as an indigenous rejection of modernity. The indigenous culture is, however, Islam. The secularization of education and the acceptance of cultural pluralism threaten both "the old ways" and the power of the clerics to enforce them. He points out that the critical civil rights issue in Iran today is not personal privacy and lifestyle, as it is in the West, but the need for peaceful political dissent. For four years Iran has executed more of its own citizens than the rest of the world combined, and he expresses no optimism about the immediate future for civil rights in Iran.

Edith Wyschogrod's "Mass Death and Autonomous Selves" is critical of the idea of the self as independent thinker and actor. Wyschogrod is less concerned with the philosophical concept of the autonomous self as articulated in the history of philosophy than she is with the role it plays in our current common-sense view. In the first part of her essay she describes two characteristic forms of manmade mass death: the concentration camp and nuclear war. In the second section of her essay she turns to various models of the self, emphasizing the sea change that has taken place in Western philosophy as a result of manmade mass death, especially in regard to agency.

Wyschogrod notes that earlier Western views of selfhood have all interpreted the self as a substantive entity of some sort which has thoughts, intentions, desires, habits, and the like. This self is the subject of cognitive, productive, and moral acts. She is sympathetic with those who see the self as relational, but admits that pure relationality undermines the individual boundedness of each self. She turns to Heidegger, who argues that "what makes selves individuals is the relation of each self to its own death." This is rather different from John Smith's view that a self is defined by relation to its own purposes. But if one takes death as self-definitive, then the experience of manmade mass death will radically alter self-conception.

She argues that the death-world of the concentration camp and nuclear war both diminish the agent's capacity to affect future events. The threat of nuclear war limits the freedom of all individuals, so a limited benevolence is called for, since "the transactional social self that desires to persevere in existence includes a relational field of others in its wish. Once the whole human community is threatened, the self must wish for the survival of everyone in wishing for the preservation of a few."

Is there, then, something "realistic" to be said for utopians after all? Sissela Bok thinks so. She is skeptical about the moral possibility of a just war and turns instead to utopian advocates of perpetual peace. Her essay deals with "Early Advocates of Lasting World Peace: Utopians or Realists?" She notes that the just war theory assumes that war is an immutable aspect of the human condition. But in the nuclear age nations cannot run the risk of a major war. Bok argues that previous assumptions about the impossibility of perpetual peace are now untenable.

She turns to Erasmus and Kant for challenges to the common assumption that war will always be with us and for suggestions about a social climate conducive to the forging of a stable peace. Erasmus, in his *Adages* of 1500, wrote that "War Is Sweet to Those Who Have Not Experienced It." He later proposed a "congress of kings" who would sign a peace treaty, and he wrote *The Education of the Christian Prince* to guide the young Prince Charles of Spain, soon to become Charles V. Erasmus was not a pacifist but argued that war appeals to dreamers, not realists; it promises good, but produces "the shipwreck of all that is good."

Kant's essay on "Perpetual Peace" in 1795 furthered Erasmus's argument. Although Kant held that peace was more difficult to achieve than Erasmus had assumed, he nevertheless held that it was possible.

Bok's essay is a sympathetic historical account of utopian views, in the sense of a society that is possible but at present merely visionary. She does not argue that they are right. She argues only that we have no choice but to take them seriously. "Only time will tell whether a cumulative process and principled efforts at domestic and international change can, in the long run, disprove the age-old assumption that war will always be with us."

Our second section, "Religion and the Search for Values," begins with an especially vivid example of renewed confidence and seriousness in the philosophy of religion, Eliot Deutsch's "Knowing Religiously." Eschewing the old defensiveness, he argues that aesthetic religious considerations are not peripheral to philosophy but are at the heart of the philosophic enterprise. In the past, issues such as causality and the nature of language have been held as primary and then applied to problems of aesthetics and the philosophy of religion. Deutsch goes at it the other way around. "If we can understand creativity, we might then be able to understand causality; if we can understand what religious language is, we will then be able to understand better what a proposition is." His basic thesis is one William James would have found sympathetic. Our most fundamental experience of knowing comes not when we have clarified the cognitive status of specific concepts. It is not factual or formal or strategic or praxis-oriented. "Knowing religiously" is not a skill; it does not grasp empirical truth or logical rules and systems. It does not conceive strategies or achieve goals. Knowing religiously is an attentiveness to one's world in the spirit of what Aristotle called philosophic wonder. This fundamental awareness is not subject/object-bound, and it conjoins idea with feeling in the knowing process. For Deutsch, religious knowledge is not characterized by its object but by the style and manner of knowing, which involves wonder, openness, insight, and love. It is the key to human creativity because it transforms ordinary knowledge and leads to the kind of "unknowing knowing" which is necessary for the direction of creative instinct.

Knowing religiously is nonegocentric. Whereas most modern Western epistemologies present individual minds hard at work grasping and shaping sense impression to structure concepts and create knowledge, Deutsch turns to Śaṁkara and the Hindu philosophy of Advaita Vedānta for a realization of the simplicity of being, once we stop setting our ego over against its world of objects. When one adds care or concern to this nonegocentric approach to experience, the thinking process becomes liberated for creative imagination, which is as much a form of play as it is work. Deutsch also turns to the Chinese tradition to argue that truth and the nature of language are both dependent upon the personhood of the knower, at least in those utterances arising from the liberated creativity of knowing religiously.

Huston Smith is principally a philosopher of religion, but his interest in science was sharpened during his years teaching philosophy at the Massachusetts Institute of Technology. Smith is experimental; and in the fearless tradition of William James, who often found himself in odd philosophic company, Smith regularly finds himself learning from those with irregular views. In his paper on "Two Evolutions" he contrasts the view backed by modern science, that the human self can be understood naturalistically as an organism in an environment, with the Judeo-Christian view that humankind is created in God's image with an immortal soul, occupying a place in nature between the beasts and the angels. He finds these two views incompatible but notes that most of us accept parts of both, and he sets out to fashion some resolution. En route, he challenges Darwinism, and finds himself in the uncomfortable company of the Creationists. That they have muddied the waters with simplistic theology and sometimes bogus science he has no doubt. He admits that in some ways they have his respect, because they have sensed that Darwinism is not compatible with what Stephen Toulmin has called a universe "intrinsically hospitable to human life and the human heart," but Smith is no Creationist. His proposal is much broader. His Great Origins thesis argues simply that humankind has derived from that which exceeds us. Since such metaphysical propositions do not admit of proof, he takes the negative path of showing that Darwinism does not serve our need for feeling at home in the universe and that such felt need is a scientifically legitimate way of approaching the metaphysical issue. He is concerned to overcome the self/world divide of modern Western thought, and he points out that the Great Origins thesis, in answering the question about the origins of humankind, must include the answer to the origins of everything else. "Reality and the life that is set within it are charged with meaning throughout by virtue of being, at heart, whole."

Marx Wartofsky's essay on Feuerbach will strike many readers as unusual, coming as it does from a Marxist in search of a viable materialist conception of religious transcendence. He begins by sketching Feuerbach's formulation of the problem, first negatively and then positively. He then discusses what is meant by Feuerbach's notion of "religious materialism." He goes on to sketch philosophical and theological alternatives to traditional conceptions of transcendence. In conclusion, he argues that the Hegelian notion of dialectic in its transformation by Feuerbach and Marx provides a clue to a materialistic conception of transcendence. He does this first in terms of a dialectic of consciousness and then as a dialectic of praxis.

Those readers informed by the Judeo-Christian tradition of theological reflection will, I suspect, be intrigued by Wartofsky's use of the term *materialism*. Because of the Marxist critique of religion, the initial response of these readers is likely to be characterized by a hermeneutics of suspicion. As the essay progresses, however, what Wartofsky means by *material* may seem increasingly congenial to what the Judeo-Christian tradition has regularly meant by *historical*. Wartofsky outlines the spirit of revolutionary praxis as one which "has as its animating spirit a vision of human possibilities which sees the divine as within the grasp of our own creative activity, and as the object of our hope. Such a theory of belief, as a materialist theory, ex-

ceeds the bounds of contemporary materialism, which has as yet
no consistent theory of hope, or of this sort of recognition of the transcendent. But the transcendent, thus conceived, is within the realm
of human possibility. And a theory of hope as active, practical, efficacious belief in such human possibilities, is needed." Here a materialist understanding of religion finds common ground with other
traditions of world religion, as well as fundamental elements of human
experience.

Many Christian thinkers are now concerned to do justice to those
folk whom an imperial Christianity has previously ignored, neglected,
and put down. The easiest way to solve the problem of interreligious
conflict, of course, would be to give up religion altogether, as many are
doing. George Rupp confronts the issue of commitment, acknowledg-
ing that the foundations for faith have been severely shaken. With the
collapse of traditional authorities, Rupp has a pragmatic concern not
just for individual spiritual fulfillment but rather for "commitment to
more inclusive causes." He gives voice to the concern which Josiah
Royce had for the spirit of loyalty, and Ernest Hocking discussed under
the general theme of human morale. He develops his thesis with
specific reference to feminist concerns for more inclusive religious imagery and institutions, and the ecological concern for limiting growth
in our biosphere in order to preserve a viable planet.

Rupp's call is for an inclusive commitment rather than the
narrower traditional ones. He is concerned for a religious life which
seeks the salvation of the whole world, but he is especially mindful that this comes only from a commitment within particular communities, where the full range of contemporary experience is taken
seriously.

Elizabeth Kamarck Minnich asks "Can Virtue Be Taught?: A
Feminist Reconsiders." Her feminist perspective on the question is
informed by a mode of resistance, of ongoing critique of dominant
thought patterns. If we do not approach questions such as virtue and
the goals of education "with all our feminist-critical senses awake, we
are liable to be led down well-trodden paths, which . . . remain within
the maze of a world of meanings defined in male terms claiming to be
universal." Because of the continuing effects of male dominance, we
need to be aware of old mistakes, perpetuated in the present. Mistakes to be recognized and exorcised include faulty generalization,
from a few men to all of humankind; mystified concepts, "such as that

of virtue that . . . [makes] women subject to a separate and distinctly unequal notion of womanly virtue that is not human virtue"; and definitions which dissociate Man from women, from nature, and from "lesser men"—indeed, from elements within himself which he has in common with all those "others."

Minnich calls for a reconfiguring which will respect and bring to the center those whose experiences and values have been ignored and marginalized. She speaks particularly of women—women of different races and classes—but she notes the convergence of feminist critiques with those from Third World people and proponents of environmentalism, pacifism, and multiculturalism. Recovering the virtues of those who have been dissociated from Man will lead to a *transformation* of Man's virtues. Minnich cites the image used by Larry and Sande Churchill of ethical theory as a collage embracing diverse perspectives.

Leroy S. Rouner's essay "Can Virtue Be Taught in a School?: Ivan Illich and Mohandas Gandhi on Deschooling Society," takes up Minnich's issue from a different point of view. Rouner's central question for today's students about their teachers is Socrates' question: "What will they make of you?" Can teachers in college and university settings aid their students in finding out who they are and how they might live a good life? The question is not whether the intellectual discipline of ethics can be taught, because ethics "is only the tuneless prescription of social thought," whereas "virtue is a song. One has to get the tune right." Virtue, like courage, needs to be learned with the heart as well as the head. "The purpose of teaching someone about courage is to make them courageous."

Rouner analyzes three models of how to teach virtue: Ivan Illich, Socrates, and Mohandas Gandhi. Illich views schools and teachers as unnecessary—even as obstacles to learning—because teachers wrongly fall into or are forced into the authoritarian roles of custodian, preacher, and therapist. Illich theorizes that schools should be done away with, and people will then automatically learn from life outside of school—from families, the work place, the larger community. But Rouner finds Illich unsatisfactory, because knowledge must be worked at to be achieved, and school is the place where we work at attaining knowledge.

Socrates and Gandhi, unlike Illich, both approve of people especially identified as teachers. Both of them, however, also realize that a true, life-changing understanding of virtue "is finally discovered by individuals in their own souls, rather than imposed by someone else from outside. So one can't 'teach' virtue, but one can help people get to the place where they can learn it for themselves." Socrates' method of trying to get people to that place relied almost entirely on rational argumentation, and Rouner recognizes that the powers of rationality are no longer trusted as they were in Socrates' time.

Gandhi's way of teaching virtue was to personify it. As Rouner points out, Gandhi understood the educator's role as that of guru, and he lived that role in relation to the whole of India. His goal was that the teacher's (his own) insight into virtue would be transferred to the student (the nation of India).

Rouner is drawn to Gandhi's personalizing of teaching, but he finds Gandhi's model, in the end, too authoritarian, and he reminds us that not only is virtue a song; "it is a song sung in one's own voice." Thus the goal of teachers in higher education should be to help students find their own voice—as artists, as scientists, and as human beings attempting to live virtuously. The route to this personal transformation, suggests Rouner, is to personalize education, by focusing on the "inwardness" of both students and teachers, by recognizing the dimension of *spirit* in learning and teaching virtue.

John Mack's "Psychoanalysis and the Self: Toward a Spiritual Point of View" deals with the values which undergird psychoanalytic practice. He proposes that a spiritual point of view is now required in order to understand the psyche more fully, and to interpret the conditions of contemporary human life. He points to a host of problems which have eluded treatment based on traditional, limited views of the psyche. They include addictive disorders, child abuse and other forms of domestic violence, and increased reliance on drugs. He also notes that many people are turning toward "holistic" or "alternative" therapies as a result of unmet hunger for spiritual elements in their treatment.

Definition of the *spiritual* is admittedly difficult because of the complexity of the idea and the inevitable subjectivity of any definition. He quotes Barbara Marx Hubbard on the increase of mystical experience in our time, but admits that most spiritual experience is less dramatic and more subtle. His point of departure is the realization that there is a realm of the numinous, "an other reality beyond that which is immediately manifest to our senses or reason." Further, our world has design, even intention, and is not random flux or a chance creation. One difficulty with entering the spirit world, however, is the disturbing emotions, such as great fear or sadness, which are associated with that experience. Another is that we have not been educated in the language of spirituality, even though virtually all other peoples throughout history have experienced its central importance to their lives. He lists six elements of a spiritual point of view: an attitude of appreciation or awe toward the mysterious in nature; an openness to the cosmos as sacred; the application of a cosmological (nonmaterialist) perspective on reality; a subjective hesitancy, expressing consciousness of the mystery of being and the dignity of every person; a distrust of all human institutions; and an attitude toward the emotionally troubled which is focused less on pathology and more on the shared fate of what it means to be human.

Mack calls for a wider human identity in which our individual core self is connected to diverse others. The spirituality he proposes is therefore not one of personal inwardness alone. It is a principle of social interaction as well. The widespread phenomenon of mass death, and the ecological crisis of global survival, demand a new spirituality. Here Mack echoes the same call for selflessness-in-community which is characteristic of so many of our authors. "Human beings grow when, in the confrontation with death, they are enabled to discover a new personal perspective, sacrificing their egoism before it is the body's time to die."

Charles Griswold writes on what it means to be happy, and notes that philosophers in the Western tradition have had relatively little to say about happiness in spite of its enormous importance to human life. After a brief survey of that literature he turns to his own definition of happiness as tranquillity. He means happiness in the long term, not some momentary experience. And tranquillity is not some static emptiness. It is indeed more like rest than motion, and it is an end state, but it differs from contentment. Happiness is tranquillity in the sense of "reflective integration over time." In this sense happiness has overcome any deep anxiety in one's life which would lead one to doubt "the fittingness of one's basic stance." This is not to deny the turbulence attending one's many passions, attachments, and commitments; it is only to undergird this turbulence with the tranquil assurance "that basically one would change nothing in one's life" and that one is fundamentally at peace with oneself.

Griswold distinguishes his view from that of Epictetus, who argued that the loss of a child need not provoke any emotional response if one's inwardness is tranquil. Griswold, on the other hand, admits that one would suffer tremendous grief, but that one's essential tranquillity would not be shaken, "for I will still say that it was right and good that I had this child." He is not making the extreme claim that one could still be happy while being tortured on the rack, but he turns to Socrates as an example of tranquillity within our grasp even in the midst of great misfortune. This is different from contentment, as Griswold sees it, not only because contentment is momentary but because it is "a state of mind severed from an appraisal of the truth of the matter." Hence contentment and unreflectiveness are natural allies. Griswold's tranquillity is both reflective and related to what the ancients knew as a life of virtue. It is this "reflective arrangement of one's life" which quells any deep anxiety about what sort of life is worth living, and makes tranquillity the definition of happiness.

The importance of a common conversation on such critical issues as these was underscored by President John Silber of Boston University in his 1995 commencement address. Silber pointed out that there are three areas of our common life. One is governed by law, where we must do what the law decrees. Another is determined entirely by personal choice, where we can do anything we want. Between these two is that critical area which is not determined by law, but where we have moral responsibilities and are therefore not free to do whatever we like. This middle area is where the morale of any culture flourishes or dies, and in times of cultural stress the advocates of law and the advocates of personal freedom are both destructive as they try to take over the middle. Silber argued persuasively that we cannot legislate the morality of this middle ground; nor can we forsake moral responsibility for it by mindless arguments for personal freedom.

In calling for a renewal of moral responsibility in this middle ground of American life Silber focused on a theme which has long been a concern of ours. The Institute and its publications are our modest attempt to engage various viewpoints on critical issues in a civil conversation. Better understanding of these issues will promote that sympathy for opposing views which alone makes common bonds possible in a pluralistic culture.

PART I

Public Philosophy
and the
Common Good

Public Philosophy and Public
Theology in America Today
ROBERT N. BELLAH

HAVING BEEN INVOLVED for almost seven years in a project that is in part a contribution to both public philosophy and public theology, and which has just been published,[1] this seemed a good occasion to step back and look at the larger issues of the place of public philosophy and public theology in America today. I will consider first some recent predecessors: John Dewey, Reinhold Niebuhr, and Walter Lippmann. I will then look at two books that clearly pose the terms of the current discussion: William M. Sullivan's *Reconstructing Public Philosophy* and Richard John Neuhaus's text *The Naked Public Square*.[2] Finally I will relate the discussion to my own most recent work, to the Catholic Bishops' draft Pastoral Letter on Catholic Social Teachings and the U.S. Economy, and to some other recent developments. Throughout I will be concerned with the following issues: the necessity of public philosophy and public theology; the content of public philosophy and public theology; and the difficulties which the present state of our intellectual life and of our public life poses for these undertakings.

Alexis de Tocqueville's classic *Democracy in America* posed the problem starkly and in terms quite different from any of our twentieth-century authors. For Tocqueville Christianity was simultaneously our public philosophy and our public theology. It provided the secure basis of our freedom and our capacity to experiment and innovate in the economic and political fields. He went so far as to say that religion should be considered "as the first of their political institutions," not because it is established by law or intervenes directly in government, but because it provides the secure principles of our public life. "Christianity," he wrote, "reigns without obstacles, by universal consent; consequently, everything in the moral field is certain and fixed, although the world of politics is given over to argument and experiment."[3]

Our twentieth-century authors differ from Tocqueville in two important respects. The first is that they do not expect or hope for a consensus quite so "universal" as Tocqueville described (we will have to consider what they do hope for as we go along) and which was probably not quite accurate even for the America of the 1830s. The second is that they are dismayed by the lack of even a minimal and nuanced consensus such as they feel is necessary for the survival of free institutions. Instead they describe an individualism, a privatism, a liberalism, a secularism, or a utilitarianism that has all but destroyed the basis of our common life. The images are quite striking and reinforce each other. I have already noted Neuhaus's image of "the naked public square." Walter Lippmann, writing in 1955, spoke of "the hollow shell of freedom." He said that "the citadel is vacant because the public philosophy is gone, and all that the defenders of freedom have to defend in common is a public neutrality and a public agnosticism."[4]

William Sullivan spoke of "the exhaustion of political imagination." He found that the philosophical liberalism which is common to both liberals and conservatives in contemporary American politics is "deeply anti-public in its fundamental premises" and "denies meaning and value to even the notion of common purpose, or politics in its classic sense."[5] Reinhold Niebuhr found in 1944 that modern secularism "creates a spiritual vacuum" and that "it stands on the abyss of moral nihilism and threatens the whole of life with a sense of meaninglessness."[6] John Dewey in 1930 said that "the loyalties that once held individuals, which gave them support, direction, and unity of outlook on life, have well-nigh disappeared." In consequence such individuals are "lost, confused, and bewildered."[7] Indeed the litany of woes stretches back far enough that we might well ask how come the game has not been lost long before this.

We must note that the jeremiad, which continues, as it has since the seventeenth century, to be a common form of American public discourse, is always admonitory. The overt message is that things have come to a sad pass but the real message is that *if* things go on as they are *then* indeed all will be lost. John Courtney Murray offered a consummate example of the genre, precisely apt for our present concern, when he wrote in 1962:

> And if this country is to be overthrown from within or from without, I would suggest that it will not be overthrown by Communism. It will be overthrown because it will have made an impossible experiment. It will have undertaken to establish a technological order of most marvelous intricacy, which will have been constructed and will operate without relations to true political ends; and this technological order will hang, as it were, suspended over a moral confusion; and this moral confusion will itself be suspended over a spiritual vacuum. This would be the real danger resulting from a type of fallacious, fictitious, fragile unity that could be created among us.[8]

If our three older authors, Dewey, Niebuhr, and Lippmann, share a common diagnosis, they differ, and differ instructively, in the directions they would turn to for a cure. In the very title of the book I am using as a key to Dewey's position, *Individualism Old and New*, we can discern his key contrast. The old individualism is rooted in an outmoded form of society in which a *laissez faire* economy went hand in hand with a rugged individualism that virtually ignores society. The new individualism of which Dewey speaks is that not-yet-realized individual flowering that would develop in a genuinely cooperative corporate society toward which we are moving. For Dewey the "merely traditional," the "beliefs and institutions that dominate merely because of custom and inertia,"[9] are precisely the things that are holding us back from the creation of a new, more satisfying society. For Dewey natural intelligence, which is never merely technical, but is also moral and even emotional, can show us the way to the future by sloughing off the past and building on the methods of natural science, so that we can consciously create a new society in conformity with the possibilities of the modern world. In that new more collective and corporate society American individualism will be fulfilled: "equality and freedom expressed not merely externally and politically but through personal participation in the development of a shared culture."[10]

Walter Lippmann looks in precisely the opposite direction from John Dewey for a cure to our lack of public coherence: he looks to the old, not to the new. For Lippmann the very meaning of the term *public philosophy* is close to the perennial philosophy of classical antiquity which was the common sense of the educated throughout the history of the West, at least until the end of the eighteenth century. At the core of his project Lippmann wants to resurrect the idea of natural law and the reason that instructs all persons of good will as to its teachings. For Lippmann, even more than for Dewey, this reason is far from a merely technical rationality. It is not so much Dewey's natural intelligence that actively intervenes in the world to bring about a desired result as it is a moral reason that instructs us about our rights and our duties. Far from seeing modernity creating the conditions for a new sociality, as Dewey does, Lippmann tends to blame modernity for the radical subjectivism and relativism that has almost destroyed our ability to understand the teachings of the public philosophy.

It is interesting that neither Dewey nor Lippmann can do public philosophy without doing public theology. They are thus both characteristically American, as Bruce Kuklick argues in his *Churchmen and Philosophers: From Jonathan Edwards to John Dewey*.[11] But the way in which they do theology is characteristically opposed.

In *Individualism Old and New* Dewey merely derides the impotence of contemporary American religion, but in *A Common Faith*, published in 1934, Dewey offers a constructive alternative. He differentiates between religion and the religious. Religion is tied to the dogmas and superstitions of the past, chief of which is the idea of the supernatural. Dewey sees the idea of the supernatural as inevitably belittling the natural intelligence, as reinforcing the status quo, and, even against the intention of believers, taking an essentially *laissez faire* attitude toward the problems of this world. In place of the old static religion Dewey sees the religious attitude carried into all the spheres of life, an open-ended quest to realize the highest ideal values of our common humanity, which would make explicit what "has always been the common faith of mankind."[12]

If the originally Protestant John Dewey ends up with a faith in naturalistic historicism the originally Jewish Walter Lippmann could hardly have taken a more opposed route. In *The Public Philosophy* Lippmann is clearly flirting with a Catholic Neo-Thomism to give religious depth to his perennial philosophy. Lippmann affirms what Dewey denies: a "realm of the spirit," a vision that "is not of this world but of another and radically different one."[13] For Lippmann it is just such a sensitivity to the spiritual realm that supports morally serious men and women in their search for the good life. And far from calling for the end of the traditional religions and their replacement by a generalized religious faith in the ideals of humanity, Lippmann would strengthen the traditional church as a critical balance to the state:

> But while the separation of the powers of the churches and of the state is essential to a right relationship between them, the negative rule is not the principle of their right relationship. Church and state need to be separate, autonomous, and secure. But they must also meet in all the issues of good and evil.[14]

For all of these contrasts it will not do to characterize Dewey simply as a liberal and Lippmann as a conservative. There are Puritan and even Aristotelian aspects of Dewey's thought that prevent him from being classified as a liberal. As Daniel Bell has recently pointed out, neither conservatives nor liberals really understood Lippmann's book *The Public Philosophy*. The first thought he agreed with their ideas more than in fact he did. The second were merely charmed by his style. In their views of property and of the relation between the economy and society both men transcend the dichotomy between neocapitalists and welfare liberals that has characterized our political spectrum for some decades.

Dewey in 1930 decried a number of weaknesses of American economic life that the New Deal and the Great Society would greatly mitigate. In particular he called for unemployment insurance, old age insurance, and medical insurance, none of which existed in Hoover's America. But moving beyond those immediate needs Dewey raised issues that are still not resolved, indeed still barely discussed in American political life: democratic participation in economic decisions and whether our economy is to be organized for private profit or for public use. He was certainly not a state socialist but he did favor a number of experiments and innovations that today we might classify under the rubric of economic democracy.

When we turn to Lippmann we discover that the very first example that he gives of the process of "the renewal of the public philosophy" is to call into question the absolute sanctity of private property that has developed in recent times. He sees many of our current social and economic problems as arising from a system of private property in which the rights of ownership do not have concomitant duties to the public good. In place of the "sole and despotic dominion" that Blackstone would give the individual property owner, Lippmann takes the Thomist position that "the ultimate title does not lie in the owner. The title is in 'mankind,' in *The People* as a corporate community." He goes on to say:

> Because the legal owner enjoys the use of a limited necessity belonging to all men, he cannot be the sovereign lord of his possessions. He is not entitled to exercise his absolute and therefore arbitrary will. He owes duties that correspond with his rights. His ownership is a grant made by the laws to achieve not his private purposes but the common social purpose. And, therefore, the laws of property may and should be judged, reviewed, and, when necessary, amended, so as to define the specific system of rights and duties that will promote the ends of society.[15]

On still another point Dewey and Lippmann seem to be opposites but in the end may not be so far apart. Dewey seems at first glance to be as resolutely historicist as Lippmann is ahistorical. For Dewey everything changes according to the historical context. For Lippmann the public philosophy would seem to be true at all times and all places. Yet it is hard to reconcile Dewey's stalwart commitment to specific moral virtues — compassion, justice, equality — with a radical historicism from which they could never be derived. And Lippmann's insistent use of the qualifier *Western* seems to give his ahistorical reason a local habitation. At one point Lippmann seems to be moving toward a more specifically historical understanding when he speaks of tradition:

But traditions are more than the culture of the arts and sciences. They are the public world to which our private worlds are joined. This continuum of public and private memories transcends all persons in their immediate and natural lives and it ties them all together. In it there is performed the mystery by which individuals are adopted and initiated into membership in the community.

The body which carries this mystery is the history of the community, and its central theme is the great deeds and the high purposes of the great predecessors. From them the new men descend and prove themselves by becoming participants in the unfinished story.[16]

Yet even here it is tradition and history in general that are being celebrated. Throughout the book we get little sense of a concrete history of which we might be a part. Both Dewey's historicism and Lippmann's ahistoricism are equally abstract. Neither situate us in a specific history or tie us to traditions that actually operate in our society. In this regard turning to Reinhold Niebuhr is a refreshing change.

Our exemplar of Niebuhr's public philosophy and public theology is *The Children of Light and the Children of Darkness* of 1944. The problem with which Niebuhr is concerned is similar to that of Dewey and Lippmann. He too wishes to offer a defense of free institutions more adequate than those currently available:

The thesis of this volume grew out of my conviction that democracy has a more compelling justification and requires a more realistic vindication than is given by the liberal culture with which it has been associated in modern history.[17]

And like the others he mixes philosophy and theology. He offers up the book as "political philosophy," whose religious and theological basis he does not seek to elaborate. Nevertheless he concludes the foreword by saying,

It will be apparent, however, that [these pages] are informed by the belief that a Christian view of human nature is more adequate for the development of a democratic society than either the optimism with which democracy has become historically associated or the moral cynicism which inclines human communities to tyrannical strategies.[18]

Related to Niebuhr's greater historical specificity is his greater willingness to deal in his Christian political philosophy with the reality of conflict and difference, compared to Dewey's common faith or Lippmann's public philosophy. Dewey, of course, believed in discussion and experiment as essential to the public process. Yet he saw the implicit historical direction that he discerned as inevitably winning out. Lippmann specifically disavows the idea that the public philosophy of a free society could be restored "by fiat and by force." Instead he sees the necessity of a form of moral education:

> To come to grips with the unbelief which underlies the condition of anomy, we must find a way to reestablish confidence in the validity of public standards. We must renew the convictions from which our political morality springs.[19]

But the inevitable antinomies of social life are as obscured by the notion of socialization into a common culture as they are by the idea of the progressive triumph of a single historical tendency. For Niebuhr on the other hand there is always the yes and the no, the light and the dark, the contending forces. Christian political philosophy does not offer any perfect resolution of these struggles but only the hope of enough common ground and enough perspective so that the conflict does not become self-destructive.

Central to Niebuhr's discussion of the conflicts between the individual and the community and between the community and property is his conviction that the bourgeois liberal alternative on these questions has run its course but that the Marxist collectivist alternative is, in any absolute sense, intolerable. He thus sees our common life as moving back and forth, upholding individual rights but also the common good of the community, defending economic decentralization but intervening firmly where private economic forces lead to grave injustice.

In his discussion of the conflict between secular universalism and religious particularity Niebuhr's observations are profound and especially relevant to our present situation in America. He is equally negative toward a secular universalism that ends in the emptying out of all meaning and a religious triumphalism that would assert something like a "Christian America." His own position is what he calls a "religious solution of the problem of religious diversity":

> This solution makes religious and cultural diversity possible within the presuppositions of a free society, without destroying the religious depth of culture. The solution requires a very high form of religious commitment. It demands that each religion, or each version of a single faith, seek to proclaim its highest insights while yet preserving an humble and contrite recognition of the fact that all actual expressions of religious faith are subject to historical contingency and relativity. Such a recognition creates a spirit of tolerance and makes any religious or cultural movement hesitant to claim official validity for its form of religion or to demand an official monopoly for its cult.
>
> Religious humility is in perfect accord with the presuppositions of a democratic society. Profound religion must recognize the difference between the unconditioned character of the divine and the conditioned character of all human enterprise. . . .
>
> Religious toleration through religiously inspired humility and charity is always a difficult achievement. It requires that religious convictions be sincerely and devoutly held while yet the sinful and finite corruptions of these convictions be humbly acknowledged; and the actual fruits of other faiths be generously estimated. Whenever the religious groups of a community are incapable of such humility and charity the national community will be forced to save its unity through either secularism or authoritarianism.[20]

Richard John Neuhaus and William M. Sullivan have quite recently published books which sharply pose the issue for public philosophy and public theology today and which draw in interesting ways on the writers and positions I have already discussed. Richard Neuhaus in *The Naked Public Square* clearly stands in the tradition of Reinhold Niebuhr in trying to recover a public discussion of fundamental religious and political truths even when we do not expect complete agreement. He calls to task both the liberal mainline churches and the conservative evangelicals for undermining this essential common task.

Particularly impressive is the sharpness with which Neuhaus criticizes the Christian right, in view of his own growing identification with political and religious conservatism in recent years:

> Fundamentalist leaders rail against secular humanists for creating what I have called the naked public square. In fact, fundamentalism is an indispensable collaborator in that creation. By separating public argument from private belief, by building a wall of strict separationism between faith and reason, fundamentalist religion ratifies and reinforces the conclusions of militant secularism.[21]

In this tendency Neuhaus finds that religious conservatives are ironically following the lead of religious liberals who for some time have abandoned the effort to relate Christian truths to current reality in favor of embracing uncritically some current version of liberal or radical ideology. Neuhaus attempts to recall both sides to faithfulness to their traditions and the public relevance of those traditions, but in the spirit of humility and contrition of which Niebuhr wrote. Neuhaus fears that in their various sectarian fervors the religious left and the religious right will withdraw so totally from the public square that it will be invaded by some form of authoritarianism or totalitarianism. It is this eventuality to which Niebuhr also warned a triumphant secularism would lead.

In an important chapter entitled "Critical Patriotism and Civil Community" Neuhaus makes a move in his fervent criticism of the religious left that I think is in serious need of rebuttal. He quite rightly suggests that when elements of the religious left reject the United States as totally corrupt, and perhaps also idolatrously praise some doubtful foreign regime, they have removed themselves from the public discussion and have undermined the possibility of our recovering a viable public philosophy. He correctly suggests that a critical patriotism is a necessary condition for a fruitful public discussion. But he makes a most un-Niebuhrian move when he offers a kind of loyalty test for admission into the public discourse.

The proposition to which he would have us all agree is one he calls "carefully nuanced." It reads: "On balance and considering the alternatives, the influence of the United States is a force for good in the world."[22] Yet, I would argue, adherence to such an empirical proposition, one almost impossible to test, would tie the critical patriot into a kind of civil orthodoxy that would irreparably rupture the Niebuhrian dialectic. I would agree that the critical patriot must *hope* that the United States will be an influence for good in the world. If there is no hope then one must withdraw into apolitical sectarianism or revolutionary mania. But Neuhaus misses the Niebuhrian irony of history that it may be precisely the best nation in history that does the worst thing that humans have ever done. It is as though Neuhaus has suddenly forgotten about sin. The critical patriot must hope that the United States will be a force for good in the world but must fear that it may be a force for evil. After all the United States is the only nation in the world to have used the atom bomb, and that against civilian populations in two large Japanese cities. It is certainly possible — it is a possibility toward which the critical patriot must exercise a salutary fear — that that same United States would set off a catastrophe which could destroy civilization if not life itself. For the critical patriot who is also a Niebuhrian Christian it is life lived in the tension between that hope and that fear that will make the greatest contribution to our recovery of a public morality, not some enforced patriotic orthodoxy, however "nuanced." Yet finally I want to emphasize the service that Neuhaus has done us in attempting to recall us from our sectarian enthusiasms of recent years to engage once again in a public discussion about the most important things.

If Neuhaus continues the Niebuhrian strand of the discussion, William M. Sullivan, in *Reconstructing Public Philosophy*, in interesting ways combines the traditions of Dewey and Lippmann. (Even the title suggests as much, for "reconstructing" is a Deweyan term while "public philosophy" recalls Lippmann.) Sullivan clearly agrees with Dewey that we are moving into an ever more interdependent world that demands greater corporate responsibility, not a return to atomistic individualism. He also raises the possibility that economic democracy should return to the agenda of our public discussion. But he does not believe that an ahistorical "natural intelligence" of the sort Dewey relied on is the appropriate vehicle to meet our present need. Indeed it is precisely Dewey's inability to differentiate such a natural intelligence from the purely technical or scientistic rationality that seems to be the cause of many of our problems that limits Dewey's relevance to our present discussion. Instead Sullivan turns to something much closer to what Lippmann describes, namely, the tradition of civic republicanism, which is rooted in Platonic and Aristotelian political philosophy but has been in subsequent centuries developed by Christian insights and the experience of republican and democratic societies. Sullivan's approach is more historically specific than Lippmann's, in that he seeks to trace the presence of civic republicanism in the formative phase of American history as well as in its survivals in the present day. Sullivan argues that only a rootedness in the classical tradition will help us avoid turning any effort at present reconstruction into one more experiment in disintegrative modernization.

Sullivan's contribution is critical as well as constructive. Neuhaus warned of the danger of the disintegration of our public life into warring religious and political sectarianisms. Sullivan warns us of the dangers in our intellectual life of an alliance of technical reason and psychological individualism that entirely precludes a serious consideration of public life. Increasing academic specialization has led philosophers and social scientists (and often theologians as well) to turn away from public discourse to the discussion of technical issues with fellow experts. It is partly for these reasons that we do not have today a journalist like Walter Lippmann, a theologian like Reinhold Niebuhr, or a philosopher like John Dewey, each combining the highest intellectual seriousness with full participation in public discussion.

It is only a step beyond Sullivan's book to recognize that recovering a notion of social science as public philosophy and even as public theology may be a part of our effort to reconstruct those enterprises. In fact Sullivan is one of my collaborators in the effort to do just that that I mentioned at the beginning of this essay. Before briefly summarizing our efforts and some related ones, let me discuss some of the obstacles to this task. There has been a great tradition of social science as public philosophy, without which our own efforts would have been impossible. Tocqueville is the classic exemplar, but he has been followed not unworthily in the twentieth century by such works as the Middletown studies of Robert and Helen Lynd and David Riesman's book *The Lonely*

Crowd.[23] Even as recently as 1976 we have the powerful example of Kai T. Erikson's *Everything in Its Path: Destruction of Community in the Buffalo Creek Flood*, which is a moving meditation on the inadequacies of an individualistic culture in the face of catastrophe.[24]

Yet throughout the twentieth century another notion of social science has been growing in prestige, one that sees social science not as a process of social self-understanding,[25] but as a quasi-natural science, one that produces purely factual "findings" that are value-neutral but can be "applied" by whoever can, or can afford to, apply them. Social scientists as public philosophers have always kept a critical distance between themselves and their society, in part because they are loyal not only to their own society but to traditions of social reflection that transcend their own society in time and space. But for technical social scientists the link is severed altogether. There is simply no relation between the scientist as scientist and the scientist as citizen. Not only do they not see social science as contributing to public discussion, they think of their profession as one more interest group in the competition for scarce resources.

This conception of social science was forcibly borne in on me when a colleague, with the best of intentions, sent me a copy of an article that had appeared in the January 1985 issue of *Footnotes*, the bulletin published by the American Sociological Association to carry news of the profession. The friend had seen a newspaper article about *Habits of the Heart* and commended me for doing what the article recommended. Upon looking at the article in *Footnotes* I discovered that it concerned the dissemination of sociological research findings in the media. It quoted a report of the ad hoc Task Force on Sociology and the Media as follows:

> On balance, we believe the arguments for informing the public outweigh those which argue against such action. The gains that can be produced by an active, sustained public relations program, in our judgment, will be greater than the losses that may be incurred. Moreover, the growing competition for students and research/training funds plus the continuing political attacks on social research dictate the development of an effective and ongoing public relations program that is aimed

at building support for sociology in special and general publics. In this effort, our presentation of self in the mass media is of maximum importance.[26]

In looking through the entire article, though there is much about the "profession's image in the eyes of the public," there is nothing at all to indicate that sociologists have anything to contribute to public discussion — or anything to learn from it either.

This is not the place to summarize the data or the argument of *Habits of the Heart.* All I can do is indicate briefly why the five of us who wrote it believe it is a modest contribution to public philosophy and even perhaps to public theology.[27] The focus of our study is on the classic problem of citizenship: why do some Americans become involved in civic life? what meaning does it have for them when they do? why do they sometimes withdraw from it? why do other Americans never become involved at all? We wanted to know whether Americans are still citizens because the answer to that question, if the traditions of social thought and political philosophy upon which we draw are at all right, will tell us something significant about the possibilities for the survival of free institutions in our society. In carrying out our study we used the oldest methods known to social science: participant observation and the interview. In short we spoke as citizens to other citizens about matters of mutual concern. We did not try to hide our own beliefs nor were we hesitant in probing the bases of theirs. And then we brought the public discussion which was the data of our study into the book itself, so that it could provide the basis of a still wider public discussion.

Our book drew on many of the writers discussed in this paper but our conclusions are somewhat different. We avoided, or I hope we avoided, the tone of the jeremiad. We did not find the public square naked or the citadel vacant, though we did find those occupying those places feeling more than a little beleaguered. We found many volunteers, some of whom know deeply what it is to be a citizen, but we also found many for whom the public sphere is baffling and alien. We saw not just one tradition in America but several, sometimes related in fruitful complementarity but sometimes related in destructive attrition. We took our stand that the biblical and the civic republican traditions are the ones most in need of nurturing today.

We did not hesitate to draw conclusions from our work, though we have no political program nor even any specific policy suggestions. One thing we noted repeatedly: the destructive consequences of the way our economic life is organized on all those commitments in private and public life that hold us together as a free people. We found the destructive forces of modern economic life everywhere at work and the challenge to democratic reconstruction in the face of those forces greater than ever.

Among a number of other recent works that deserve comment let me single out the just published *Varieties of Religious Presence* by David A. Roozen, William McKinney, and Jackson W. Carroll,[28] because it is an example of social science as public theology very congenial to the approach of *Habits of the Heart*. The authors studied ten congregations in Hartford, Connecticut, through participant observation and interviews, and came to understand and to bring into the larger public discussion the views of those to whom they spoke.

In conclusion I would like to turn to an example of another kind of public philosophy and public theology that helps us understand our present situation, and that also uses social science in doing so: the first draft of the Catholic Bishops' Pastoral Letter on Catholic Social Teaching and the U.S. Economy.[29] Again this is not the place to summarize a long and complex document. Let me merely indicate a few of the reasons I believe it is significant and admirable.

Needless to say the bishops in this document are going against the current of the times, as the great exemplars of public philosophy and public theology often do. This means they have gotten an exceptionally bad press and that unless you have read the document itself you are almost certain to have a very inadequate understanding of it. The first thing to note, in spite of some press commentary to the contrary, is the extraordinary humility and openness of the document. It brings to the discussion of matters of great public concern the resources of the Bible, the tradition of Catholic social teachings, a sensitivity to the Protestant dimension of American culture, and the arguments and data available to secular reason alone. The document is, wherever particular policy matters are concerned, tentative and open to further discussion. It is firm only in the assertion that morality is as applicable to our economic life as to any other aspect of our life together and that it is possible to discover criteria in the economic sphere that a good society should meet, even though actual societies are not likely to approximate them very closely.

In my view, and in the view of the drafters of the document itself, it is Part 1, Biblical and Theological Foundations, that is most important. The press has ignored Part 1 and concentrated on the policy suggestions of Part 2, on the assumption that Part 1 consists of platitudes in which we all believe. Part 1 is a clear critique of radical American individualism. It asserts that "the dignity of the human person, realized in community with others, is the criterion against which all aspects of economic life must be measured."[30] It balances an absolute commitment to the dignity of the person, based on the fact that we are created in the image and likeness of God, with the fact that that dignity is only realized in community. "Communal solidarity is at the heart of the biblical understanding of the human condition."[31] I would say on the basis of our research for *Habits of the Heart* that most Americans do not understand that and that the greatest service the bishops could render would be to help more of us to do so.

I think in Part 2, again in contrast to much opinion in the media, it is the sober and judicious use of social science to flesh out tentative policy suggestions that is most impressive. The call for a new experiment in economic democracy drew the greatest fire, though I believe it is well thought through and well argued, because it is most out of step with the popular mood of the moment. Here the bishops are indeed ahead of their time, but perhaps not as far ahead of their time as some suggest. The bishops are accused of serving up warmed-over Mondaleism, of advocating welfare liberal programs that have been tried and failed. But economic democracy has never been tried in America, at least not since the rural towns of Puritan Massachusetts. There is something reminiscent of the 1920s about the present moment in America. Untrammeled capitalism is offered as the answer to all our problems. Babbitt is again our national hero. One looks in vain to the White House for a seriousness to match that of the bishops (or to match that of earlier chief magistrates who were sometimes teachers of our public philosophy and sometimes, as in the case of Lincoln, of our public theology as well). Instead one finds an offhand and highly selective biblicism[32] on the one hand and an unrestrained confidence in science and technology as the solutions to all our problems, foreign and domestic,[33] that would have appalled every writer cited in this paper.

In short our public philosophy and public theology are in peril, as distinguished Americans have been pointing out for over fifty years. Yet in religious and civic organizations we have many among us who understand the truth of our traditions and of our present condition as well as Americans ever have. If that is not ground for optimism it is at least ground for hope.

NOTES

1. Robert N. Bellah, Richard Madsen, William M. Sullivan, Ann Swidler, and Steven M. Tipton, *Habits of the Heart: Individualism and Commitment in American Life* (Berkeley, Calif.: University of California Press, 1985).

2. William M. Sullivan, *Reconstructing Public Philosophy* (Berkeley, Calif.: University of California Press, 1982); Richard John Neuhaus, *The Naked Public Square: Religion and Democracy in America* (Grand Rapids, Mich.: Eerdmans, 1984).

3. Alexis de Tocqueville, *Democracy in America*, trans. George Lawrence, ed. J. P. Mayer (New York: Doubleday & Co., Anchor Books, 1969), p. 292, with omissions.

4. Walter Lippmann, *The Public Philosophy* (New York: Mentor, 1956), p. 88.

5. Sullivan, *Reconstructing Public Philosophy*, pp. xi, xii.

6. Reinhold Niebuhr, *The Children of Light and the Children of Darkness* (New York: Charles Scribner's Sons, 1944), p. 133.

7. John Dewey, *Individualism Old and New* (New York: Putnam, 1930), p. 52.

8. John Courtney Murray, "Return to Tribalism," *Catholic Mind*, January 1962, as cited in Neuhaus, *Naked Public Square*, p. 85.

9. Dewey, *Individualism Old and New*, pp. 70, 71.

10. Ibid., p. 34.

11. Bruce Kuklick, *Churchmen and Philosophers: From Jonathan Edwards to John Dewey* (New Haven, Conn.: Yale University Press, forthcoming).

12. John Dewey, *A Common Faith* (New Haven, Conn.: Yale University Press, 1934), p. 87.

13. Lippmann, *Public Philosophy*, p. 115.

14. Ibid., p. 119.

15. Ibid., p. 93.

16. Ibid., p. 105.

17. Niebuhr, *Children of Light and Children of Darkness*, p. xii.

18. Ibid., pp. xiv, xv.

19. Lippmann, *Public Philosophy*, p. 88.

20. Niebuhr, *Children of Light and Children of Darkness*, pp. 134–35, 137–38.

21. Neuhaus, *Naked Public Square*, p. 37.

22. Ibid., p. 73.

23. Robert S. Lynd and Helen Merrell Lynd, *Middletown: A Study of Contemporary American Culture* (New York: Harcourt, Brace, 1929); and *Middletown in Transition: A Study in Cultural Conflicts* (New York: Harcourt, Brace, 1973); David Riesman, with Nathan Glazer and Reuel Denney, *The Lonely Crowd: A Study of the Changing American Character* (New Haven, Conn.: Yale University Press, 1950). It is interesting that John Dewey draws on the Lynds' Middletown studies for data in support of his arguments in *Individualism Old and New*.

24. Kai T. Erikson, *Everything in Its Path: Destruction of Community in the Buffalo Creek Flood* (New York: Simon & Schuster, 1976).

25. On social science as social self-understanding see the title essay in Edward Shils, *The Calling of Sociology and Other Essays on the Pursuit of Learning* (Chicago: University of Chicago Press, 1980). See also Robert N. Bellah, "Social Science as Practical Reason," in *Ethics, the Social Sciences, and Policy Analysis*, ed. Daniel Callahan and Bruce Jennings (New York: Plenum Press, 1983); and Norma Haan, Robert N. Bellah, Paul Rabinow, and William M. Sullivan, *Social Science as Moral Inquiry* (New York: Columbia University Press, 1983).

26. Carla B. Howery, "Public Relations Program Features Multifaceted Efforts," *Footnotes* 13, no. 1 (January 1985): 1.

27. See the Appendix, "Social Science as Public Philosophy," in Bellah, *Habits of the Heart*.

28. David A. Roozen, William McKinney, Jackson W. Carroll, *Varieties of Religious Presence: Mission in Public Life* (New York: Pilgrim, 1984).

29. "Catholic Social Teaching and the U.S. Economy," *Origins, NC Documentary Service* 14, nos. 22–23 (November 15, 1984).

30. Ibid., par. 23.

31. Ibid., par. 69.

32. *San Francisco Chronicle*, 5 February 1985, reports that Reagan quoted Luke 14:31 in support of his call for a continuing military buildup. *San Francisco Chronicle*, 22 February 1985, reports Reagan as

saying that he found "that the Bible contains an answer to just about everything and every problem that confronts us, and I wonder sometimes why we won't recognize that one book could solve our problems for us."

33. *San Francisco Chronicle*, 22 January 1985, reports Reagan in his second inaugural address as saying: "There are no limits to growth and human progress when men and women are free to follow their dreams." *San Francisco Chronicle*, 7 February 1985, reports that in his State of the Union Address Reagan stated that "manned space stations" will provide "new opportunities for free enterprise" in manufacturing "crystals of exceptional purity to produce super computers, creating jobs, technologies, and medical breakthroughs beyond anything we ever dreamed possible."

The Moral Crisis of Capitalism

PETER BERGER

I AM A SOCIOLOGIST who has moral nightmares; and it is out of the compulsion of dealing with those nightmares that I find myself constrained to deal with topics which twenty years ago would have been unthinkable for a sociologist. These nightmares are not idiosyncratic; they are shared by many people with moral concerns in our world. The fundamental nightmare which we all share is about the amount of human misery in the contemporary world.

Future historians looking at our age may well be puzzled by a very curious phenomenon: the remarkable successes of capitalist economics in achieving vast gains in the standards of living of masses of people, and the equally remarkable failures of capitalism to inspire the admiration of many of these same people. It is a paradox that was first commented on by Joseph Schumpeter who, contrary to Marx, believed that capitalism would be brought down not by economic failures, but by economic success. The same paradox has been much pondered over, recently, by various interpreters of contemporary society from Left to Right.

What are we talking about when we say "capitalism"? If we speak of capitalist and socialist societies, we are not speaking of exclusive categories. The most useful way of looking at the phenomenon of capitalism is to see it in a continuum. While human beings have shown remarkable ingenuity and imaginativeness in thinking up the most diverse social arrangements, the range of economic possibilities is not terribly large. There are some exceptions to this, but if one considers human history, basically we are dealing with two kinds of mechanisms to solve the economic problem. There are market mechanisms on the one hand, and various mechanisms of political allocation on the other. In other words it is either the market which decides who gets what in a society, or it is some process of allocation by some kind of authority;

presumably at least in the modern society that will be a political authority. We cannot point in the present world, and perhaps never could have, to any society which is either a case of pure market mechanisms, or pure political allocation. Every society which we call capitalist in the world today has massive processes of political allocation, and even the oldest societies which have called themselves socialist have massive underground market economies which, in some of these countries, play an enormous role.

A more sensible way to think of this is to look at various national societies in a continuum between two empirically unavailable ideal poles. In that way one can certainly say that the United States is a more capitalist society than the Soviet Union; we can say that Sweden is a more capitalist society than Yugoslavia; and various other societies can be placed on this continuum. It obviously follows from this that where you draw the dividing line is, to some extent, arbitrary, but I suggest that in most concrete cases, certainly outside the Third World, it is never empirically doubtful. Hence it would be very hard for me to accept an argument which would put Sweden on the socialist side of the divide and put Yugoslavia on the capitalist, though clearly they are approaching this divide.

In these terms we can speak empirically of an international capitalist system. In fact, one of the best ways of placing societies within this continuum is to ask about their relations to this international capitalist system. The moral assault on this international capitalist system has come from organized socialist states and movements, of course, but also from a broad coalition of intellectuals and educated people in the capitalist societies themselves. They make five principal charges against capitalism, which will be compared here with principal empirical facts as we know them. The charges are, first, that capitalism fosters inequality within a society. Secondly, that it fosters inequality between societies. Thirdly, that it fosters political oppression. Fourthly, that it fosters ecological dangers. And, fifthly, that it has a dehumanizing effect.

The first charge of inequality within a nation is very interesting because it is relatively new in the moral critique of capitalism. To some extent at least it results from the failure of the anti-capitalist charge which was much more important in earlier periods. The classical Marxian phrase is miseration. In other words, the Marxist prediction was that capitalism would create an increasing misery of larger and larger numbers of people which would lead to inevitable revolution. This did not take place. Far from miseration being the effect of capitalism in Western societies, these societies have seen the most remarkable and dramatic increase in the standard of living of the great majority of the population in human history. Thus the charge of miseration did not hold, and if one had a basic antagonism to capitalism, one had to think of something better. In terms of political psychology, therefore, the importance of inequality issues is due to the failure of the earlier moral critique of capitalism.

Income and wealth distribution statistics are notoriously complicated and even economists, especially economists, engage in endless quarrels over how to interpret them. Yet most economists would agree that, in the earlier stages of economic growth in a capitalist economy, there is indeed very great inequality. Then, after a certain period of time, a leveling out of this inequality occurs, resulting in what some people call "the tyranny of the bell-shaped curve." After a certain stage of development, income distribution seems to follow this bell-shaped pattern, and apparently does so regardless of, or in spite of, various political attempts in different countries to modify it. Now, this does not mean that more advanced capitalism becomes egalitarian. The bell-shaped curve is not a picture of equality, although it is more egalitarian than earlier stages of the process.

There is no empirical way of saying whether any degree of equality is or is not enough. When one asks about equality in our type of capitalist society, a very crucial question is: What is the present reality of income distribution, wealth distribution, and other attributes of inequality, and with what is this present reality being compared? Is it compared with an ideal of equality? Then obviously the reality will come out very badly. Do you compare it with the past of Western societies? In that case, it comes out very well. But, do you compare it with other societies, in which case it also comes out remarkably well? If you compare our society to the Third World, we are much more egalitarian than most. Empirically, therefore, the charge that capitalism in advanced industrial societies of our kind produces a high degree of inequality is a very dubious charge unless, of course, you compare it with an ideal which has no empirical realization anywhere in the world.

The second charge against capitalism is that of inequality not within a nation, but between nations. Historically this is also very interesting because it is a further development of the Marxist miseration theory, and has become central to that series of assertions made by Third World countries which is sometimes loosely called the Third World ideology. This view admits that the proletariat, the working class in advanced capitalist societies, did not become more miserable. It argues, however, that there was an external proletariat which did. The advanced capitalist societies as a whole could be considered the exploiting bourgeoisie while the poor countries of the Third World constituted the proletariat. The misery of the Third World was thus the foundation of the wealth in what we now call the First World.

The evidence for this is, if anything, more complex than the evidence for the issue of domestic inequality. It is extremely difficult to verify either in terms of history or contemporary realities. In terms of history, there is no doubt that colonial powers exploited some of their colonies. Whether, say, for a country like France or the Netherlands, the benefits of colonial domination exceeded the costs for those societies is very hard to establish and it is unclear how it would come out. Historically, it is also very interesting that some of the absolutely most wretchedly poor countries have had no history of colonial or imperialist penetration at all, while some of the countries which are doing very well indeed are those which were introduced into the capitalist system by imperialist force. The most dramatic example of this is of course Japan, which was brought into this system in the most violent way possible when Commodore Perry and his warships sailed into Tokyo Bay in the 1850s and, at gun point, forced Japan to trade with the United States and other Western countries. In 1868, the modernization of Japan began, and by 1905, Japan was a country capable of defeating Russia in a war. An unbelievable process of economic growth, modernization, catching up went on, opened up by an act which anyone would call imperialist aggression. The historical facts are much more complex, then, than the Third World ideology would maintain.

As to the contemporary realities, to be sure, there are relationships between advanced and less advanced countries which are exploitive. They do not constitute the norm, however. The characteristic relationships are enormously more complex. My view of them is determined by the moral nightmares of which I spoke at the outset. How can we do something about the more degrading and unspeakable kinds of wretchedness in the world—poverty, degradation, early death, disease, and so forth? The positive way of asking that question is: What is a successful model of development? Here we cannot simply speak of economic growth. One can have enormous economic growth and still have continued wretchedness, with very few people benefitting from that economic growth, and there are many cases of this. Success must also mean some ways by which large and increasing numbers of people begin to enjoy the benefits of this economic growth.

What, then, is a successful model? What are success stories? There are some things we know and some things we do not know. We know that there are no socialist success stories. There is not a single socialist success story given the above definition of success. The only success stories are capitalist success stories. There are not very many. They also, which is uncomfortable morally, tend to be centered in Eastern Asia. The reasons why this is uncomfortable is that it suggests at least a possibility of an importance of cultural factors. If these are decisive, their success does not help the Africans or the Latin Americans.

Thus one hopes that there are further factors, other than cultural, which are related to the increasing success of East Asian capitalist societies. There is also, obviously, a very large number of non-success stories in the capitalist world. If one understands not the ideology, but the institutional mechanisms of socialism, the reason for the economic fiascos that socialism invariably brings about are not very hard to understand. What is not clear yet, and is desperately important to understand, is why capitalist models fail. Or, to put it very simply, why does something that succeeds, in say Taiwan, not succeed in a large number of other countries? That is a very burning intellectual and practical question with very great moral weight.

A third very important charge brought against capitalism is that it is supposedly linked with political oppression. The critiques of capitalism habitually contrast the political oppressiveness of capitalist systems with the alleged socialist linkage with liberation of one sort or another. The root facts again are very interesting. If one speaks of democracy as being distinguished from regimes of political oppression, there is not a single case in the world of a society which one could reasonably call socialist which is a democracy. There are no socialist democracies. All the democracies in the world are states that are part of the international capitalist system. There is a large number of capitalist nondemocratic states. In other words, the distribution here of facts has a certain formal analogy to the distribution of success stories noted above. What it suggests, at least hypothetically, is that capitalism, while clearly not a sufficient condition for economic success, seems to be a necessary condition. In the same way, just as capitalism clearly cannot be identified with democracy (otherwise one could not explain the cases of capitalist societies with no democracy), there seems to be a propensity of capitalist systems toward democracy.

Socialism, on the other hand, shows a very clear propensity in the other direction. This is no great mystery, but can be systematically analyzed in terms of the political implication of economies that are largely allocative, as against market-oriented, in organization. This is not to espouse the Wilsonian view, for I do not believe that democracy is the only morally acceptable form of government, although I would personally go to great lengths to defend it in my own country. In my view there are benevolent societies which are not democratic. Leaving aside democracy for a moment for purposes of analysis and looking simply at where one finds the grossest violations of human rights, and where one finds something approximating institutionalized respect for human rights, what one finds is a remarkable correlation between institutions that organize respect for human rights and democracy. Thus, the question of whether capitalism is or is not conducive to democracy is a question very much related to the question of human rights; and if one gives any moral stature to the question of human rights, one must take that correlation very seriously indeed.

There are, briefly, two charges which are frequently made. One is that capitalism, particularly because of its emphasis on economic growth, produces peculiar dangers to the environment and therefore to the future survival of the human race. There is a confusion here of capitalism with technological civilization as such, and it is doubtful that a change in the economic arrangements of societies towards the allocated pole would do anything about dangers to the environment.

Finally, as to the alleged dehumanizing effects of capitalism in terms of materialism and greed, there is a very fundamental confusion between capitalism and the human condition as such. It is curious that people in North America or Western Europe sometimes say that our societies in this part of the world are peculiarly materialistic. I have traveled around in many countries quite extensively, societies of enormous differences in terms of social-economic system, culture, and degree of development. The attachment of human beings to material objects is, in most places, very much the same. One could even make the argument that the more affluent the society is, the less materialistic it tends to be; not because affluence makes for virtue but mainly because people have less to worry about to survive from one day to another, and therefore there is a somewhat greater chance for altruism.

Finally, let us return to the paradox of the empirical facts about capitalism as they relate to the moral reputation of it. This time, however, I want finally to come out from under this mass of detachment and comment as an unabashed moralist. Why has capitalism had this bad press, especially among intellectuals in capitalist countries? (Incidentally, it is almost impossible to find Marxists in socialist countries. A visitor to Poland or Hungary who speaks of Marxism is usually laughed at; no one takes it seriously. It is in the nonsocialist countries that people dream of socialism.) In any case, why this anti-capitalist animus among Western intellectuals, many of whom had benefitted from the affluence of their own societies?

One thing that we should have learned from Marx is that if you analyze human motives, always begin with the most vulgar ones. In other words, if you ask why somebody does something, begin by asking what is in it for him. At least part of our answer, not the entire answer, has to do with vested interest. Political elites everywhere have been interested in anti-capitalist policy, which is particularly important in the Third World countries. Capitalism creates and depends upon entrepreneurship and this in turn creates wealth. This is not in the interest of political elites because peasants who become wealthy have a tendency to become uppity, which political elites do not like. The most revolutionary force in the world today is poor people who become less poor. Political elites want to remain in power and have a vested interest in preventing this revolutionary process.

As far as Western countries are concerned, a very important aspect of anti-capitalism has to do with what some people have called the new class, the knowledge class. They do not make their livelihood out of the manufacture and distribution of material goods, but of symbolic knowledge, such as education, media, counselling, and planning. These people tend to be quite educated and think of themselves as intellectuals, even though some outside people may not want to give them that title. Ever since the nineteenth century, intellectuals have always been very much opposed in their basic attitude to capitalism. Capitalism was vulgar; it did not give them sufficient place in society. Rather it elevated merchants and tradesmen. Intellectuals have a built-in aristocratic tendency. As long as intellectuals were a very small group, this was a colorful phenomenon on the fringes of society. Today there are millions of these people in a society like ours and the anti- capitalist animus is therefore much more important.

While vulgar motives take us a long way, they do not take us all the way. There are other reasons for the persistent attraction of what one may call the socialist vision. These, I think, are rooted not in vested interests, but in some very fundamental discontents of modernity. Modernity, while it has modernization, while it has produced enormous benefits for human beings, has also created very sharp discontents. It has created a loss of essential belonging; it has created a destruction, a weakening of the traditional structures which provided solidarity and identity to human beings. It is not altogether a mistake to identify this process with capitalism in so far as capitalism has been a central motive force of modernization. Socialism is, at its deepest level, a dream of solidarity. It is a dream of a new kind of belonging among human beings across the dividing lines of a complex and modern world. It is this vision which gives it its quasi-religious, profound appeal. That this vision empirically is very unlikely to be realized is another question, but in the history of myths and poetic visions, empirical success has never been a decisive criterion.

I have not tried to hide my feelings even up to now, and it may be clear that I am not altogether opposed to capitalism. A pro-capitalist attitude is one that one ought to take. Let me emphasize as strongly as possible that one should not do this uncritically. Let me stipulate that all kinds of morally repulsive things have happened under the aegis of capitalism. Let me stipulate that capitalists as a class have done morally, and are doing morally, reprehensible things. We live in a very ugly world. If we think by political doctrine we are going to make it a beautiful world in our own lifetime, we are the most dangerous people around because we will sacrifice limited possibilities of improvement for an impossible dream. So let me stipulate this: First, one should not be uncritically pro-capitalist, either in the American society or anywhere else. Second, there are moral reasons for being pro-capitalist, and underline moral with a red pencil. Essentially there are three, of which the first is the most important.

The most important moral argument for capitalism is its power for dealing with human misery. It is astonishing that the Left in Western societies, the political Left, parades around the moral arena as the party of compassion, while the Right is always painted as the party of cruel, selfish, profit-seeking insensitivity. If one is serious about compassion, the most important thing to be compassionate about in the present world is starvation, early death, infant mortality, disease, of which there is an intolerable amount in this world. Who is doing anything to eradicate these afflictions of humanity? If you want to be morally outraged by one thing, if there is one thing that we know about socialism, as close to certitude as you can come empirically, it is that it totally fouls up agriculture. Even if in other sections of the economy socialism may fumble along, it makes a mess in agriculture—everywhere, without exception. That is not an abstract, morally neutral, empirical statement; it has moral implications. To make a mess out of agriculture is people dying of starvation. You have the unbelievable fact that a country like the Soviet Union, sitting on top of some of the richest agricultural soil in the world, is unable to feed its own population, let alone people in other countries. If you look at the number of human beings who are kept alive by the agricultures of the United States, Canada, and Australia, that is a moral as well as an empirical fact. The most important reason why there is a moral dimension to a pro-capitalist bias is this: the power of capitalism in eradicating misery.

The second one is the correlation of capitalism with political liberty and human rights. I say the correlation, not the identification, and again you bring up torture and Latin American dictatorship, violations of human rights, and things of this sort; I stipulate all of these. I speak of correlation. Where is the best bet of achieving democratic systems of institutionalizing respect for human rights? Capitalism creates dynamics which point in that direction, not inevitably, but with some empirical force.

The third reason is the relationship of capitalism to a plurality of values. Capitalism, precisely because it creates a market, also creates market conditions for human beliefs and values. This is a double-edged sword; it creates many problems. Capitalism creates economic, social, and political conditions in which a uniformity of values is not politically established. This is particularly important in the Third World because of tradition; the chance of traditional values to survive within the process of modernization. Many people in Third World countries are very rightly concerned about the tremendous crisis into which traditional ways of thinking and living have been placed by the process of modernization. There is an enormous concern in many parts of the Third World to protect these traditional values. They may be changed but they should somehow survive this great transition. What are the conditions under which they are more likely to survive and under pluralism is more likely to exist? It is under more capitalist rather than more socialist models that there is the better chance.

What is the outlook for the future? The vested interest in anti-capitalism is not likely to disappear, especially on the international scene where it is supported by the immense power of the Soviet Union. Also, the socialist vision is persistent, and it is remarkable how one disaster after another of socialistic experiments in the world seem to be absorbed, explained, adapted, by socialist sympathizers in the Western world. First you get some new country like the Soviet Union and then there was China, and then you find some new country. *That* is where it is really happening. And then that produces some disaster, and then we look for some other one—Nicaragua, Mozambique, whatever; Albania was fashionable for a while in Europe, the most improbable case one might think of. Then the argument is always, "Well, this also was not yet true socialism; we have to wait for true socialism." This, I think, is a major fantasy of our age, but fantasies of such emotional and poetic strength do not easily disappear.

On the other hand, the voice of reason is quiet but persistent. What Freud called the "Reality Principle" imposes itself sooner or later, especially in economic life. Apart from those realities which are hard to deny, there is a continual appeal of liberty. Liberty is another myth of our age, and is very powerful. More than any other country in the world, the United States has carried the image of liberty, not necessarily politically, but in its culture. The enormous appeal of American culture, even in politically anti-American countries, perhaps especially in anti-American countries, is very interesting. Analysis of this music, or these jeans, reveals that these are symbols of liberty, freedom of the individual, against various collective entities, be they traditional or modern. This is a myth with some power of its own.

Fundamentalism and Civil Rights in Contemporary Middle Eastern Politics

MANSOUR FARHANG

FACED WITH THE CHALLENGE of the modern world and subjected to the pressures of historical forces, the Muslim societies are currently undergoing profound transformations. The personal and political crises caused by this situation exhibit two contradictory tendencies: (1) a progression in the consciousness of freedom as manifested in the rise of popular demand for participation in the political life of the community; and (2) an unprecedented expansion in the coercive apparatus of the state along with the emergence of religious fundamentalism as a major ideological current. These developments are related to the integration of the Middle Eastern economies into the world market system as well as to the Western cultural penetration of the Islamic societies. Indeed, all the major political upheavals and ideological conflicts in the Middle East since the turn of the century have been variously influenced by the Western challenge to the native culture patterns in the region. Emulation and fascination as well as resentment and resistance characterize the attitudes of Middle Easterners toward this historic encounter.

Like nationalism, liberalism, socialism, and Marxism, the contemporary idea of civil rights is essentially a Western import into the Middle Eastern countries. It is a preconception of the Universal Declaration of Human Rights that in spite of the diversity in cultures and differences in existential conditions in the world, a common standard of rights can be established for all peoples and nations. Thus the Declaration claims that "all human beings are

born free and equal in dignity and rights", that some basic rights
are inherently human. Among the civil and political rights included
in the Universal Declaration are rights to freedom from discrimination, to life, liberty, and security of the person, to freedom from
slavery, to freedom of assembly and association, to freedom from
torture and cruel punishment, to equality before the law, to freedom from arbitrary arrest, to fair trial, to protection of privacy,
and to freedom of movement.

From a theoretical perspective, one could interpret Islamic
doctrines in a manner largely consistent with the letter and spirit
of the Universal Declaration. But historically — that is to say, in
Islam as a cultural system — governments have generally ruled with
arbitrary power and the individual has lived at the mercy of the
state. Thus, before analyzing the fundamentalist view and treatment of civil rights, it is necessary to outline the general Islamic
concepts regarding such rights. In Islam, the rights of individuals
constitute obligations connected with the Divine. The state must
enforce the *shari'a* (the laws derived from the Qur'an), the *sunnah*
(normative practices associated with the Prophet), *ijma* (the consensus of the community) and *ijtihad* (the counsel of judges on
a particular case). In the Islamic state, sovereignty belongs to God
alone and legislation is restricted within the limits prescribed by
the *shari'a*. The Islamic state is charged with maintaining a balance between the rights of individuals and the duties of government; it must prevent individual freedom from threatening the
interest of the community. The liberal notion of freedom from
external restraint is incompatible with Islamic theology because
freedom in Islam is not an inherent right. Individual freedom is
perceived as personal surrender to God. It is only in relation to
obligations that human rights are recognized in Islam.

Yet Muslims do not have a unified and monolithic perception
of their faith, any more than do the followers of other religions.
For example, the contemporary interpretations of the Qur'an by
various Muslim thinkers range from extreme left to extreme right,
or any combination of themes from the two polar positions. Discourse on such controversies often revolves around the meaning
of revelation or the intentions of the Prophet, but it is in fact a
manifestation of deep-rooted conflicts and contradictions in the
socioeconomic structure of the society. For contrary to the recent

media/academic assertion that ascribes to Islamic societies a special proclivity to link religion and state power, separation between state and religion has been the norm in the Muslim world for much of its history. Muslims, for the greater part of their history, have lived under regimes which had only the most tenuous link with the *shari'a* or the religious law.

Despite the *shari'a*'s grasp of nearly all aspects of individual and social life, there is no unified Islamic legal system, enshrined in integrated codes and accepted by all Muslims. Besides the sectarian divergences in interpreting the *shari'a*, the willingness of the state in the application of the law, which is often a function of its ideological and political underpinnings, is also a determining factor. For example, Saudi Arabia, Libya, Pakistan, and Iran all consider themselves as Islamic states but none of them is recognized by the others as authentic. To the extent that Islamic doctrines have been instrumental in the formulation of criminal or private codes in the four nations, it has stemmed only from what their leaders perceive to be true Islam — a perception shaped by a host of political, psychological, social, economic, and historical factors.

In the century-old cultural encounter between the West and the Islamic Middle East, four response patterns have tried to meet the challenge:

- *The secularists* — they perceive their societies as backward, both economically and socioculturally, and maintain that only scientific education, economic development, industrialization, and modernization can remedy the ills of the society.
- *The traditionalists* — they reject modern ideas and wish to retain the political authority structure as well as the sociocultural values of the past.
- *The religious modernists* — they favor a liberal and scientifically based interpretation of Islam and call for radical reform in both the socioeconomic and political order of the society. They maintain that the progressive aspects of Western thought already existed in original Islam.
- *The fundamentalists* — they portray Islam as a civilization superior to the Western tradition, including both Marxism

and capitalism. They are convinced that Islam will defeat the West in the ongoing confrontation between them. They present Islam as the only moral order and regard themselves as the exclusive representatives of the Divine on earth.

The emergence of Islamic fundamentalism as a popular movement has to be comprehended in the context of the failure of the secularists and religious modernists to reach a functioning synthesis between Islam and modernization. In Iran, for example, Islamic fundamentalism could not thrive until the Pahlavis' blind Westernization drive produced massive sociocultural alienation and the secular alternatives to the Shah's dictatorship were fatally suppressed. As the economic gap between the privileged few and the wretched many increased, so did the cultural gap. The enclaves of wealth and power in Tehran, Shiraz, and Isfahan also became enclaves of imported cultures and lifestyles. One could make a reasonable case that the rapidity of political disintegration in Iran in 1978 was primarily due to the lack of minimal capacity on the part of the regime to contain or accommodate a peaceful popular challenge. Indeed, the Pahlavi state proved to be much weaker than expected, not only in its relations with the society at large but, more importantly, within itself. The arbitrary rule of one family could no longer be maintained in the face of new socioeconomic realities which, besides causing cross-class disaffection, entailed a massive increase in the urban poor population.

To understand the Islamic fundamentalist view of political life in general and civil rights in particular, it is essential to acknowledge the desperate existential conditions of its principal constituency—the urban poor. As a society moves away from its traditional setting, people often find themselves in unexpected situations. Individuals and groups respond to this challenge in diverse ways. The mediating or intervening mechanism is the internalized cultural orientation. As Barrington Moore has explained in his classic study of modernization, "The residue of truth in the cultural explanation is that what looks like an opportunity or a temptation to one group of people will not necessarily seem so to another group in a different form of society."[1]

It is due to the intervening variable of native culture that modernization as a concept and as a policy can be seen to be either a hope or a curse. For example, whatever else it might be and regardless of its equity or inequity, modernization historically has involved a change from conservative toward liberal values in the realm of culture. Almost everywhere, this process seems to produce disturbances because it dramatically threatens the habits, customs, living conditions, and values of individuals and social classes. The nature of such disturbances cannot be generalized simply because there are variations in premodern conditions. Diversity in experience, past and present, leads to different results. Thus each society produces its own distinct response to the challenge or demand of modernization. When the inevitable traditional resistance to cultural change is combined with feudal politics and the deepening of relative deprivation, as was the case in Iran under the Pahlavis, then the social disruptions caused by the process of modernization could create anomie in the classical sense, which often results in the growth of anxiety, hostility, and fantasy.

Under these circumstances, the fundamentalist preachers and organizers can be quite effective in appealing to the disaffected sectors of the population. Since the problem of cultural identity is an instance of the crisis of national disillusionment, the fundamentalists can easily transform the disorientation of the individual into a collective hatred toward the *other*. Hatred toward the enemy, both internal and external, real or imagined, is an indispensable characteristic of the fundamentalist political consciousness. Indeed, it is hard to see how a fundamentalist regime or movement can function without an intense and hateful confrontation with the *other*.

The great revolutions of the past sought, at least theoretically, to create a new society. The fundamentalist revolutionary movements, in contrast, seek to reestablish a sacred utopia presumed to have existed in the distant past. For the fundamentalists maintain that their project is to restore the Islamic institutions and beliefs to their original pristine purity. They reject any attempt to interpret Islamic doctrines in modernist terms. Thus, in pursuing their political objectives, they inevitably run into violent conflict not only with the secularists but also with Islamic modernists and traditionalists. They believe that they alone are able to resolve the problems facing the world today.

The fundamentalist view of society and history is derived from

a supposedly timeless struggle between good and evil. The attitude of the fundamentalists toward the world revolves around the
question of how things have deviated from the sacred principles.
They contend that the Islamic laws and doctrines as revealed in
the Qur'an were enacted by Prophet Muhammad 1400 years ago
in the first divinely inspired state in history. This conception of
the past, it should be noted, is an invention of the fundamentalist
imagination, not an accurate portrayal of history. To be sure, the
Islamic state under the leadership of Muhammad was a progressive experience in the life of the Arabian peninsula, but the subsequent mythology about this state was a by-product of the fantastic territorial expansion and military successes of Islamic forces
during the century following Muhammad's death in 632 A.D.

History or theology aside, the ongoing fundamentalist current in the Middle East is primarily a nativist response to the crisis environment at home and the cultural challenge from abroad.
The word *native* is used here without normative connotation because, as we have learned from the revolutionary experience in
Iran, native values do not necessarily serve the interests or aspirations of the community. Furthermore, even though the fundamentalist currents in the Islamic societies have certain important characteristics in common, each movement has to be understood in
the context of its national environment. Needless to say, the establishment of the Islamic Republic of Iran has provided impetus for
militant action by both Shiah and Sunni fundamentalists throughout the Islamic world, but such a source of inspirational influence does not change the significant differences in the nature of
the crises which fuel the fundamentalist current within each nation. In this regard, it is also worth mentioning that contrary to
Khomeini's claim that he leads a transnational movement beyond
national boundaries or identification, the Ayatollah is an *Iranian*
Shiah fundamentalist par excellence. He preaches Islamic universalism but pursues a messianic form of nationalism with the purpose of extending Iran's influence in the region. In a more general
sense, the emphasis on Islam, or any particular interpretation of
it, as the overriding motivational force behind the current upheavals in the Middle East is analytically misleading.

Islamic fundamentalist thinkers in various Middle Eastern
countries have written extensively on the issues and problems fac-

ing their respective societies. Their primary effectiveness is in providing emotionally satisfying answers to the existential and sociocultural concerns of certain strata of population caught up in the disruptive processes of disorganic development. For example, the urban poor and the newly rich petty bourgeoisie are attracted to fundamentalism because it promises to end all deprivation and alienation in the framework of a moral language and psychocultural symbolism rooted in their deepest sensibilities, fears, and hopes.

It is now clear that in all his anti-Pahlavi postures Ayatollah Khomeini was expressing not so much an opposition to political or economic inequities as a reaction against the observable consequences of Westernization in the cultural sphere. Indeed, it is only on cultural matters such as education, art, entertainment, courtship, and sociosexual mores that Khomeini has a coherent idea of what he wants — a quick return to an imagined puritanical past. In each of these spheres of activity he prescribes behavior down to the last details. Khomeini maintains that the corruption of the Islamic Iranian culture began with the success of the constitutional revolution at the turn of the century. It was the constitutional movement that paved the way for secular reform in the judicial and educational institutions of Iran. Thus the fundamentalist clerics regard the reestablishment of Islamic cultural and judicial standards and practices as the principal goal of the 1979 revolution.

The sociocultural policies of the Islamic Republic are astonishingly consistent with the specific concerns and priorities expressed in Ayatollah Khomeini's first political treatise, *Kashf al-Asrar* (Key to the secrets), published forty-five years ago. In this book Khomeini repeatedly refers to the unveiling of women, mixed swimming pools, coeducation, dancing parties, and the drinking of alcohol as the most undesirable and destructive reforms of Reza Shah's period. He vehemently condemns the permissive government policies with respect to such vices and asks the authorities to suppress the violators as well as the critics of the Islamic moral codes. He wrote:

> We expect the Islamic government to support the religious ordinances, prevent the publication of antireligious material, and publicly execute the responsible persons. These seditious

characters who corrupt the earth must be done away with
so that others like them will not indulge themselves in treach-
erous agitation and discussions against the sacred religion.[2]

The dominant issues in *Kashf al-Asrar* are the general impact
of Western values on the society, unveiling, the emergence of woman
as a public person, the practice of liberal manners in courtship,
and male-female contacts. There is hardly a page in the book without an execrating remark about these issues. The following is quite
typical:

> The mixing of the newly pubertized men with the young li-
> bidinous ladies, atrociously exposing their hair, legs, jewelled
> chests, and listening to joyous and lustful music played on
> the radio. . . . [The] poisonous education given to them by
> the lecherous instructors. . . . What corruptions they cause
> in the country.[3]

Kashf al-Asrar illustrates the nature of the fundamentalist
response to the value transformations in Iran under the Pahlavis.
It is important to note, however, that the book was virtually unknown to the general public before the rise of Khomeini as the
leader of the 1979 revolution. Even most of Khomeini's clerical
followers did not begin to take the book seriously until the
mid-1960s. For during the 1940s and the 1950s there was no up-
rooted or dramatized social class whose alienated members could
be attracted to the lure of religious fundamentalism.

Thus, given the fundamentalist view that secularization of
education and acceptance of cultural pluralism threaten the moral
authority of the clerics, it is understandable why the present rulers
of Iran regard the re-Islamization of the country's sociocultural
institutions as the first priority of their domestic agenda. They reject all secular studies of humankind and society as unnecessary
at best and blasphemous at worst. Thus even in the universities
most of the social science, humanities, arts, and music departments
have been abolished. Books considered contradictory to Islamic
doctrines or values have been destroyed or removed from libraries
and bookstores. The fundamentalists simply believe that their version of Islam contains perfect and eternal knowledge about all aspects of individual and social existence. They reject the very no-

tion of objective investigation of human conduct. Even students applying for admission to engineering and medical colleges must pass a comprehensive examination on *feqh* or religious law.

The Islamization of the elementary and secondary schools is complete. Textbooks have been rewritten to reflect the Shiah fundamentalist view of society, science, and history. Just as was the case under the Pahlavis, the new interpretations of Iranian history in the official texts suffer from much distortion and inaccuracy. Faith and belief are supposed to compensate for evidence and proof. Virtually all secularly oriented teachers have been dismissed; even the mathematics and geography instructors have to pass examinations on *feqh* to keep their jobs. Schoolchildren are subjected to daily indoctrination. Some are interrogated to provide information about their parents' private lives; others are persuaded to spy on their neighbors.

Ayatollah Khomeini has repeatedly emphasized the crucial importance of complete Islamization of the country's educational institutions. Once he said to a group of students visiting him at his house:

> My dear ones, we are not afraid of economic sanctions; we are not afraid of military invasion; what frightens us is cultural dependency. We are afraid of the imperialistic universities which train our youth to become servants of the West or communism.[4]

Parallel with the transformation of the schools and universities, the fundamentalist rulers of Iran have acted decisively in re-Islamicizing the country's judiciary, particularly in the area of criminal law. The Islamic Code compels judges to base their sentences on the edicts of the Qur'an and the supposed sayings and practices of the Prophet. Thus prostitutes have been stoned to death, and fingers of petty thieves have been cut off. With thousands of minor officials claiming to speak in Khomeini's name, each with an individual interpretation of Islamic norms, it is difficult to escape the puritanical wrath of the regime. The very arbitrariness of law enforcement is a source of terror and uncertainty. Thousands of Iranians have been arrested and publicly whipped for drinking or playing cards. The Ayatollah has gone so far as to issue a *fatva* (religious judgment) holding that chess, which some believe originated in Iran, is a sinful game; players can be punished by the Islamic justice system for pushing a pawn.

The detailed examination of such developments in the Islamic Republic of Iran is essential for an adequate comprehension of the intentions and the potential of the fundamentalist currents in the Islamic world. For Iran is the first country where the fundamentalists have established their hegemonic control over the state and society. Before this historic achievement, the only other fundamentalist organization which exerted great influence on society was the Egyptian Brotherhood, which was founded in 1928. Between the two world wars, Egypt was plagued with socioeconomic crises and conflicting ideological currents. This situation created a favorable environment for the appeal of the Brotherhood. Hasan al-Banna, the leader of the Brotherhood, was a charismatic leader with a message of spiritual and sociopolitical salvation. By the mid-1940s, the Brotherhood had a million followers and was perceived as the most formidable contender for power against the monarchy.

Members of the Brotherhood were totally devoted to their cause and the organization controlled all aspects of their lives, including family affairs, athletics, and finances. By the late 1940s, the Brotherhood had virtually established a state within the Egyptian state. The relationship between the Brotherhood and civil society was explained by Hasan al-Banna in a famous statement addressed to his followers:

> My brothers, you are not a benevolent society, nor a political party, nor a local organization having limited purposes. Rather, you are a new soul in the heart of this nation to give it life by means of the Qur'an; you are a new light which shines to destroy the darkness of materialism through knowing God; and you are the strong voice which rises to recall the message of the Prophet.[5]

The Brotherhood's violent activities brought a reign of terror to Egypt, leading to Hasan al-Banna's assassination in 1949. His successor, Sayyid Qutb, the most influential fundamentalist theoretician in the Arab world, was accused of plotting to assassinate President Nasser in 1965. He was tried and hanged in the same year. The Brotherhood continues to be the most significant source of influence on the current fundamentalist movement in Egypt.

Before coming to power, the fundamentalists, like other anti-status quo political formations, criticize their governments for civil rights abuses and present a rather humane conception of Islamic laws and values. This tactic can be used in a credible fashion because the sources of *shari'a* are open to diverse interpretations. Ambiguity is in the nature of all religious texts and traditions. Muslim theologians and judges are perfectly capable of interpreting their laws and doctrines in such a way that the absolute domination of the society by the state is seen as legitimate. Iran is a vivid example.

Unlike the West, where civil rights are largely focused on lifestyles and matters of privacy, concern for civil rights in the Middle East centers around the need for peaceful political dissent. Only a tiny segment of the urban population think about civil rights in terms of choices in the private sphere. In the countryside and in the urban slums, where the vast majority of the people live, consciousness of individual or collective rights revolves around basic human needs and resentment of privilege. The distinct absence of respect for civil rights on the part of the state has to be seen more as a problem of political culture and socioeconomic inequalities than as a manifestation of religious dogma. Secular Syria is at least as repressive a state as traditionalist/religious Saudi Arabia. Radical nationalist Iraq is more tolerant of dissent than fundamentalist/theocratic Iran.

Nearly all Middle Eastern countries are ruled by armed minorities who do not recognize any rights for their opponents. There is a tragic scarcity of political civility in the societies of the region. Amnesty International Reports of the 1970s and 1980s portray the Middle Eastern states as the worst violators of human rights in the world. These reports document the sorry fact that throughout much of the region freedom of expression is nonexistent and torture of political prisoners is routine. Since the 1979 revolution Iran has executed more people than the rest of the world combined. In both Iran and Iraq to question the wisdom of continued conflict in their seven-year-old war is regarded by both regimes as a crime against the state. The war magnifies the unresolved sociopolitical contradictions which underlie the uncivil politics of the region. The absurd and tragic theater of the war, which is characterized by the use of human wave tactics and poison gas, has become a place where the psychopathology of politics and the pathology of the cult of personality, in both their secular and religious varieties, can be watched and studied.

Even though in the position of power fundamentalists do not seem much different from their secular rivals, the impact of fundamentalism on the civil rights situation in the Middle East has a unique significance of its own. The essence of this uniqueness lies in the fact that the fundamentalist rulers truly believe in their justifications when they abuse the rights of others. Khomeini is an *authentic* man. But authenticity is not necessarily a virtue, a realization that can be existentially painful in certain circumstances. The agents of the Shah's secret police were ashamed of what they were doing. Khomeini's executioners feel proud. Since the fundamentalists deny the very humanity of their critics, they naturally perceive them as opponents without rights. Under these circumstances, the ends always justify the means.

The fundamentalist project does not differentiate between politics and daily life. In the past when Iran was under traditional despotism like that of the Pahlavis, politics was merely one component of life; it did not interfere with the thought and being of the passive or uninterested citizen. But under the totalitarian regime of the fundamentalists, politics provides the method of constructing a supposedly organic society in which every aspect of life is to be integrated with the basic purpose of the state. As the fundamentalists define this basic purpose, no citizen is allowed to stand apart. Constant propaganda, pervasive terror, character assassination, the presence of organized gangs in the streets, and the perpetuation of big lies — all tools of modern totalitarianism — are used to maintain order and exalt the cult of personality. This is a great leap backward because in the Middle East restraining the cult of personality is a precondition for the development of civil society.

Yet Muslim fundamentalists must be seen in their sociohistorical environments. Simply to label them as fanatics, as if that would be an adequate characterization of their being, is an emotional condemnation of a mode of behavior without any effort to understand the causal relations that produced it. The fanatic is always the *other*. This is why in the mass media Muslim fundamentalists are presumed to be frenzied, irrational, thoughtless and brutal. Paraphrasing John Stuart Mill, this picture is at best a falsehood that contains an element of truth. Fanaticism is an enduring ingredient of history and thus those who wish to comprehend their motives and actions ought to refrain from substituting labels for analysis. For fanatics of destruction or rebirth have played a decisive role in inventing our religions, our countries, and our revolutions.

NOTES

1. Barrington Moore, Jr., *Social Origins of Dictatorship and Democracy* (Boston, Mass.: Beacon Press, 1966), p. 485.

2. Imam Khomeini, *Kashf al-Asrar* [Key to the secrets] (Tehran: Ministry of Islamic Guidance, 1980), p. 105. This book was originally published in 1942 and is currently available only in Persian.

3. Ibid., p. 249.

4. Imam Khomeini, *Imam va Enghelab-e Farhangi* [Imam and the cultural revolution] (Tehran: Teachers Training College, 1983), p. 21. This book consists of a collection of statements by Ayatollah Ruhollah Khomeini on cultural issues; it is currently available only in Persian.

5. R. Hrair Dekmejian, *Islam in Revolution: Fundamentalism in the Arab World* (Syracuse, N.Y.: Syracuse University Press, 1985), pp. 81–82.

Mass Death and Autonomous Selves

EDITH WYSCHOGROD

THE DEATHS OF VAST NUMBERS of persons brought about by human agency is the most significant historical event of our time. This is because if we fail to neutralize or eliminate at least one especially threatening form of mass death, nuclear war, the opportunity to resolve other problems, famine in underdeveloped countries or the AIDS crisis, may never arise. To be sure, developing the means to circumvent nuclear disaster and, by extension, chemical and biological warfare, does not assure progress toward the elimination of hunger or a cure for a fatal disease. Nor can we be certain that these or unforeseen alternative catastrophes might not strike us down first. But it is at least arguable that, among the intractable phenomena mentioned, manmade mass death is of our own making and therefore easier to understand, epistemologically cleaner, and more open to alteration by human agents. The common-sense perception is summarized in Vico's remark in the *New Science* that human history and natural history differ in that we have made the one but not the other. Another way of describing this view is that history is the sphere of human freedom. I define freedom as the ability of an agent to affect some future event or events together with the belief that the agent can bring about the outcome intended. The freedom of agents is altered both by internal and external constraints on his or her action.

I have no quarrel with the common-sense view that it may be possible to avoid nuclear war if appropriate measures are taken. Nor do I think such measures are, as Chernus has argued, either facilitated or forestalled because nuclear weapons have acquired a negative sacrality.[1] Instead, the source of my worry is a theory of the self as independent thinker and actor that is bound up with the common-sense view. The received theory, although widely held, has been significantly modified by farsighted anti-Cartesian philosophers for conceptual reasons, and now, in a manner that remains to be specified, is changing under the impact of mass death. The most recent alterations occurred within the comparatively brief compass of the present century and can conveniently be dated as beginning with World War I and continuing to the present.

In what follows, I show how manmade mass death bears on our views of self, freedom, and moral action. In the first section of this paper, I describe two characteristic forms of manmade mass death, the concentration camp system and nuclear war, together with some difficulties that arise in connection with this account of types. In the second section I turn to some models of the self, first the pattern underlying some earlier conceptions of self held by otherwise different thinkers of the Western philosophical tradition, then a later modification of this design, and finally the sea change in the concept of self that is only now coming into focus as a result of manmade mass death. I show that some redescriptions of agency are suggested by the two manifestations of manmade mass death — the camp system and nuclear war — and that these new views are not only consistent with a changed view of self but inseparable from it. In the third section I consider the consequences for moral action that are bound up with these shifts in self-concepts.

TYPES OF MASS DEATH

Wars and natural calamities have decimated whole populations in the past. What is unprecedented in the phenomenon considered here is that the deaths of millions are the result of a rational calculation of *means,* bureaucratic techniques applied to new technologies. Scale is no longer reckoned by head count alone but in terms of the compressed time frame in which the liquidation of persons occurs. But the phenomenon is only loosely described when these features are attributed to it. Close inspection reveals that humanly contrived mass death characteristically shows itself in two quite different ways. The first is a complex of practices and policies that isolate whole populations, herd them together in enclosures or camps, and consign them to slave labor or extinction *tout court*. The second is nuclear war, to be considered later.

Elsewhere I have referred to the first form as the death-world in order to contrast it with what Edmund Husserl called the life-world — the given, taken-for-granted, everyday natural and social world that is the backdrop for all our activities.[2] Spatial and temporal compression and a foreclosing of future options characterize the death-world. This manifestation of manmade mass death aims at the destruction of a specific group of persons and may occur apart from the context of war. Accused (often falsely) of having aims inimical to the interests of the larger embedding society, a group becomes the negative symbol of such social ideals as the Aryan race, the perfect revolutionary, the spirit of the military junta, white supremacy, and the like. It is cordoned off as tainted, impure, and often also morally corrupt. The phenomena generated by this pattern include not only concentration and extermination camps at the far end of the spectrum but also branch forms of varying degrees of severity. Thus hard labor as a technique for reeducating the urban population in Hungary after the revolution of 1956 can be seen as a branch form when compared with the Draconian measures having an allegedly similar aim pursued by the Khmer Rouge after the occupation of Phnom Penh. There is little disagreement that the full force of what lies at the far end of the spectrum — degradation, death, and human suffering on an unprecedented scale — is signified by the term *Auschwitz*. In the technical sense *Auschwitz* refers to the concentration camp located near Oswiescem. The name *Auschwitz*, however, has come to symbolize the vast Nazi extermination program.

It is neither useless nor unimportant to consider other historical phenomena that belong to the complex of events targeting a specified group within an embedding society. It may be helpful to think of these other events as puzzle cases.[3] In doing so a way is cleared for pondering a whole range of phenomena without prejudicing this special character of *Auschwitz*. The events I shall consider are not puzzling in regard to their morally repugnant character or the human suffering inflicted. But they are enigmatic in another way. They raise questions about whether they are phe-

nomenologically identical, the same in every significant respect —
whether, in fact, this can be determined, and, if not, whether one,
both, or neither of these events belong to the death-world *unam-
biguously*. Consider the government-sanctioned disappearance and
murder of some nine thousand civilians by the military government of Argentina that came to an end with its fall from power
in 1983.[4] Although entailing the death of large numbers of "internal enemies," this event is not Auschwitz, the extreme of the death-
world. Is it the same, however, as the detention, torture, and death
of blacks in smaller numbers in prison blocks connected with the
South African government's apartheid policies? Do both count as
death-world events? Is there a point at which the death-world ceases
to exist, a border where one case merits inclusion and the other
not? It is hard to believe that the difference between inclusion and
exclusion could consist in the small differences described between
the South African and the Argentinean cases. It is, to borrow a
term from Derek Parfit, an empty question. Is Argentina but not
South Africa to count as a death-world phenomenon? The claim
that South Africa does not but that Argentina does is neither true
nor false but indeterminate. We can decide arbitrarily to assign
it a place, but doing so in no way changes the description of the
events involved. South Africa and Argentina are simply equiva-
lent to the multiple constituent continuities and connections that
make up these events. This analysis is useful in the present context
because it helps us to grasp the full force and significance of the
far end. Auschwitz is the standard of reference for the death-world.
There are, however, two undesirable possible outcomes of this claim
(a claim I do not dispute) which this analysis helps to defeat. On
the one hand, when the uniqueness of Auschwitz is interpreted
to mean that nothing else is like Auschwitz, this may have the
paradoxical and unintended effect of diminishing rather than increasing its power as a symbol. This view may encourage people
to tolerate extreme injustice because such injustice still falls short
of Auschwitz. On the other hand, if a large number of intolerable
acts are compared to Auschwitz, the enormity of Auschwitz is at-
tenuated or lost. But on the present analysis, Auschwitz remains
sui generis, the darkest of dark death-worlds. Other events need
not be compared with it. At the same time, they need not be forced
into an identity or lack of identity with one another so as to in-

clude or exclude them from the death-world. There need be no answer to the questions that try to do this; they are *empty* questions. The South African and Argentine cases simply are what they are made up of, the arrest and deportation of persons, interrogation under torture, and torture *tout court*. Once the question of whether a worrisome case is still part of the death-world is mooted, each event retains its negative moral force. The result is a certain fluidity among puzzle cases but not a diminishing of the moral significance of each. At the same time, the extraordinary character of the sui generis phenomenon at the far end remains. This is important to my argument because I believe that smaller scale cases reinforce the memory of Auschwitz without attenuating its power or having to establish their credentials in its light. Taken together, present-day events and Auschwitz as a living symbol erode our received notions of self and freedom in a manner still to be interpreted.

Consider now the second type of manmade mass death, nuclear war. It does not help any in trying to grasp the impact on our view of self and freedom to think of nuclear war in terms of gradations in which ambiguous cases arise. This is because nuclear war must be viewed as a *total phenomenon* threatening planetary survival. It is generally agreed, as Lord Zuckerman argues:

> There would be no neutrals in a nuclear war. Nuclear explosions have no regard for national boundaries. That was proved by Chernobyl — a relatively minor nuclear accident compared to what the explosion of a nuclear warhead could do. Whereas in the past the destruction caused by war has been suffered only by the contestants, this would no longer be so in a war in which nuclear weapons were used.[5]

Even if (as is highly improbable) this conclusion is wrong, nuclear conflict is never *imagined* as *une petite guerre*. Even survivors of Hiroshima and Nagasaki, the *hibakshi*, who had no foreknowledge of the bomb's power, describe an eschatological and apocalyptic *grande guerre* in which the whole earth seemed to be coming to an end. Unlike the character of the death-world for which ample detail can be supplied, for obvious reasons there could be no experiential account of present-day nuclear war. But even survivors of the earlier bomb reported that they thought of a nuclear world as futureless in the sense that time had run out.[6]

Earlier it was suggested that the camp system and phenomena linked with it are bound up with notions of *taint* and *impurity*. Nuclear war, however, should be interpreted in a different framework, that of military history. The earliest extended accounts of the *ethoi* of war found in various epic traditions stress the virtues of courage and cunning. Achilles and Odysseus taken together constitute the might of the Hellenes. Because they embody the same martial virtues, the sons of Priam were worthy, if less accomplished and less divinely favored, adversaries. Conflict is aimed at settling a dispute and is played out against the backdrop of Olympian politics. Similarly the biblical book of Samuel establishes ancient Israelite martial tradition, especially in its account of the war against the Philistines. David's exploits, bold and tactically astute, are underwritten by a transcendent power. To be sure, what is holy is holy because loved by God, but God's love comes to rest on one already marked by sagacity and daring. The Indian epic tradition, despite the wavering of Arjuna and some fatalistic aspects of the *karma* tradition described in the *Bhagavad Gita*, endorses daring and cunning within the framework of caste and family. Even when Greek and Israelite perspectives are modified by Israelite prophecy and the Gospels, changes later reflected in the just war tradition, the concept of martial virtue is maintained.

This brief historical sketch is intended only to suggest that the earliest accounts of war are bound up with some specific notions of self and freedom. Individuals are the initiators of actions which are aimed at deciding a disputed issue. The constraints on agency are theological, customary, and calculative. The first two types of constraint establish the framework of agency: the leeway sanctioned by divine power in the deployment of force and the limits imposed by social roles. Within these boundaries calculation and cunning are given free rein. Apart from the dispute to be resolved by war, the allowable intentions and practices of adversaries are roughly symmetrical. But later, when hostilities are extended, there is less and less agreement about more and more. The thinning of consensual ties forces adversaries to trade on what each believes is common to all. (Compare Herodotus' account of the Greeks in the war between Athens and Sparta with

Tacitus' view of Roman citizenship in the campaigns against the Armenians or Syrians.) As agreement about self and freedom based on shared folkways diminishes, it is supplanted by a reflective view. Individuals are increasingly defined in terms of a fundament of rationality taken to be normative for thought, utterance, and action.

Beginning with World War I, events occur which change this picture. Wars are still intended to resolve disputes, but the means for waging war conflict with its stated purpose. War's principal aim becomes depriving the enemy of its armies. The destruction of persons depends on sophisticated weapons systems rather than on tactical genius or relationships in the field. In recent wars, visible adversary lines are drawn among recognizable sociopolitical entities that align bureaucratic and technological power. But invisible undeclared lines exist between those who collectively control these technologies and those who lack effective counterforce. Nuclear war obliterates these boundaries as well in that it is more than likely that those who directly control nuclear arsenals, as well as those who do not, will become its victims.[7]

In one important respect the effects on self and freedom of nuclear war and the death-world converge. Human beings naturally anticipate the future. When war, disease, and natural catastrophe strike, hope for species continuity persists. Even millenarian movements, past and present, assume that for the most part a saving remnant will remain and, if not, someone loosely continuous with a preceding self will arise from the ashes. Both the camp system and nuclear war frustrate this natural anticipation, each in a distinctive way. The camp system replicates imagined conditions of negative postmortem survival, an eternal present complete with torturers and fiery furnaces. Inmates experience themselves as the living dead. Hope centers on the unlikely survival of some few who might establish collective continuity, either symbolic or biological. In the event of full-scale nuclear war such hopes would lack all plausibility. It can be argued that, so long as it is not in any individual's power to prevent nuclear war, perhaps it is better simply to live in the present and so avoid the anxiety of anticipation. If worry about the future ceases, concern for one's own death which cannot be avoided in any case would also fall away.[8] Not only does this argument issue from a misunderstanding about the future-directed aims of present action; it also encourages despair and inhibits constructive response. Because the death-world and nuclear war maintain these negative tendencies come what may, they already play an important part in altering our self-concepts and the uses we make of them. Consider the case in Garrison Keillor's fictional account of the young girl about to be confirmed in the Lutheran Church. "She turned on the TV and lost her faith. Men in khaki suits were beating people senseless, shooting them with machine guns, throwing the bodies out of helicopters . . . and she thought, 'This could happen here.'"[9]

THE STRUCTURE OF SELVES

Accounts of the self in its life circumstances, in the present context those of ancient and modern wars and the death-world, are bound up with the general features attributed to selves by philosophers. Only by observing our everyday comportments can the structure of selves be brought to light. There is widespread agreement about the connectedness of the self in action and the self under philosophical scrutiny even among philosophers who agree about little else. Heidegger's account of the *Dasein*, the existing human being, stands or falls on the notion that its way of being can only be brought out by exhibiting it "in its average everydayness [*Alltäglichkeit*]" as it is first encountered in primordial experiences of the world, time, language, and other persons.[10] Similarly Bernard Williams claims, in the spirit of Wittgenstein, that "how truthfulness to an existing self or society is to be combined with reflection" cannot be explained in the formulations of ethical theorists. Instead such a question might be answered through "reflective living [but not] in the way that [ethical theorists] require an answer, as a piece of philosophy. To suppose that, if their formulations are rejected, we are left with *nothing* is to take a strange view of what in social and personal life counts as something."[11]

The term *self* has fallen into philosophical disrepute because it has often been interpreted substantively as an entity alongside of the thoughts, intentions, desires, habits, and actions that, taken together, make up a unified stream of experience. Despite important differences in Plato, Descartes, Kant, and others, this interpretation of the self as thinglike is entrenched in the history of philosophy. The self is seen as the subject of cognitive, productive, and moral acts. For some philosophers—Locke is an example—the self is said to be the same when the same body accompanies a stream of mental acts unified by memory. For others like Plato, the self's identity is strongest when memory, not of experienced facts but of rational principles alone, perdures in the absence of the body. On both interpretations the self initiates its social relations but is prior to them and can exist apart from them. Hegel, despite the difficulties attached to his philosophy of the Absolute, recognized that consciousness of self arises through the connectedness of selves with one another. The self becomes aware of itself when it learns that it is the object of another's experience. Selves are simply the rich network of social relations in which they engage.

But if selves are relational in the sense described, the boundedness, the individuality, of selves is undermined. Recognizing this difficulty, Heidegger argues that what makes selves individuals is the relation of each self to its own death. I cannot substitute my death for that of another nor can another substitute for mine. I can sacrifice my life for another, but this only buys time. On this view, the self is bound up with body, for even if something outlasts the body, the body must certainly come to an end. To be sure, some philosophers have recently begun to imagine how various techniques that would insure bodily continuity, such as cloning, memory cell transplants, and the like would affect the way we think about whether or not one is the same person. Such strategies may be useful when considering formal questions connected with personal identity but have little bearing on the actualities of the death-world. Those who have survived a death-world event and who say that they are no longer the same connect this claim not with bizarre bodily alterations they may have undergone but with the damaged health and psychological changes their suffering has caused.

In the context of the death-world the body takes on significance in another way. Not only does it become the actual object of violence, but it becomes the symbol for vulnerability to violence.[12] The body also acquires meanings that generally are attached to objects of use. Whereas in everyday life tools are extensions of the body, in the death-world the body again becomes an actual or symbolic tool. In the absence even of the simplest equipment, the hand can both become and symbolize a hammer, the torso and limbs a cart, and the like. At the same time the corporeal aspect of selves should not obscure the self as a transactional network of social relations.

It can be argued against the account of a transactional social self that thoughts, beliefs, intentions, and desires are private. Unless I express what I think or inadvertently give myself away through gestures or slips of the tongue, other persons have no access to my experiences. Even when I speak or gesture, my silent thoughts remain private. There is no denying that others cannot gain direct access to my stream of experience, but this is not a definitive argument against the transactional view. Although there is a stream which remains private, available to me alone, the self to whom the stream is open must be constituted first. Were there no awareness of the stream, there would be nothing for the flow of experiences to relate itself to. This self assumes the standpoint of another to the ongoing rush of experiences. But to be other than another presupposes standing apart in social existence from the start.[13]

It may be useful to use the pronouns *I* and *me* to distinguish functionally awareness of the stream from the stream itself, so long as the *I* is not interpreted as thinglike, a position criticized earlier. The *I* is not something timeless but flashes by to join the *me* and thus to become integrated into the stream. In turn, the flux of experience is always in the process of moving into the past. The *me* grows, lengthening as first person flash points are integrated into the past. The content of the *me* can be communicated to others through language.

It may seem as if the body belongs to the *me* because it is something tangible. This is only partly true. There is an aspect of the body that never becomes objective, because it is through the body — its orientation in space and time, the positioning of the sense organs, the organs themselves — that persons and objects communicate themselves to me. The ensemble of *I* and *me* relate harmoniously as long as the self's transactions with its social and physical world allow it to affect further events. Thus its sphere of freedom as defined earlier is intact although its freedom may vary in degree. But in the death-world physical conditions hostile to life and psychological degradation work together to force an identification by victims with those already dead. In the case of nuclear war, however, human extinction as a result of human acts is envisioned as possible or even likely. For those who have not survived a death-world or the use of nuclear weapons, the two work together to form a background of morbidity against which other experiences are played off. The result is the deterioration of the active *I* with an attendant loss of the self's robustness. This decline of the *I* means not that people are inactive but that the self's relations to the future have been impaired.

BOUNDLESS AND BOUNDED ALTRUISM

While nuclear war and the death-world reinforce the background belief that there will be no future, some distinctions may help clarify the relation to the future of each of these phenomena. For victims of the death-world, projection into both the near and the distant future is curtailed. Because immediate hardship overrides other concerns, there is little thought about the far future except for the often feeble hope that at least some will survive. For those few who emerge alive, wishes bound up with the future come into conflict. On the one hand, survivors believe they should recount their experiences as a way of honoring the dead and warning the living about a possible recurrence of past events. This entails projecting into the far future. A Tibetan monk interviewed at Drepung reports, "I spent 21 years in prison. . . . I know what electric shocks are like. . . . We say if you kill us, the Dalai Lama is still alive."[14] But after release from the death-world, the survivor encounters the nuclear fears common to all. Whatever he or she may believe about future lives, a Tibetan Buddhist who has experienced the deaths of large numbers of other Tibetans faces the general threat of nuclear annihilation. All who are now alive are threatened, so that vast numbers of people share this fear in varying degrees.

The fear of death and the desire to remain alive are not new. Aristotle and Spinoza thought the desire for self-preservation was an expression of a living thing's essence. Hobbes made it the foundation of his ethical system while Nietzsche and Schopenhauer attributed cosmic power to the will to live. For the most part these earlier views took for granted that the natural outcome of the desire for self-preservation is an ethic of self-interest. Nuclear fear for the future reinforced by the death-world's impact on the self does not do away with the desire to remain alive. Instead it overturns the self-interest interpretation of the will to live.

Because the transactional self described earlier is already social, the desire to persevere in one's existence includes other people — if not directly, at least indirectly. The wish for self-preservation under ordinary circumstances encompasses the hope for the continuation of one's social world as well as for oneself since the self as social and transactional is a collective term. In the context of nuclear war, the self so threatened has become a *we* that includes everyone without exception who is now alive as well as future generations. The proposition "I want to remain alive in the nuclear age" cannot be strictly interpreted to mean "I want to survive together with my family." Because the threat of total nuclear war exempts no one, the demand to remain alive must include this newly introjected collective whole. The result is that I am required to consider the fate not only of others to whom I have emotional or prudential attachments, but of all others. The result is that in committing myself to anyone's survival in the context of full-scale nuclear war I am obliged to commit myself to furthering everyone's survival.

Dostoyevsky in *The Brothers Karamazov* makes this point with his parable of the onion. A wicked peasant woman dies leaving no good deeds behind her. When she is plunged into the lake of fire, her guardian angel reminds God that once she gave a beggar woman an onion. God tells the angel to let her grasp the onion and be pulled out on the condition that the onion does not break. Just as the angel is about to succeed, one of the other sinners notices that she is being rescued. They catch hold of her but she hurls them back. "I'm to be pulled out and not you. It's my onion, not yours," she cries. With this, the onion breaks and she is hurled back into the burning lake.[15]

Paradoxically, in the context of nuclear war the very reason for commitment to the whole human community — its possible destruction — is a key factor in creating the backdrop of morbidity, despair, and hopelessness. But an important change has occurred.

Once the self-preservation demand has become other-inclusive, selves are in transition from psychological to ethical selves. This does not assure the ability to withstand the pressure of manmade mass death, especially in the light of the diminished force of the *I*. But the self-emptying that decreases the *I*'s power may have two quite different consequences. On the one hand, without the harmonious balance of *I* and *me* of a more robust self, people may continue to pursue private pleasure, where this is politically and socially feasible; and where it is not they may simply surrender to crushing pressures. In fact, these are the responses of most. The effect of the diminished power of the *I* may result in depersonalization, a privation of the force to initiate activity. On the other hand, it may alter self-concepts so that impersonality, a detached objectivity that permits the destitution or need of the other to come to the fore, may motivate one's own acts. Person predicates are translated into impersonal terms.[16] Such a change is anticipated in the Buddhist view that person predicates are harmful because they reinforce egoism and selfishness. A loosening of this language could have the effect of encouraging benevolence and self-sacrifice.

It is useful in pursuing this point further to consider again the distinction between nuclear war and the death-world. In the context of the death-world, resistance to it from within is nearly impossible, since even extreme acts of sacrifice such as the willingness to surrender one's life for another have little hope for success. In that context acts of generosity such as giving up food or equipment, or willingness when possible to substitute oneself for others when "punishments" are being meted out, count as acts of extreme unselfishness. The scope of the self's freedom is, however, radically curtailed in that victims can hardly affect future events. Because room for action is close to the null point, the amount of effort required on the part of individuals to have an effect is inversely proportional to the rigidity of the system. Still, the destitution of others may motivate acts of extraordinary self-sacrifice. Such acts may miscarry, but, if their intent is understood, they can have paradigmatic force. An example is giving away food to save a life although the victim dies anyway. Some acts that appear selfish, such as staying alive under odious circumstances, may actually be altruistic if they are intended to bring these circumstances to light later. This is because successful acts may be measured not in terms of immediate success but in terms of consequences for a more remote future. Franz Jagerstatter, a German Catholic peasant who refused to be conscripted into the German army during the Nazi period because he believed the war to be unjust, had no effect on the war's outcome, but his act affected the postwar self-evaluation of some German Roman Catholics.[17] The opportunity to act occurred, however, because his freedom was only partially curtailed. Quixotic acts, striking out wildly in a fashion that may unnecessarily injure others, are not exemplary. But in actual situations it is not easy to tell whether acts claimed to be absurd and useless are genuinely so or whether the claim itself reflects a disguised reluctance to act.

The important point is that when the sphere of freedom is radically curtailed, boundless altruism is desirable but is rarely feasible. It does not follow that the right to persevere in existence *excludes* oneself. It cannot become mandatory that one sacrifice one's life. But when the *I* self is transformed into an impersonal, but not depersonalized, self, exceptional individuals may be moved to boundless altruism by the extreme distress of others. Because the simplest altruistic acts are often punished with death, when such acts occur they may become boundlessly altruistic. The impact of such acts may alleviate immediate distress, but on the other hand they may become paradigmatic only in the future.

When egocentrism diminishes in the death-world, the other's suffering is brought to light in a new way, as soliciting benevolence. The other's need does not appeal to sympathy and compassion, because these emotions begin with the self as their affective center and radiate toward the other. As such they cannot provide a starting point for altruism. Instead, the other's plight appears as a language-like appeal in the imperative voice. The other's destitution is not given in the form "X is destitute," but rather as "You *must* help X because she is destitute."[18]

In the case of nuclear war no appeal issues from another to the self. One problem bound up with nuclear threat is our difficulty in picturing it. By touching everyone's life it appears to touch no one's. Individual action to thwart nuclear destruction seems useless. Although the sphere of freedom is far larger than in the death-world, the effect of any one person's efforts is unnoticeable, and individual efforts that are conspicuous may seem quixotic, such as the protest of Matthias Rust, the young West German pilot who landed his small plane on Red Square as a peace protest. The relative ineffectiveness of individual action does not rule out the possibility that large numbers of persons acting in concert might produce perceptible change. However, it can also be argued that, because nuclear arsenals are in the hands of governments, even collective action may prove futile. But governments are made up of social transactional selves and so are not immune to influence. In any event, the threat is sufficiently great to make taking steps worthwhile.

My reason for pursuing the point about collective action is not to advocate any specific course of policy but to provide a backdrop for seeing an important difference between the death-world and nuclear threat as this difference bears on the problem of altruistic action. Boundless altruism, which I link to the death-world, is, odd as it may seem, structurally closer to egoism than to bounded altruism because it presupposes an asymmetry between self and other. The egoist places self-interest ahead of others' interests; the boundless altruist, others' interests before those of self. Bounded altruism, which I link to nuclear war, is based on the parity of selves impersonally considered. Individual action is undertaken in the interest of the human community as a whole rather than in response to the distress of extreme situations.

CONCLUSIONS

Twentieth-century manmade mass death falls into two distinctive categories: the death-world and nuclear war. The first is made up of enclaves in which large numbers of persons are subjected to physical and psychological suffering and death. Auschwitz is the extreme case, but the status of other morally repugnant cases must be considered. Both the death-world and nuclear war reinforce one another in diminishing the self's capacity for spontaneous action. Depersonalization and diminished effectiveness in the face of pandemic death are the result. But freedom, an agent's capacity to affect future events, requires separate analysis in each context. In the death-world exceptional individuals may not suffer depersonalization. Instead, egolessness may take the form of impersonality that, together with minimally enabling circumstances, may allow the agent to put aside selfish claims and act with boundless altruism. Such individuals interpret another's destitution as a moral claim for which they are answerable. Indicative statements about the suffering of others are taken as imperatives demanding moral responses. Restrictions on freedom, however, make all action perilous.

The threat of nuclear war affects all persons alive as well as future generations. Even if the sphere of freedom in which action is possible is enlarged, the effect that any one person's actions can have is limited. Under these circumstances, limited benevolence is called for. This follows from the claim that a transactional social self which desires to persevere in existence includes a relational field of others in its wish. Once the whole human community is threatened, the self must wish for the survival of everyone in wishing for the preservation of a few.

NOTES

1. Ira Chernus, *Dr. Strangegod: On the Symbolic Meaning of Nuclear Weapons* (Charleston, S.C.: University of South Carolina Press, 1985).

2. Edmund Husserl, *The Crisis of European Sciences and Transcendental Phenomenology*, trans. David Carr (Evanston, Ill.: Northwestern University Press, 1970), pp. 142–43.

3. The notion of *puzzle cases* is developed in Derek Parfit, *Reasons and Persons* (Oxford: Oxford University Press, 1986), pp. 213, 239.

4. Figures cited are from "The Pope and the Victims," *Topics of the Times, New York Times*, 15 April 1987.

5. Lord Solly Zuckerman, "The Nuclear Hope," *New York Review of Books*, 7 May 1987, p. 44.

6. Robert J. Lifton, *Death in Life: Survivors of Hiroshima* (New York: Basic Books, 1982), esp. chap. 1.

7. For a more extended analysis of this point see Edith Wyschogrod, *Spirit in Ashes: Hegel, Heidegger, and Man-Made Mass Death* (New Haven, Conn.: Yale University Press, 1985), pp. 52–57.

8. In support of the position that worry about the future is undesirable see Parfit, *Reasons and Persons*, pp. 174–77.

9. Garrison Keillor, *Leaving Home* (New York: Viking Press, 1987), p. 234.

10. Martin Heidegger, *Being and Time*, trans. John Macquarrie and Edward Robinson (New York: Harper & Row, 1962), 370, p. 421.

11. Bernard Williams, *Ethics and the Limits of Philosophy* (Cambridge, Mass.: Harvard University Press, 1985), p. 200.

12. For an analysis of the symbolic significance of torture see Elaine Scarry, *The Making and Unmaking of the World* (New York: Oxford University Press, 1985).

13. For an analysis of the self along comparable lines see George Herbert Mead, *On Social Psychology: Selected Papers*, ed. Anselm Strauss (Chicago: University of Chicago Press, 1964), pp. 242ff.

14. Edward Gargan, "In a Silent Monastery: God, Tears, and Fears," *New York Times*, 6 October 1987.

15. Fyodor Dostoyevsky, *The Brothers Karamazov*, trans. Constance Garnett (New York: Random House, n.d.), pp. 369–70.

16. Thomas Nagel, *The Possibility of Altruism* (Princeton, N.J.: Princeton University Press, 1986), p. 281. See also Parfit, *Reasons and Persons*, p. 225.

17. Jagerstatter's life is the subject of Gordon Zahn, *In Solitary Witness: The Life and Death of Franz Jagerstatter* (London: Geoffrey Chapman, 1966).

18. Emmanuel Levinas makes this point the centerpiece of his ethical metaphysics. See especially *Totality and Infinity*, trans. Alphonso Lingis (Pittsburgh: Duquesne University Press, 1969).

Early Advocates of Lasting World Peace: Utopians or Realists?[1]

SISSELA BOK

THE PLANS THAT Erasmus, the Abbé de Saint-Pierre, Kant, and others offered for moving toward a universal and perpetual peace have long been dismissed as utopian or hypocritical, at times even suppressed as dangerously heretical. These thinkers challenged the common perception of war as an immutable aspect of the human condition and of lasting peace as possible, if at all, only in the hereafter — a perception that has seemed self-evident to most commentators from antiquity onwards, whether they espouse what has come to be called a realist, a pacifist, or a just war perspective.

In the nuclear age, however, nations can no longer afford to leave that perception unchallenged. They cannot run the risk of yet another world war, even in the unlikely event that such a war could be kept nonnuclear. Today's conventional weapons would bring devastation beyond anything that humanity has experienced. Likewise, prolonged regional conflicts are increasingly seen as intolerable, given the levels of impoverishment, homelessness, and suffering that they inflict, as well as the risk that they will ignite large-scale war. The social and environmental threats that nations now face collectively, moreover, call for unprecedented levels of cooperation that will be unattainable except under conditions of lasting peace.

If, therefore, self-preservation now dictates collective efforts toward a lasting world peace, no matter how difficult to achieve, it is worth reexamining the writings of those who once pioneered such an approach. To be sure, they had more than their share of quick-fix solutions; and the particulars of even the most sophisticated of their plans can hardly be adequate for today's international relations. But two aspects of the best among their writings are as relevant today as in the past: first, their intrepid challenges to the common assumption that war will always be with us; and second, their suggestions for how to create a social climate conducive to the forging of a stable peace.

In the works of Desiderius Erasmus and Immanuel Kant, these lines of reasoning are pursued with special subtlety and force. They are as relevant to practical choice by contemporary governments, organizations, and individuals as to theories of war and peace. By now, many proponents of realist, just war, and pacifist theories have come to agree on the necessity of working toward the goal of lasting peace, while continuing to differ about the means. It will help, in debating the means, to consider the coordinated, practical measures explored by these two thinkers in the light of all that we have later learned about which ones work best and why. In turn, such a study will require a rethinking, from within each of the three theoretical perspectives, of the role and the demands of morality in international relations.

I

It will be enough for me, however, if these words of mine are judged useful by those who want to understand clearly the events which took place in the past and which (human nature being what it is) will, at some time or other and in much the same ways, be repeated in the future.

Thucydides, *The Peloponnesian Wars*

The conflict between Athens and Sparta depicted by Thucydides has been reenacted time and again over the centuries. Most thinkers since his time, whether they have gloried in war, tolerated it, or denounced it, have taken for granted that it will remain a constant in the human condition. To be sure, they have argued, it can be staved off for a time or fenced away from one or more regions of the world; but experience shows that it cannot be eradicated for good. To think otherwise is to be caught in an illusion.

They have explained the perennial nature of war by referring, as did Thucydides in the passage cited above, to incorrigible traits in human nature such as pugnacity, vindictiveness, partisanship, and the lust for conquest and power. They have also invoked the external circumstances of scarcity and hardship that drive communities to fight one another in order to survive. These traits and circumstances have in turn often been seen as inflicted on human beings by fate or some supernatural power. Thus Homer portrays the gods as prolonging the Trojan War by using participants for purposes of sport or intrigue or amusement. And the biblical God has been interpreted as imposing hardship and tribulation to punish human beings, to test them, or to separate the just from the unjust.

The debate about how to respond to such a predicament was, for centuries, largely three-cornered. Against the common background of war as a constant in the human condition, the responses accorded with one or the other of what we now call the realist, pacifist, and just war traditions.

Realists, often invoking Thucydides, held that it was useless and perhaps even dangerous to rail against the cruelty and immorality of anything as perennial as war. What mattered, rather, was to act according to the best available strategic estimates of what would serve a ruler's or nation's self-interest. In this way, engaging in wars for the sake of preserving or increasing a nation's independence, wealth, or power was acceptable, even commendable. Moral judgments about the rights and wrongs committed in starting any particular war or in its conduct were, according to such a view, at best beside the point.

Tertullian, Origen, and other early Christian pacifists argued, on the contrary, that morality and religion commanded human beings to renounce war and all killing. No matter how prevalent war might be and no matter what interests any one war might serve, the Christian's duty was to refuse all participation. Otherwise the biblical injunctions to love one's enemy and to turn the other cheek would lose all meaning.

Just war theorists, from Augustine and Thomas Aquinas on, advocated, on similarly religious and moral grounds, limiting rather

than renouncing the recourse to war. Among the causes these thinkers regarded as justifying going to war were, variously, wars fought
in self-defense, wars in defense of an ally, and wars of conquest
and crusade to punish wrongdoing and to convert unbelievers. But
justice also required careful scrutiny of the conduct of the warring forces, no matter how just the cause to which they laid claim.

Beginning in the sixteenth century, a fourth pattern emerged
among the responses to the prevalence of war—that of Erasmus
and other advocates of specific, practical steps toward what they
called "perpetual peace." They challenged, not only the commonly
accepted thesis regarding war's perennial nature, but also the specific claims of thinkers in the existing three traditions regarding
when, if ever, war was legitimate. Because the proposals for a lasting peace were often summarily dismissed or even suppressed, they
did not constitute a lineage of well-known fundamental texts, nor
give rise to the wealth of commentary generated by the other traditions. As a result, advocates of perpetual peace were rarely seen
as contributing to a tradition separate from that of pacifism. By
now, however, it is becoming increasingly clear that they were
shaping a new tradition of thinking about war and peace fully
as worthy of study as the three others. To this tradition belong,
among others, Erasmus, William Penn, the Abbé de Saint-Pierre,
Immanuel Kant, and Jeremy Bentham.[2] Among its interpreters
and critics are Leibniz, Rousseau, and Hegel.[3]

Thinkers in this fourth tradition had no illusions that peace
was somehow a natural state for the human species. And they could
hardly quarrel with the historical record of recurrent aggression,
injustice, and warfare. They meant, rather, to challenge what they
saw as the unthinking extrapolation from that past experience to
the future, the unwarranted inference from what has been to what
must always be. Over time, they argued, nations could break away
from the destructive patterns of the past. But they had little faith,
unlike a number of utopians, in some convulsive political or religious transformation that would bring permanent harmony—the
more so as they had seen at close hand the corrupting and brutal-
izing effects of unrestrained violence both on perpetrators and on
victims, no matter how humane the original motives.

The synthesis arrived at by these thinkers was eloquently
voiced by Erasmus and formulated with greater precision, clarity,

and scope by Kant. It employs both the realist language of strategy and the normative language common to pacifists and just war theorists. According to this view, nations can only achieve lasting strategic benefits by respecting fundamental moral constraints. But it does little good merely to stress these constraints without setting forth concerted, practical steps to facilitate and reinforce their observance. War may indeed continue to be our lot, they admit; but we are free to choose differently. Each generation, far from being condemned to reenact the errors of the past, has the opportunity to learn from the mistakes and disasters of previous generations, and thus the capacity to move toward a state of perpetual peace.

II

> What is more brittle than the life of man? How short
> its natural duration! How liable to disease, how exposed
> to momentary accidents! Yet though natural and inevi-
> table evils are more than can be borne with patience,
> man, fool that he is, brings the greatest and worst ca-
> lamities upon his own head. . . . To arms he rushes at
> all times and in all places; no bounds to his fury, no end
> to his destructive vengeance.
>
> Erasmus, *The Complaint of Peace*, 1517

Few have spoken out more forcefully than Erasmus about the folly and cruelty of war. Already in his *Adages*, published in 1500 and reportedly more widely circulated at the time than any other book save the Bible, he had inveighed against war in an essay entitled "Dulce bellum inexpertis," or "War Is Sweet to Those Who Have Not Experienced It."[4] Between 1514 and 1517, when a brief interval in the near-constant wars between European powers made a more lasting peace seem at least possible, Erasmus devoted himself wholeheartedly to helping bring it about.[5] He suggested summoning a *congress of kings* — a *summit meeting* among the kings of Europe — for the purpose of signing an indissoluble peace agreement. He revised and expanded his essay on the sweetness of war to the inexperienced for the latest edition of the *Adages*. And he wrote a manual for princes — *The Education of the Christian Prince* — to guide the young Prince Charles of Spain who was shortly to become Charles V.[6]

This book presents a striking contrast to Machiavelli's *Prince*, written a few years earlier but still unpublished.[7] Where Machiavelli had broken away from the stress on virtues so common in previous books of advice for princes, and urged the prince to resort to violence, deceit, and betrayal whenever necessary to gain or retain power, Erasmus emphasized moral virtues as prerequisites to a good reign. And whereas Machiavelli had urged the prince to study war above all else, Erasmus gave precedence to learning "the arts of peace": how to establish and preserve a rule of just laws, improve the public's health, ensure an adequate food supply, beautify cities and their surroundings, and master the diplomatic alternatives to war. A last, brief chapter, entitled "On Beginning War," counsels the prince never to go to war at all, save as a last resort; but "if so ruinous an occurrence cannot be avoided," then the prince should wage it with a minimum of bloodshed and conclude the struggle as soon as possible.[8]

A year after publishing his *Education*, Erasmus returned to the charge with *The Complaint of Peace*.[9] This time he sent his book to all the rulers of Europe rather than addressing it to one prince alone. Peace, speaking "in her own person, rejected from all countries," is the protagonist of this book. Her complaint addresses the irrationality and inhumanity of war. Of all the evils that beset humanity, she argues, surely war is the most puzzling, because it is self-chosen. If the insults and indignities heaped upon her went along with advantages to mortals, she could at least understand why they might persecute her. But since they unleashed a deluge of calamities upon themselves through engaging in war, she has to speak to them of their misfortune even more than complain of her own.

In these several works, Erasmus gives short shrift to the realist and just war schools of thinking that ruled the day at the courts of Spain and other European powers. At the same time he distances himself from pacifist calls for nonresistance at all times. However attractive a war may seem at the outset, first of all, Erasmus argues, it appeals to dreamers, not to realists. From war "comes the shipwreck of all that is good and from it the sea of all calamities."[10] Claims about the benefits of war result, he argues, from inexperience. Those who have had to live through war are too rarely consulted. As a result, each generation foolishly undertakes to learn about war's costs from scratch. Even on the strictest strategic grounds of national self-interest, Erasmus insists, a truly realistic look at the costs of war should dissuade a prince from just about all recourse to arms.

Second, Erasmus is skeptical about claims that particular crusades and wars are just. He writes scornfully of the spectacle of clergy on both sides of so many wars declaiming the just cause of their own rulers. When does one not think one's own cause just? he asks, warning that the likelihood of bias and corruption is so great in seeking reasons for going to war that "the good Christian Prince should hold under suspicion every war, no matter how just."[11] This suspicion, he held, was the more necessary since so many conquests and crusades were being fought in the name of the Christian Church, even though "the whole philosophy of Christ teaches against it."[12]

Third, Erasmus addresses pacifist concerns by holding that wars in self-defense are, indeed, legitimate, but only after all other alternatives, including arbitration, have been exhausted; and only after obtaining the consent of the people, who will, after all, suffer so much more directly from any war than their rulers. If such procedures were taken seriously, it is doubtful whether any war would remain to be fought. But the decision to avoid going to war would then be made on pragmatic as well as religious and moral grounds, rather than constituting an absolutist rejection of all war no matter what the costs.

In *The Complaint of Peace*, Erasmus advances a carefully reasoned attack on the underlying assumption widely shared in his day as in our own: that violent conflict and organized war are somehow inherent in the human condition. He discusses each of the three most common explanations for why human existence should be so burdened with the ravages and deaths that war brings: that war will always be with us because of indelible deficiencies in human nature, unrelenting outside pressures, or divine intention — perhaps because of all three.

To those who embrace the first explanation and point to aggression and vindictiveness as human traits so pervasive that they

eliminate all chances of a lasting peace, Erasmus responds by asking, What is it in human beings that predisposes them to war? Are
they saddled with indelible personality traits that preclude all
chances of a lasting peace? How do we have to envisage human
nature for this to be true? If it carries with it traits that make wars
inevitable, Erasmus begins, they cannot be traits shared with animals, since animals show no organized hostility to members of their
own species. The conduct of human beings can be so much baser
than that of animals that the word *bestiality* bestowed upon the
worst forms of human conduct is unfair to animals.[13] Neither the
viciousness that human beings can show one another nor the increasingly destructive machinery they were coming to employ in
combat had equivalents elsewhere in nature.

What about the traits which distinguish persons from animals? Surely they are not such as to predispose us to war. Our
human capacity to reason, our inability to survive alone that
makes us dependent on family and society, and our "power of
speech, the most conciliating instrument of social connexion and
cordial love"—these traits, he argues, need hardly be conducive
to war. On the contrary, they should predispose human beings to
living with one another in peace, not war. It is only our familiar-
ity with everlasting feuds, litigation, and murder, that produces
the conduct that we mistake for a natural predisposition to war—
the more readily so if leadership, education, and social reforms
offer no counterbalance.

To the second standard explanation—that outside pressures
of scarcity and hardship and natural calamities inevitably cause
recurrent conflicts—Erasmus answers that it is surely madness to
add to these undoubted outside pressures all the suffering that wars
bring. The corruption into which human societies have fallen has
rendered them unable to deal in the most reasonable way with
conflicts engendered by such hardships. For the state of affairs in
his own period, Erasmus holds rulers responsible above all others.
In their greed and folly, they repeatedly and mindlessly drag their
peoples into the tragedy of war. But rulers cannot wreak this havoc
by themselves. Hatred and conflict have become endemic. Erasmus catalogues the groups which harbor such traits. There are
citizens given to strife and dissension; courtiers poisoning the climate with their intrigues and grudges; scholars and theologians

at daggerheads with one another; clergy and monastics tearing one another to pieces through their partisan disputes; mercenary soldiers feeding as vermin on the miseries they inflict on human communities.

The third explanation common since antiquity — that the human predisposition to war is due to divine intention — could in principle account for the first two and undercut all proposals for reform. While human nature may not by itself be destined for perennial warfare and while outside pressures might not of their own precipitate it, God may have seen to it that these conditions would nevertheless persist. In response to such theological claims, Erasmus invokes Scripture. Christ's central message is one of peace, forgiveness, and nonviolence. If anyone has intended the brutal, near-constant warfare which admittedly beset Europe in his time, he suggests, it must rather be Satan.

Having countered the three explanations most often brought forth to buttress ancient dogmas about the inevitability of war, Erasmus turns to the future. Though a lasting peace is possible, great changes are needed to bring it about. Peace cannot simply be ordained by religious or political authorities, nor can it be mandated merely through treaties and alliances alone. Rather, it has to be undertaken at every level of society. Kings must work together for the good of their citizens and consult them before embarking on any war. And citizens must grant kings "just so many privileges and prerogatives as are for the public good and no more."[14] Erasmus, who never ceased criticizing kings for their exploitative and brutal schemings at the expense of their peoples, here hints at the alternative of government limited by democratic consent — hard to envisage in his time and dangerous for anyone to promote. If nations submitted, further, to an international court of arbitration, they could avert many wars; if need be, peace should be purchased to prevent still others.

Bishops and priests must likewise unite against war and cease appealing to just war theory to excuse every war their king or the pope undertakes. The nobility and all magistrates must also collaborate in the work of peace. To each of these groups, and to "all who call themselves Christians," Erasmus pleads: "unite with one heart and one soul, in the abolition of war, and the establishment of perpetual and universal peace."[15] But beyond Christianity, Erasmus also wishes to suggest that the hostilities between faiths and nationalities could be tempered if only people reflected that they are, above all, members of the same human race: "If name of country is of such a nature as to create bonds between those who have a common country, why do not men resolve that the universe should become the country of all?"[16]

During the remaining decades of his life, Erasmus saw the world move relentlessly in the opposite direction. Wars of conquest succeeded one another, religious and ideological persecution spread, and the religious conflicts that would later culminate in the Thirty Years' War intensified. Though frequently reprinted, Erasmus's writings on war and peace fell out of favor in many quarters. To militants of every persuasion, his insistence on arbitration and other peaceful means of resolving conflicts seemed an endorsement of cowardice and vacillation. Over time, his work was deprecated, even outlawed. As a result, later advocates of perpetual peace too often ignored the depth and scope of his proposals. They tended, rather, to stress purely diplomatic methods for achieving lasting peace. Thus the Abbé de Saint-Pierre proposed, in 1712, a permanent league of European rulers under common laws.[17] Even today, most texts dealing with issues of war and peace mention Erasmus only in passing, if at all.

III

Wars, tense and unremitting military preparations, and the resultant distress which every state must eventually feel within itself, even in the midst of peace — these are the means by which nature drives nations to make initially imperfect attempts, but finally, after many devastations, upheavals, and even complete inner exhaustion of their powers, to take the step which reason could have suggested to them even without so many sad experiences — that of abandoning a lawless state of nature and entering a federation of peoples in which every state, even the smallest, could expect to derive its security and rights. . . .

Immanuel Kant, "Idea for a Universal History with a Cosmopolitan Purpose"

It was not until Kant published his essay on "Perpetual Peace" in 1795, building on earlier works such as his article on "Universal History," that individual and institutional change were once again brought into public debate as prerequisites for arriving at a lasting peace.[18] Like Erasmus, Kant argues that such a state of peace is fully achievable, even though war, thus far, has been a constant factor in the human condition. But Kant sees greater obstacles to achieving such a peace than Erasmus ever conceded.

Kant shares, first of all, the Hobbesian view of international relations as anarchic. Nations exist in a "lawless state of nature" where "the depravity of human nature is displayed without disguise," whereas, within civil societies, it is at least controlled by governmental constraints.[19] Unlike Erasmus, Kant also agreed with those who held that wars had served important purposes throughout history and had most likely even been intended for such purposes by nature. Without the incentives provided by competition, lust for power, and conflict, human beings might never have developed their talents or their technology much beyond the animal stage. But wars had become increasingly destructive and risked becoming even more so, to the point where a war of extermination could bring about "perpetual peace only on the vast graveyard of the human race."[20] As a result, the time had come when nations would have to break out of the state of nature or perish.

Given Kant's concessions to the holders of the majority thesis, how did he envisage that such a change might be brought about? To begin with, he saw grounds for hope that nature has intended such a shift for human beings. We cannot prove that this is so, nor even infer it, but it is "more than an empty chimera."[21] Each individual life is brief and flawed, but through experience, human beings may eventually achieve a sufficient degree of rationality and the capacity to cooperate in achieving security for themselves and their descendants. That it is *possible* for human beings, thus equipped, to change is clear. Kant acknowledges that human beings do exhibit a propensity to evil and to war, but they also possess a predisposition to good. They are at all times free to choose to act according to what they recognize as right and to guide their lives differently. Though peace will not come of its own accord nor from some oversupply of human goodness, it can be instituted, if chosen.

But bringing peace about will require far more than the piece-meal reforms too often advocated. Plans such as those of the Abbé de Saint-Pierre have been ridiculed as wild and fanciful, Kant suggests, in part because their proponents took for granted that the necessary changes were imminent, easy to institute, and unproblematic. Any realistic approach would have to be based on the recognition that change would be slow to come, that it would require reforms at every level of national and international society, and that such reforms would be bound to fail over and over again unless measures were first taken to change the very atmosphere in which negotiations are carried out.

Accordingly, Kant began his essay on "Perpetual Peace" by proposing a set of "preliminary articles" to help prepare the social climate for the larger institutional reforms. Some of these preliminary articles set forth steps that governments could take right away to reduce the distrust standing in the way of all meaningful cooperation. If governments could negotiate peace agreements without secret reservations concerning future wars; if they could abstain from forcible interference in the affairs of other nations; and if they could, even when at war, discontinue what he called "dishonorable stratagems" such as the breach of agreements or treaties, the employment of assassins, and the instigation of treason within one another's states, then they would, at the very least, not be poisoning the atmosphere for peace negotiations.[22]

By stressing basic moral constraints not only within but also between nations Kant does not mean to say that these constraints, by themselves, will provide all that is needed to ensure a lasting peace.[23] He merely insists that so long as they are not taken into account, there can be no chance whatsoever of instituting such a peace. Distrust, as Hobbes had pointed out before him, undermines the incentive to cooperate. Little wonder, then, Kant argues, that a lasting peace has been out of reach. The *reasons* for such debilitating distrust have never been carefully addressed. But at the same time, we need not imagine that peace will continue to elude humankind, once the constraints are taken seriously and once it becomes clear that they are indispensable to long-term collective survival.

Along with creating a climate that allows for institutional reform, Kant sees three "definitive articles" as necessary for a perpetual peace among nations. The first calls for the achievement, over time, of a world in which more and more states have representative governments elected by free citizens equal before the law. Such a form of government will do much to cut back on the wars of any state, since citizens tend to be far less enthusiastic about wars they know they will have to pay for and fight in than autocratic leaders who impose taxes and give orders from the sidelines. But of course, citizens in such states can still be persuaded to concur in wars of conquest by skillful propaganda. As a result, additional international measures are necessary. The second article proposed by Kant calls for the joining together of states in a federation capable of keeping a just peace. The third calls for respecting the human rights of visitors or outsiders to such states so as not to enslave or conquer them.

Kant may well have been thought utopian to speak of the spread of representative government as conducive to lasting peace at a time when only the young American republic could lay claim to a stable form of such governance, and to invoke "a universal right of humanity" in condemning slavery and imperialistic conquests in a period when these practices were so widespread. But he insisted that such an idea was not "fantastic and overstrained." "Only under this condition can we flatter ourselves that we are continually advancing toward a perpetual peace."[24]

IV

In your hands rests our future. By your labors at this conference we shall know if suffering humanity is to achieve a just and lasting peace.

President Harry S. Truman, speaking to delegates
at the opening session of the UN Conference
in San Francisco, April 23, 1945

In 1953, President Dwight D. Eisenhower spoke of the change that the Cold War had brought since that "hopeful spring of 1945." At that time, "the hope of all just men . . . was for a just and lasting peace. The eight years that have passed have seen that hope waver, grow dim, and almost die. And the shadow of fear again has darkly lengthened across the world."[25] That shadow has continued to lengthen. By now, over seventeen million people, most of them civilians, have died in wars since the end of the Second World War, and many more have been driven from their homes. The great powers have built up vast stockpiles of nuclear weapons with unprecedented destructive potential, and still more nations stand poised to follow suit. As a result, Kant's warning that a war of extermination could bring perpetual peace on the vast graveyard of humanity has taken on a directness in the nuclear age that even he could hardly have predicted.

The full horror of such a prospect has decisively shifted the incentives with respect to war. It has become a commonplace for world leaders to speak of the necessity of lasting peace. In principle, if not yet when it comes to implementation, they have agreed to make every effort to avoid unleashing, even accidentally, another major war.

So it is no wonder that we are also witnessing a realignment within the several traditions of thinking about war and peace. Their exponents are moving closer to one another, and in turn — often without knowing it — to the principled yet practical stance by which thinkers in the perpetual peace tradition combined moral and strategic considerations.

Already during the nineteenth century, many pacifists adopted the language of the perpetual peace tradition, its stress on step-by-step efforts to strengthen conditions for lasting peace, and its support for international organizations. Thus British Quakers founded a "Society for the Promotion of Permanent and Universal Peace" in 1816.[26] They disagreed among themselves, as did other pacifists, about whether to endorse complete nonresistance in all wars or to accept resistance in clear cases of self-defense when all other methods have failed. This disagreement still persists among pacifists today. Many who, like Tolstoy, were once in favor of unilateral disarmament and noncooperation with all military activities, including strictly defensive ones, have had to weigh whether such a stance with respect to nuclear weapons might not increase, rather than decrease, the risks to humanity. "Do what is right though the earth should perish" has taken on an entirely new and more literal meaning since Hiroshima and Nagasaki.[27]

Only a minority of those active in contemporary peace movements adopt such an absolutist stance. But the threat to collective survival posed by nuclear weapons has induced many to focus their attention on weapons systems and government military strategy. Their research and advocacy has at times reflected back, as in a mirror, the priorities of their opponents; and the underlying moral debate has centered on issues of violence and nonviolence. But as the events beginning in the late 1980s continue to unfold, it is becoming increasingly clear that the chances for peace depend on a complex linkage of individual, domestic, and international policies. Shifts in military strategy do not lead but rather follow upon a restructuring of such policies, as seen in the present thawing of the Cold War. A more comprehensive moral framework is needed, in which nonviolence plays a central but not exclusive role. In the Philippines, in East Germany, in Czechoslovakia, and in Hungary, "people power" has shown itself victorious in the face of massively armed governments. As Václav Havel long continued to insist at great personal risk, citizens who are "living in truth" can overthrow dictatorships by nonviolent means.

Realists, whether of a practical or a theoretical bent, are increasingly driven to reconsider their most fundamental presuppositions in the face of the present predicament. Many among them once argued that strict national self-interest should dictate foreign policy, quite apart from what might be desirable for other nations, and that morality was beside the point in international relations. By now, the first argument has had to be sharply modified and the second abandoned. National self-interest now clearly mandates a concern for comprehensive international security. International security, in turn, is affected by such factors as hunger, deforestation, and population growth the world over.

Even from a strictly strategic point of view, therefore, it matters to attend to these factors. Doing so necessitates being alert to the role of moral claims, such as those voiced the world over regarding fundamental human rights. References to human rights abroad were once dismissed by many realists as sentimental, given political realities in most nations, and as potentially counterproductive efforts to interfere with sovereign states. But the political power of calls for human rights can no longer be denied, nor their importance to foreign relations. The same is true with respect to the action or inaction on the part of governments in matters of environmental or nuclear strategy. It is not surprising, therefore, that George Kennan, who has long argued against the assumption "that state behavior is a fit subject for moral judgment," does not hesitate to express such moral judgments when it comes to nuclear weapons. In *The Nuclear Delusion*, he cries out, in a tone that Erasmus would not have disowned, against the readiness to use nuclear weapons against other human beings, thus placing in jeopardy all of civilization, calling it a blasphemy and "an indignity of monstrous proportions."[28]

Contemporary just war theorists, unlike those in the realist tradition, have consistently advanced moral claims in the context of war and peace. If the nuclear balance of terror has accelerated a shift, on their part, in the direction of Erasmus and Kant, it has been in reducing the range of wars seen as potentially just ones. It is hard, at present, to see many wars as likely to serve the cause of justice. Whereas Augustine and Thomas Aquinas argued in favor of certain wars to avenge wrongs, the U.S. Catholic Bishops stated, in 1983, that "if war of retribution was ever justifiable, the risks of modern war negate such a claim today."[29] They restate the just war position so as to exclude, in the contemporary world, nearly all wars as unjust except those of strict self-defense or defense of others under attack, and only then as a last resort. And, like Erasmus and Kant, they emphasize the monumental injustice of governments in channeling such a vast proportion of the world's scarce resources into armaments, calling it "an act of aggression upon the poor."[30]

Marxists have also been narrowing the very different criteria that V. I. Lenin and Mao-tse Tung elaborated for when wars are just. Lenin held that wars against oppressors by wage earners and enslaved or colonized peoples were fully legitimate, progressive, and necessary. "Whosoever wants a lasting and democratic peace must stand for civil war against the government and the bourgeoisie."[31] Mao likewise argued that the only just wars are nonpredatory wars, wars of liberation. "Communists will support every just and nonpredatory war for liberation, and they will stand in the forefront of the struggle."[32] But it has become increasingly difficult to maintain that the fanning of regional wars has promoted justice. The faith that a lasting peace is bound to result from such warfare is faltering even among many committed Marxists. Similarly, Marx's castigation of moral claims as "ideological nonsense" is undergoing impassioned rejection throughout much of the Communist world.[33]

In all these respects, Kant's essay on "Perpetual Peace" bears rereading. Nearly two centuries after its publication, and especially after the events of 1989, it no longer seems fantastic or overstrained to link the chances for peace with the respect for human rights and with the growing cooperation between nations in which those rights are protected by representative forms of government.

Just as contemporary thinkers who once rejected fundamental moral claims as irrelevant or postponed them as premature have been led to take them into consideration on strict realist grounds, so, too, have many who once based their position on strictly normative claims had to acknowledge that strategic realities affect their choices. While the goal of lasting peace may still seem out of reach, it no longer makes either strategic or moral sense for governments, policy advisers, or theorists to fail to move in the direction of that goal.

But if so many have come to take such a goal seriously as at least worth striving for, however utopian it seemed when first advocated by thinkers in the perpetual peace tradition, then there is reason to take equally seriously the ways of moving closer to that goal that they suggested. Clearly they could not have foreseen the kinds of negotiations required by today's weapons and international alignments, nor the present social and environmental threats to humanity. These developments call for responses of a complexity that no one could have predicted centuries ago. But the tradition of perpetual peace may be much more helpful when it comes to exploring the crucial role of the social climate that determines whether or not adequate levels of cooperation will be possible, and the framework of moral constraints needed at every level of society to keep that climate from deteriorating.[34]

Our century has seen the development of new strategies for bringing about change in ways that respect the social climate. The tradition of nonviolent resistance to oppression that began with Mohandas Gandhi in India and continued in the civil rights struggle led by Martin Luther King, Jr., in the United States has influenced political change in countries as different as South Korea and East Germany. During the past year, we have witnessed a striking contrast. While peaceful revolutions produced astounding successes in one country after another in Eastern Europe, fighting dragged on with no end in sight in Lebanon, Ethiopia, El Salvador, and too many other nations, producing only further suffering. Few have doubted that nonviolent resistance is more respectful of human rights and less likely to brutalize and corrupt its participants. What is becoming increasingly clear is that, with the help of modern communications media, such resistance can also bring speedier and more far-reaching results. Being more protective of the social climate, it is also more conducive to the cooperation that is so desperately needed once the struggle is over.

To be sure, nothing guarantees that those who lead such movements to victory can govern well, or that changes wrought with nonviolent means will not once again succumb to violence. Nor do all efforts at nonviolent resistance succeed, as Tiananmen Square and too many other examples demonstrate. But even when the latter efforts meet with repression, as did Solidarity for years, nonviolent movements have a better chance of ultimately succeeding than groups that resort to a violent uprising.

Only time will tell whether a cumulative process of nonviolent and principled efforts at domestic and international change can, in the long run, disprove the age-old assumption that war will always be with us. Much that Erasmus, Kant, and others suggested, such as giving citizens a voice with respect to whether or not to undertake a war, convening international parleys and federations, and submitting disputes to arbitration, must have seemed highly improbable — indeed utopian — at the time. The word *utopia* can have two meanings. One indicates an excellent place or society that is possible but at present merely visionary; the second refers, rather, to an unattainable society advocated by impractical idealists. In arguing that it is possible for human beings to establish a lasting world peace, Erasmus and Kant may well have been utopian in the first sense; but we have everything to lose by not trying to disprove the claim that they were also utopian in the second.

NOTES

1. This essay was published in *Ethics and International Relations* 4 (April 1990): 145–61.

2. For the works by Erasmus that contributed most to this tradition, see notes 3, 5, and 7 below. See also Edwin D. Mead., ed., *The Great Design of Henry IV from the Memoirs of the Duke of Sully* (1559–1641) (Boston: Ginn & Co., 1909); William Penn, "An Essay Towards the Present and Future Peace of Europe" (1693) in *The Witness of William Penn*, ed. Frederick B. Tolles and E. Gordon Alderfer (New York: Macmillan & Co., 1957), pp. 140–59; Abbé de Saint-Pierre, *Selections from the Second Edition of the Abrégé du Projet de Paix Perpétuelle* (1712) (London: Sweet & Maxwell, 1927); Immanuel Kant, "Perpetual Peace: A Philosophical Sketch" (1795) in *Kant's Political Writings*, ed. Hans Reiss (Cambridge: At the University Press, 1970), pp. 93–130; Jeremy Bentham, "Essay on Universal Peace: Essay IV: A Plan for an Universal and Perpetual Peace," (written in 1789; first published in 1843), reprinted in *Jeremy Bentham*, ed. Charles W. Everett (London: Weidenfeld & Nicolson, 1966), pp. 195–229.

3. Gottfried Wilhelm Leibniz, "Observation sur le projet d'une paix perpétuelle de M. l'abbé de St. Pierre," in *Opera Omnia*, ed. L. Dutens (Geneva, 1768), vol. 5; Jean-Jacques Rousseau (editing and commenting upon the work of the Abbé de Saint-Pierre), *A Project of Perpetual Peace*, trans. Edith M. Nuttall (London: Richard Cobden-Sanderson, 1927); Friedrich Hegel, *Philosophy of Right* (1821), trans. T. M. Knox (Oxford: Clarendon Press, 1958), pp. 208–16.

4. *The Adages* were first published in 1500. A later edition, published in 1515, contained a greatly expanded version of "Dulce bellum inexpertis." See Margaret Mann Phillips, ed., *The Adages of Erasmus: A Study with Interpretations* (Cambridge: At the University Press, 1964), pp. 308–53.

5. In 1516, France and Switzerland concluded the Treaty of Fribourg, known as "La paix perpétuelle," which lasted until the French Revolution. The year before, Henry VIII had concluded a "permanent" but much more short-lived peace with France. For a few years, nevertheless, Erasmus, Thomas More, and other humanists had hopes for a flowering of peace that would permit the shaping of a new political and cultural order.

6. Erasmus, *The Education of a Christian Prince*, trans. Lester K. Born (New York: Octagon Books, 1973).

7. Niccolo Machiavelli, *The Prince and the Discourses* (New York: Random House, 1950).

8. Erasmus, *Education of a Christian Prince*, p. 249.

9. Erasmus, *The Complaint of Peace* (Boston: Charles Williams, 1813). For a more recent translation, though not entirely complete, see Jose Chapiro, *Erasmus and Our Struggle for Peace* (Boston: Beacon Press,

1950), pp. 131–84, "Peace Protests!" In a letter from 1523, Erasmus comments bitterly in a letter to a friend that he must "soon compose the Epitaph, rather than the Complaint, of Peace, as she seems to be dead and buried and not very likely to revive" (cited in the translator's preface, 1813 edition of *The Complaint of Peace*, p. iv).

10. Erasmus, *Education of a Christian Prince*, p. 249.

11. Ibid., p. 250.

12. Ibid., p. 251.

13. Comparisons between animals and human beings traditionally placed humans above animals in the chain of being. Cicero, among many others, had argued that the two ways of doing wrong — by force or by fraud — were both bestial: "fraud seems to belong to the cunning fox, force to the lion: both are wholly unworthy of man, but fraud is the more contemptible" (Cicero *Of Duties* 1.13.41). Machiavelli had accepted the comparison only to argue that human beings ought to learn from the fox and the lion in those respects. Erasmus intended to show, on the contrary, that force and fraud on the scale practiced by humans and with the means at their disposal were of an entirely different order, and that to attribute such aspects of human conduct to animals was merely to calumniate them.

14. Erasmus, *Complaint of Peace*, p. 51.

15. Ibid., p. 79.

16. Erasmus, "Peace Protests!" in Chapiro, *Erasmus and Our Struggle for Peace*, p. 173.

17. Saint-Pierre, *Selections from the Second Edition of the Abrégé*. See also Rousseau, *Project of Perpetual Peace*.

18. Kant, "Perpetual Peace," and "Idea for a Universal History with a Cosmopolitan Purpose," in *Kant's Political Writings*, ed. Reiss, pp. 93–130 and 41–53.

19. Kant, "Perpetual Peace," p. 103.

20. Ibid., p. 96.

21. Ibid., p. 114.

22. Ibid., p. 96.

23. For a discussion of these constraints in Kant's writings and of their role in international relations, see Sissela Bok, *A Strategy for Peace* (New York: Pantheon Books, 1989).

24. Kant, "Perpetual Peace," p. 108.

25. Dwight D. Eisenhower, "The Chance for Peace," (Address delivered before the American Society of Newspaper Editors, April 16, 1953), reprinted in *War and Peace*, ed. Kenneth E. Alrutz et al., Lynchburg College Symposium Readings, vol. 5 (New York: University Press of America, 1982), p. 621.

26. See F. H. Hinsley, *Power and the Pursuit of Peace* (Cambridge: At the University Press, 1963), pp. 93–97.

27. Kant explicitly defended this motto; but while it committed him to absolutism with respect to lying, it did not do so when it came to violence, since he regarded violence in self-defense as legitimate. See Sissela Bok, "Kant's Arguments in Support of the Maxim 'Do What Is Right Though the Earth Should Perish,'" *Argumentation* 2 (1988): 7–25; reprinted in *Applied Ethics and Ethical Theory*, ed. David M. Rosenthal and Fadlou Shehadi (Salt Lake City: University of Utah Press, 1988), pp. 191–212.

28. George Kennan, *The Nuclear Delusion* (New York: Pantheon Books, 1982).

29. *The Challenge of Peace: God's Promise and Our Response* (Washington, D.C.: U.S. Catholic Conference Office of Publishing Services, 1983), p. 39. For a secular interpretation of just war doctrine that similarly restricts the causes for just war, see Robert W. Tucker, *The Just War: A Study in Contemporary American Doctrine* (Baltimore: Johns Hopkins Press, 1960).

30. *The Challenge of Peace*, p. v.

31. V. I. Lenin, "Socialism and War," in *Collected Works* (Moscow: Progress Publishers, 1968), p. 316. See also "The Question of Peace," vol. 21, pp. 290–94, and "April Theses, 1917," vol. 24, pp. 21–26.

32. Mao Tse-tung, *On Revolution and War*, ed. M. Rejai (Garden City, N.Y.: Doubleday, 1970), p. 67.

33. Karl Marx, *Selected Writings*, ed. D. McLellan (Oxford: Oxford University Press, 1977), pp. 568–69.

34. See Bok, *Strategy for Peace*, chap. 4.

PART II

Religion and the Search for Values

Knowing Religiously
ELIOT DEUTSCH

IN HIS VERY KIND letter inviting me to participate in the Institute program this year Professor Rouner asked that I weave into my paper some autobiographical statements concerning how and why I developed the position set forth there and — that by working, as I have further been asked to do, in an intercultural framework — to indicate some of the sources of my views in various traditions.

Like many other philosophers in what William James once referred to as the "tender-minded" (Platonic) tradition, as opposed to the hard-headed, "tough-minded," empirical (Aristotelian) tradition, I have been uneasy about the conspicuous absence of the religious spirit in so much of twentieth-century philosophy. The obsessive concern for solid facts, technical subtlety, and explanatory certainty, the search for *the* method of philosophy, whether analytic or phenomenological, as though knowledge and truth were to be had like pressing buttons on a machine, betrays not only a lack of confidence in the potentialities of the creative human spirit but a view of the world that deprives that world of what is most valuable in it. I believe that philosophy has its greatest natural kinship with those spiritual activities like art and religion that address our deepest concerns and give expression to the most valuable aesthetic and ethical features of the world. This belief has motivated and informed my interest in non-Western as well as Western traditions, for it seems clear to me that human experience is not the exclusive possession of that small and historically limited phenomenon which we call Western civilization. The great traditions of Asian thought have much to teach us in dealing both with technical philosophical matters in areas such as ontology and epistemology and with the larger issues of the spirit.

In my own philosophy I have tried to work in an unself-conscious, spontaneous way from the background of both Western and non-Western traditions and in what I would like to think is a religious spirit. I have tried to see how aesthetic and religious experience, rather than being peripheral areas that one turns to after one has done one's real work, can be brought into the very center of philosophy. If one can begin to understand the deepest, richest, and most valuable of our experiences, one can then go a long way toward understanding other issues. If we can understand creativity, we might then be able to understand causality; if we can understand what religious language is, we will then be able to understand better what a proposition is; if we can understand what it means to achieve freedom of consciousness, we can understand what free will means, and so on.

I begin, then, with a quotation from that wonderful California-Cambridge philosopher Josiah Royce, who combined a kind of East-West of the times and who, in his work *The Religious Aspect of Philosophy*, wrote: "Deliberately insincere, dishonest thinking is downright blasphemy."[1]

Most often today discussion and analysis of the so-called problem of religious knowledge is concerned to determine such things as the cognitive status of religious language, the criteria for the truth of religious claims, the definition of religious belief, and the nature of religious symbolism. It seems to me that underlying them is a more basic, primordial, experiential situation — one that makes possible a dynamic bringing together of knowledge and religion — and it is that experiential situation which I am calling "knowing religiously." My general thesis is that religious knowledge doesn't so much have a distinctive or special object as it has a unique style or manner. Knowing religiously, I shall argue, is a reverential knowing that is centered in reality. It involves wonder, openness, insight, and love; it brings about a transformation of our ordinary knowledge and the achievement of a kind of "unknowing knowing" that issues in a liberated creativity.

I propose to proffer a rather concise description or characterization of "knowing religiously"; and for the sake of clarity I will present this characterization in ideal terms, realizing of course that it is something to which we only approximate in our actual experience. I will conclude the paper with some reflections on the problem of truth as it relates to this activity. I will argue that the criterion for the truth of utterances originating from knowing religiously has to do in an important way with the personhood of the (religious) knower.

I

Before presenting the descriptive characterization, however, it might be useful to relate what I am calling "knowing religiously" with other kinds of knowing in order to see, in a preliminary and rather elementary way, what it is not. Without going into elaborate or technical detail we can, I think, recognize clearly enough the meaningfulness of distinguishing between the following: factual knowing, praxis knowing, formal knowing, and strategic knowing. These are not placed in any hierarchy and are not, of course, intended to exhaust all possible kinds of knowing. In the actual world these modes overlap, intertwine, and mesh together in a variety of complex ways.

By "factual knowing" I mean simply a "knowing *what*" (like knowing the name of the capital of Brazil). Factual knowing is a public, learned, empirical, fact-oriented knowing; the sort of knowing that one can easily be tested on, for it is a kind of possession. Knowing religiously, it will be entirely evident, is not a having of a special kind of factual understanding. When knowing religiously the knower is not in any special position to announce empirical truths.

"Praxis knowing" is knowing *how* to do something or other (like knowing how to drive a car). Most praxis knowing is also learned behavior, the acquiring of certain bodily-mental skills that enable one to perform various tasks. Although knowing religiously does involve discipline and always issues in a kind of action it is not itself a praxis knowing. It doesn't reduce essentially to a skill; it cannot be taught as such; it cannot be practiced simply in a habitual way.

Neither does it involve formal principles as such. By "formal knowing" I mean a kind of "knowing *that*" (like knowing that if

A > B and B > C then A > C). Formal knowing involves rules, systems, principles. It is that mode of knowing, of reaching conclusions, that is usually taken as the paradigm of rational knowing. Now although there is nothing irrational or illogical about knowing religiously, it is clearly not itself to be placed within a category of formal knowing. Knowing religiously is not a knowing that can be carried out simply by any rational mind who has mastered various semantic and syntactic principles.

Lastly, knowing religiously is not to be identified with what I have called "strategic knowing," by which I mean a "knowing *if*" (like knowing if I move my rook three places forward I should be able to capture your queen in five moves). Strategic knowing involves a grasping of causal connections, a manipulation of objects and situations; it involves the ability to predict, to control, to seize upon opportunities, and so on. Knowing religiously, as we will see, in contrast to this, does not intend the achievement of some specific goal or the realization of some particular purpose. It is not a knowing directed toward the satisfaction of an immediate need or desire, or the resolution of what Dewey was so fond of calling a "problematic situation."

Knowing religiously is thus different in kind from these more ordinary modes of knowing and has a distinctive character of its own.

Aristotle, as we know, spoke of wonder as the impetus to philosophy. Today, with our passion for those bits and pieces of knowledge that we call information, we have reduced wonder to curiosity. Educators constantly tell their students that they should be curious about this or that — but not that they should stand in wonderment. By *wonder* I mean essentially an openness, a "letting be" in the profound sense in which Heidegger used the expression. To wonder means to acknowledge fully the mystery of being. To be in wonderment does not mean, though, that one stands unequally in awe before some overpowering reality or being (that would be a kind of astonishment); to be in wonderment means that one attends freely in consciousness to a reality to which one feels one belongs. I don't so much wonder *at* something as *with* something. In wonderment one feels a kinship with the being of that wonderful thing.

To wonder requires, then, a kind of nonegoistic availing of

self. When obsessed with oneself, one is alienated from being. With-
drawn, one is simply not available to what is.

Knowing religiously is then first of all a concentrated attentiveness — an open sensitivity to, a belonging with, being. And it
also involves, I believe, an insight into the utter simplicity of being.

This is not the occasion to elaborate an ontology or metaphysics, but it should be noted that one of the conditions for knowing religiously is precisely the realization of the utter simplicity
of being. By this I mean a non-subject/object-bound awareness of
reality. Now there have been many ways in which this awareness
has been analyzed and understood in diverse philosophical and
religious traditions. I have found that one of the most interesting
ways to understand the nature of this insight into the simplicity
of being is to be had in the analysis of ignorance (*avidyā, ajñāna*)
put forward in the classical Indian system of Advaita Vedānta.[2]

According to Advaita Vedānta, what stands in the way of
our having an insight into reality and an adequate self-knowledge
is a fundamental and pervasive confounding of self and world
which is of our own making. We incessantly — and, according to
Śaṁkara, the leading exponent of Advaita, quite naturally — misidentify ourselves, wrongly attributing to ourselves characteristics which properly belong to the nonself and attributing to the
nonself qualities which properly belong to ourselves. In our ordinary ego-based consciousness we "superimpose" (*adhyāsa*) attributes of the nonself onto the self and of the self onto the nonself.
Śaṁkara writes:

> It is a matter not requiring any proof that the object and
> the subject, whose respective spheres are the notion of the
> 'Thou' (the Non-Ego) and the Ego, and which are opposed
> to each other as much as darkness and light are, cannot be
> identified. All the less can their respective attributes be iden-
> tified. Hence it follows that it is wrong to superimpose upon
> the subject — whose Self is intelligence, and which has for its
> sphere the Ego — the object whose sphere is the notion of the
> Non-Ego, and the attributes of the object; and vice versa to
> superimpose the subject and the attributes of the subject on
> the object. In spite of this it is on the part of man a natural
> procedure. . . .[3]

This superimposition thus defined, learned men consider
to be Nescience (*avidyā*), and the ascertainment of the true
nature of that which is (the Self) by means of the discrimination of that (which is superimposed on the Self) they call
knowledge (*vidyā*).[4]

For example:

Extra-personal attributes are superimposed on the Self,
if a man considers himself sound and entire, or the contrary,
as long as his wife, children, and so on are sound and entire
or not. Attributes of the body are superimposed on the Self,
if a man thinks of himself (his Self) as stout, lean, fair, as standing, walking, or jumping. . . .[5]

In other words, we quite naturally misidentify ourselves by
wrongly mixing ourselves up as "subjects" with a world taken to
be entirely constituted by diverse "objects." We scatter ourselves,
as it were, about the world, and then come to believe that its limitations are our own. To know religiously, to gain insight into the
simplicity of being, requires that we put aside that complexity and
recollect ourselves, recovering then the silence which is at the core
of our being. We must, the advaitin says, desuperimpose ourselves
from the world and realize its profound oneness. This, of course,
demands a great deal of hard mental work, for we need to dis-
criminate away all those misidentifications of self, such as that I
am my body, or my mental capacities, or my willing, emotional
nature. Advaita Vedānta insists that it requires a complete mental-
spiritual discipline which it calls *jñāna-yoga*. This discipline of
mental concentration and discrimination is said to yield that non-
subject/object-bound awareness of reality.

But something more is needed, I believe, for "knowing religiously"— and that is care or concern. In more traditional language
we might call it simply love. In the *Bhagavad-gītā*, Kṛṣṇa, the incarnate Lord, instructs Arjuna that the one who realizes one's own
true self will at the same time achieve the highest love or devotion.

Having become Brahman, tranquil in the Self, he neither
grieves nor desires. Regarding all beings as equal, he attains
supreme devotion to Me (8.54).

Knowing religiously involves the whole person in his or her belonging with reality. The openness, the insight that we have briefly spoken of, must be thoroughly informed by love. The religious knower is not, in other words, an indifferent observer or collector of facts. Nor is the religious knower what Josiah Royce called a "theoretic knower" who wants knowledge whatever it may turn out to be; he or she is rather one who, as Royce says, wants to know the value of the truths being sought. Religious philosophy, he writes, "wants to know what in the world is worthy of worship as the good."[6] When one knows something religiously, I submit, one celebrates or affirms the thing for what it is in the fulness of its reality. One loves the being of the thing, but not as it is an object for possession or consumption; one reveres the thing as the thing that it is.

With love, knowing then becomes a kind of power — not in the coercive sense but, if I may so call it, in a transformative sense. In knowing religiously there is brought forth a fundamental change in the confidence we otherwise enjoy in the categories of our ordinary thinking and knowing, in particular in those time/space-bound, classifying, explanatory propensities of "rationality." In knowing religiously there is a transformation of ordinary knowing in virtue of the realization, in loving, insightful wonderment, of that which is incommensurable with that ordinary knowing. Simplicity is not the opposite of complexity, as it obtains at an entirely different level of being. In other words, knowing religiously is not just another kind of knowing to be set alongside other kinds, of the sort previously identified; rather it is radically different in kind from them. It opens up entirely new dimensions of being.

For this reason, in what is surely one of its highest forms, it is often referred to as a kind of unknowing. In the *Kena Upaniṣad* (2.3) it is said:

> To whomsoever it [Brahman] is not known, to him it is known: to whomsoever it is known, he does not know. It is not understood by those who understand it; it is understood by those who do not understand it.[7]

And from Meister Eckhart we hear that

> one must achieve this unself-consciousness by means of transformed knowledge. This *ignorance* does not come from lack

of knowledge, but rather it is from knowledge that we may achieve this ignorance.[8]

Knowing religiously is a kind of ignorance, a "learned ignorance," as Nicholas of Cusa called it. It is the ignorance of the wise, one which is free from all pretense. It is a knowing which is devoid of a distinctive subject matter — a knowing, however, which as part of its nature issues in a liberated creativity. By a "liberated creativity" in the context of knowing religiously, I mean a disciplined spontaneity which gives rise to a meaningful utterance that is in its own way right for itself.

Many theories of creativity in both philosophy and psychology lay stress on the self-expressive character of the creative act. Still largely under the influence of romanticism, these theories look to the creative agent as he or she embodies and expresses a unique imaginative force as the central focus for understanding creativity. The popular image of the artist as an inspired half-mad libertarian betrays this romantic notion. But this is surely an extremely naive understanding of creativity. Without having to deny that the creative process, especially in the arts, often has its roots in the shadowy recesses of one's being, we can nevertheless see how creativity at its best is a highly disciplined activity wherein the individual, isolated self, rather than being the heart and soul of the activity, turns itself over, as it were, to what is being created.

A creative person works with the material of the medium. He or she is neither a passive responder nor a forceful imposer. "Working with" implies a full cooperation, a controlling intelligence directing and, in turn, being directed by the medium — be it wood, stone, or words. I have argued elsewhere that genuine creativity always exhibits an immanent purposiveness, that "aiming at the fulfillment of only those ends which it itself defines and articulates, the creative act answers to no other guiding need or external *telos*. Its purpose is developed in the process itself; which is to say, a sense of rightness or appropriateness, within the context of the particular creative act, governs the artist's bringing his work to fulfillment or completion."[9] Creativity, then, requires discipline: the ordering of relations so as to achieve form. And it also requires spontaneity or freedom in action. Spontaneity is different from impulsiveness; for unlike impulsiveness, where one is a victim of the strongest force within one, spontaneity is a free bringing forth of one's essential nature as an expression of creative power.

Creativity at its best, then, or what I am calling in the context of knowing religiously a liberated creativity, is a non-self-obsessed sensitivity which allows a person to engage in thinking as a kind of play — not as a frivolous jumping about, but as a spontaneous activity that is carried out joyfully for its own sake. A liberated creativity is not a knowledge-gathering activity for the achieving of something else (for example, control over nature); it is rather a natural expression of that powerful harmony that obtains between the creative person and his or her world. A liberated creativity, with respect to thinking and utterance, is then as much a listening as it is a speaking. The listening is to and with that silence of being which is at the core of knowing religiously. It is a listening to and with that silence which provides a ground for all meaningful utterance and which thoroughly informs what is said.

It is not so much then a matter of "whatever is knowable is sayable," as that what is known religiously is always said in a manner entirely appropriate to it. In fact, we would have to go so far as to say that the manner of saying in knowing religiously is part and parcel of what is known. We don't, in other words, have two distinct acts, a knowing-act and a saying-act; rather the knowing and saying are part of the same creative activity. It is not that X knows Y and could then communicate, express, utter Y in a variety of different ways (as is the case to a considerable extent with simple empirical assertions); when X knows Y religiously the mode of utterance is inseparable from that which is known.

As a liberated creativity, knowing religiously is very much like poetry then in this, that its formed content is always a unique presentation, the particular how and what of speech being as-one. It is unlike poetry, though, insofar as whereas the poet may through the power of imagination create "character voices" that are not strictly speaking his or her own (for example, Shakespeare with his innumerable characters), the religious knower will always be present in the utterance. It will always reflect the knower's state of being. This is the case because that utterance is part and parcel of immediate experience. The utterance, in other words, is an integral part of the experience of the knower and will accordingly embody the degree to which he or she has achieved openness, sensitivity, insight. These are as much qualities of being as they are features of experience. Knowing religiously always culminates in expressive, insightful utterance — utterance which is inseparable from the knowing and which exhibits the state of the knower. And it is this which further distinguishes knowing religiously from pure intuition, which need not culminate in anything beyond itself. The religious knower is centered in reality, but does not simply remain there. One's knowing, one's experience, one's very being requires articulation.

II

This brings us to the problem of truth as it relates to knowing religiously. I want to argue for what will undoubtedly appear at first to be an outlandish thesis, one that goes entirely against the grain of modern epistemology, and that is that the criterion for the truth of statements originating from knowing religiously has always to do in an important way with the quality of personhood of the knower.[10] This means that the more genuine the person, the greater will be the truth-value of what he or she says, relative to knowing religiously. The latter qualification is needed, for I am not claiming that this variable truth value pertains to all forms of assertive utterance. If it is raining now outside, the statement "It is raining now" is not more or less true depending upon the quality of the person who utters it. Its meaning, as most of us now agree, might very well depend upon what the speaker intends by the utterance. One might, for example, intend it as a warning rather than as a simple factual assertion. It might even be used as a code for some entirely different kind of meaning. Its truth, however, is independent of the character of who says it.

But let us suppose that Joe Jones, an extremely unregenerate student of religious studies, were to utter "All is one" as an appropriate answer to some academic question asked by his professor. Let us further suppose that this utterance, taken propositionally, happens to convey a profound insight into reality (uttered, as it has been, by not a few sages in history). Is it not the case that in virtue of Joe Jones being the agent of the utterance the statement is not-true — or, at the least, that it cannot rightfully be taken as a statement in the first place? Or take a sentence like *tat tvam asi*, "Thou art that," one of the great *mahāvākyas* or "great sayings" of Vedānta which asserts the identity of the self and reality (*ātman* and Brahman). Is it not more or less true depending upon who says it, when, and in what manner? If the philosopher-sage utters *tat tvam asi* from the full authority of personal experience and achieved being to a well-prepared disciple, it means something very different from, say, if students in a course in Indian philosophy were asked on an examination to give an example of one of the *mahāvākyas* of Vedānta and answered *tat tvam asi*. Their answer might be correct, but it would not — if taken propositionally — be a truthful statement. Uninitiated students know not whereof they speak.

With our passion for the so-called objective and impersonal character of truth we still no doubt find this objectionable, if not downright unintelligible. But most of us are willing to accept the idea that meaning is closely related to a speaker's intention, and that the kind of utterance delivered reflects that intention. Meaning does not reside simply in the statement itself, a sentence oftentimes not involving a statement at all in its primary use or illocutionary force. If illiterate drunkard Ed Brown just before falling into a deep stupor were to utter "$E = MC^2$," we would not assume that he was in fact asserting something about the relation of energy and matter. We would, I gather, assume rather that he was mouthing some expression that he might have heard elsewhere, that he was just sounding off. We do indeed often assume that some relation obtains between who says what (in what context) in determining the meaning of what is said. I want to take this a step further and claim that with certain kinds of utterance, namely those arising from the liberated creativity of knowing religiously, the criterion for truth has to do with the quality of the personhood of the knower. We may look to a speaker's intention to determine partly the *meaning* of what is said. We may, I believe, look to the knower's being to determine partly the *truth* of what is said when what the speaker says issues from knowing religiously.

This is the case because with utterance which is an integral part of knowing religiously we don't in the first place look at some alleged isolable content of the utterance (the mere "what" that is said) in order to determine its truth. Rather, we respond to the utterance as precisely the utterance it is in the full richness of its nature. This nature, as we have seen, is a formed content (the "how" and "what" that is said being inseparable), and will necessarily embody the qualities of the being of the speaker. "Style is the person," it is often said, and the rightness of a style is grounded in the being of the person. One's religious language is thoroughly informed by who one is as a person; the manner of its utterance inescapably discloses the personhood of the speaker, the degree to which he or she is a consummate person who exhibits a loving sensitivity and has achieved freedom in being and in action.

In other words, when we respond to the utterance in the full richness of its nature we invariably respond as well to the person who utters it. We are attracted or repulsed to what amounts to an utterer's utterance as a conjoined entity. We recognize its rightness, if it possesses it, in terms of the quality of the knower as this is made evident in the utterance.[11]

The thinking, the utterance which derives from the liberated creativity of knowing religiously is not, then, concerned with making factual claims as such. Although there might be an assertive dimension present, its fundamental intentionality is that of speaking *with* reality, not *at* it. It is a speaking from the very being of the person.

This is a rather familiar position in Chinese philosophy, and so we might profitably look there for further elucidation. Confucianism in particular insists that moral utterance is true only insofar as it is spoken "sincerely." The concept of *sincerity (ch'eng)* is a very profound one in Confucian thought and points to the whole being (*jen*) of a person. It is not thus reducible to simple "honesty." In the *Chung-yung* or the *Doctrine of the Mean*, one of the major works of ancient Confucian literature, it is said:

> Sincerity (*ch'eng*) is the Way of Heaven. To think how to be sincere is the Way of man. He who is sincere is one who hits upon what is right without effort and apprehends without thinking.[12]

Tu Wei-Ming notes that the English word "sincere" does not encompass the many-leveled meanings of *ch'eng* and that the word in fact is often translated as "true." D. C. Lau, he notes, renders *ch'eng* as "true" in his translation of *Mencius*. Wing-tsit Chan likewise sometimes renders *ch'eng* as "true" in his translation of *Chungyung*. In any event, as Tu Wei-Ming also observes:

> Whether it is translated as "true" or "sincere," *ch'eng* definitely points to a human reality which is not only the basis of self-knowledge but also the ground of man's identification with Heaven.[13]

And further:

> *Ch'eng* symbolizes not only what a person in an ultimate sense ought to be but what a person in a concrete way can eventually become.[14]

Confucianism thus clearly recognizes the intimate relationship that obtains between the quality of the person in realizing the supreme virtue of *jen* and the "truth" of knowing at the deepest levels of one's being. In the *Doctrine of the Mean* it is said that

> as there is sincerity, there will be its expression. As it is expressed, it will become conspicuous. As it becomes conspicuous, it will become clear. As it becomes clear, it will move others. As it moves others, it changes them. As it changes them, it transforms them. Only those who are absolutely sincere can transform others.[15]

This passage suggests one further point about the truth of religious language, and one which also fits well into the framework of contemporary speech-act philosophy of language, and that is the importance of the hearer or listener in determining the truth value of what is said. Although there is something irresistible about the language that issues from knowing religiously, its having a kind of compelling authority, a qualified hearer is clearly essential for recognizing and determining its truth. And this is hardly surprising. "One who has ears may listen" is stated in many cultures: only one who is properly receptive will be able to respond fully to what is said.

Knowing religiously, we might thus say, is in the final analysis a social or communal act. The religious knower does not know for his or her own sake alone, as it were, but finds the consummation of experience as that experience is taken up and embraced by others. A formed content is a form *for* someone; it does not stand isolated in a rarefied, pristine space. Knowing religiously intends to be shared; it fulfills itself as it moves, changes, and transforms others.

I have dealt with a very large topic and I have, of course, been able to treat it here in only a very brief and fragmentary way. My main goal was to try to articulate a special mode of knowing, which I have called knowing religiously, which differs in many significant ways from other modes of knowing. It is *sui generis*, but it is not in conflict with these other ways. It has no special subject matter of its own and it is not a way of knowing that admits of a formula or a recipe. The best one can do, I think, is to characterize it in a broad phenomenological way as having a certain style or manner which involves wonder, openness, insight, and love. It is a manner which brings about that transformation alluded to in Confucian philosophy and issues in what I have called a liberated creativity, a disciplined spontaneity. The creativity and the knowing are of a piece. Necessarily it is the experience of a person who is reflected in that which is uttered from the experience. The truth, then, of this kind of religious language will bear an intimate relationship to the character of the speaker. It will be true to the degree to which the speaker has achieved a loving sensitivity and that freedom of consciousness which is the truth of personhood.

NOTES

1. Josiah Royce, *The Religious Aspect of Philosophy* (1885; reprint ed., New York: Harper & Brothers, 1958), p. 7.
2. Advaita Vedānta is the nondualistic (*a-dvaita*) system of orthodox Indian philosophy which has had the largest influence in the Hindu tradition and which bases itself primarily on the ancient *Upaniṣads*. It remains today as one of the most important systems for contemporary Indian thinkers.

3. Śaṁkara, *Brahmasūtrabhāṣya*, trans. George Thibaut, *The Vedānta-sūtras with the Commentary of Śankarācharya*, vol. 35 of *The Sacred Books of the East*, ed. Max Muller (Oxford: Clarendon Press, 1890), p. 3.

4. Ibid., p. 6.

5. Ibid., pp. 8–9.

6. Royce, *Religious Aspect of Philosophy*, p. 8.

7. Sarvepalli Radhakrishnan, trans., *The Principal Upaniṣads* (New York: Harper & Brothers, 1953).

8. Meister Eckhart, *Meister Eckhart*, trans. Raymond B. Blakney (New York: Harper & Brothers, 1941), p. 107.

9. Eliot Deutsch, *Personhood, Creativity, and Freedom* (Honolulu: University of Hawaii Press, 1982), pp. 69–74.

10. See ibid., chap. 1, for a fuller discussion of what it means to achieve personhood.

11. It is interesting to note that the opposite of truth in knowing religiously is thus not falsity as such, but inauthenticity, pretense, insincerity.

12. Tu Wei-Ming, *Centrality and Commonality: An Essay on Chung-yung*, Society for Asian and Comparative Philosophy no. 3 (Honolulu: University Press of Hawaii, 1976), p. 107.

13. Ibid., p. 109. The character *ch'eng*, I am told by my colleague Roger T. Ames, is constituted of "to speak" and "to complete, to realize," and therefore suggests "to realize that which is spoken."

14. Ibid., p. 122.

15. Wing-tsit Chan, ed., *A Source Book of Chinese Philosophy* (Princeton: Princeton University Press, 1963), p. 108.

Two Evolutions

HUSTON SMITH

WALKER PERCY IN HIS *Message in the Bottle* points out that we do not know who we are. There exists in the contemporary West no coherent theory of human nature, no consensus view such as prevailed in thirteenth-century Europe, in seventeenth-century New England, or in traditional societies still. Whether these views were true or false, they were viable beliefs. They animated their cultures and gave life its meaning. They were outlooks people tried to live by.

In contrast to such embracing theories, what we have today is a miscellany of *notions* as to who we are. These notions do not cohere, but they do fall into two rather clearly demarcated camps. On the one hand is the view backed by modern science, that the human self can be understood as an organism in an environment, endowed genetically like other organisms with needs and drives, who through evolution — natural selection working on chance mutations — has developed strategies for learning and surviving by means of certain adaptive transactions with the environment. Over and against this is the Judeo-Christian view that the human being was created in the image of God with an immortal soul and occupies a place in nature somewhere between the beasts and the angels. At some point humankind suffered a catastrophic fall in consequence of which we have lost our way and, unlike the beasts, become capable of sin and seek after salvation. The clue to this second scenario derives not from science or philosophy, but from two historical events — the Exodus and the Incarnation — which produced respectively a people, the Jews; and an institution, the Christian Church.

Not only do these views not mesh; they are in head-on opposition, for according to science we are the more who have derived
from the less, whereas our religions teach that we are the less who
have derived from the more. In thus contradicting each other, our
two views — one taught by our schools, the other by our churches
and synagogues — cancel each other out, leaving us without a clear
self-image or identity. It is impossible for both views to be true,
yet simply by having been born into today's West, all of us believe
parts of both of them. Even those who have abandoned the theological specifics of the religious view continue to affirm the after-
glow that lingers from its light: the belief that human beings are
endowed with certain unique properties — inherent dignity and in-
alienable rights — that other organisms do not possess, and that as
a consequence the highest value a democratic society can set for
itself is respect for the sacredness and worth of the individual.

How does one live one's life if one tries to take these two contradictory propositions seriously? The standard way is to see oneself as an organism that has evolved enough to have developed
certain values. What is not noticed, as Walker Percy points out,
is that the moment the sanctity of the individual is turned into a
"value," an act of devaluation has already occurred.

An age comes to a close when people discover that they can
no longer understand themselves by the theory their age professes.
For a while its denizens will continue to think that they believe
it, but they feel otherwise and cannot understand their feelings.
This has now happened to us. We continue to believe Darwinism,
even though it no longer feels right to us. Darwinism is in fact dying, and its death signals the close of our age.

My rationale for a negative project — deflating Darwinism —
is this: with respect to the problem at hand (our point of origin
as it bears on who we are), our need is not just to relieve an in-
consistency but to do so in the right way, with the better of the
two hypotheses triumphing. By the better hypothesis I mean the
one that is closer to the truth and more serviceable. Darwinism
is obscuring what I believe to be this doubly better answer to the
question at stake. If I could prove that we have derived from what
exceeds us I would naturally take that direct route, but metaphysical propositions do not admit of proof, so I resort to this *via
negativa*. Rabbis say that if we cannot believe in God, we might

at least try to stop believing in idols. Less faith in the Darwinian idol might help to clear a space in which the divine might appear more regularly than it now does.

We would be better off if we could believe that our origin is momentous, and Darwinism counters that belief. Peter Drucker, the industrial consultant, says he never tells managers anything they don't know. He gets them to see that what they have been discounting as incidental information is actually critical information. So it is here. Not being a scientist, I obviously have nothing to contribute to evolutionary theory in its technical aspects. My own thrust takes a different turn. I want to work on the way the entire Darwinian theory looks to us and to change that look by *gestalting* it in a different way; specifically, by placing it in the context of the premises with which this paragraph began. When it is thus placed, my project can be visualized as a triangle, as follows:

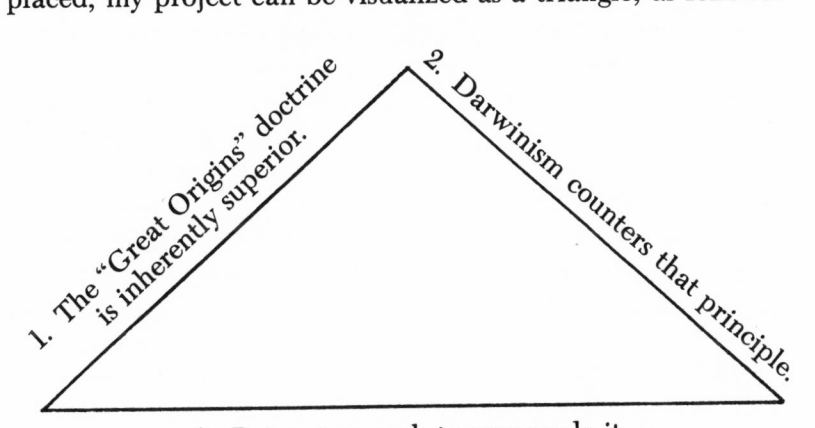

3. But not enough to supercede it.

I derive the phrase "Great Origins" from Joseph Addison's "Ode" in *The Spectator*:

> The spacious firmament on high,
> With all the blue ethereal sky,
> And spangled heavens, a shining frame,
> Their great Original proclaim.

But the point here is this: the force of my critique of Darwinism turns on its position in this triangle. There are some, to be sure, who conclude that it should be shelved for scientific reasons alone, but my point is a different one: Even if it remains useful as a working hypothesis in science, that is not sufficient reason for us to believe that its basic delivery, the Small Origins hypothesis, is true. For the game of evidence which Darwinism as a scientific theory plays is an idiosyncratic one that introduces both contraction and inflation. Contraction occurs when Darwinism sees itself as answerable only to empirical evidence; other considerations, such as metaphysical ones relating to first and final causes or the intuitive ones with which this paper will close, are discounted from the start. This reduction of the field of evidence in which it stands already exaggerates its stature. An inflationary move follows hard on its heels. To gain acceptance in science a working hypothesis does not need to show much in the way of proof; all it need do is stay ahead of its competitors. If its competitors are weak, the lead hypothesis can look strong without actually being so. And if it has no competitors? There was a period when the evidence turned against Darwinism conclusively; it didn't matter — its rating barely slipped. I refer to that pre-Mendelian moment — it extended for thirty-three years, actually — when an Edinburgh professor showed that by the mechanisms of heredity as they were then understood the emergence of new species from chance variations was logically impossible. For through admixture with the standard hereditary equipment of its mating partner, the strength of a promising evolutionary mutation would be reduced to one-half in its children, to one-quarter in its grandchildren, and so on until it vanished completely. Mendel rescinded this refutation with his discovery that genes do not blend and thus become diluted, but for a third of a century this categorical disproof scarcely tarnished Darwin's star. One is tempted to conclude with Julius Caesar that people believe what they want to believe, and there is much to this; the nineteenth and twentieth centuries wanted to believe Darwinism for its Social Darwinism and its prospect that progress would continue forever. But from the scientific standpoint there was something that was right about this tenacious clinging to a disproven theory. For Darwinism seemed (as it still seems) to be the only possible scientific explanation for life's origin and development, so it was appropriate to see how far it could succeed. That it has not succeeded enough to displace its Great Origins competitor is my conclusion, and it is time to proceed with the argument that leads up to it.

1. The Great Origins thesis is inherently superior.

Underlying this first proposition, naturally, is the supposition that notions regarding origins are important whatever their kind. Sociologically we see this in the search for roots that is cropping up in our highly mobile, transient society, while on a larger scale we find it in the cosmogonic myths that legitimize every known culture. The care with which these myths are transmitted from generation to generation and ritualistically rehearsed proves that more than curiosity is at stake in their origin. They came forward to meet a fundamental human need: the need to sense oneself as grounded in the cosmos and thereby oriented. Without orientation confusion sets in; if it persists, life loses its radar. Being ungrounded is part and parcel of this, for to be without grounding is to be adrift in ever shifting contexts that are unstable. The warning "not good if detached" applies not only to ticket stubs but to life as well. But is one surmise as good as another on this subject?

It seems unlikely. Self-image affects behavior, and to see oneself as descended from noble stock is to assume that one is made of noble stuff. This in turn disposes one to behave nobly, though of course it does not guarantee such behavior. Something like generational rub-off occurs, for where there is noble ancestry there are noble role models; also, shoddy conduct cannot be blamed on shoddy genes. Traditional societies may have sensed such things, for Marshall Sahlins tells us that "we are the only people who think themselves risen from savages; everyone else believes they descended from gods."[1]

What is difficult is to pass from everyday considerations like these to ones that are metaphysical. Two difficulties are involved. First, in our empiricistic age the metaphysical imagination has to a large extent atrophied. The scientific account of origins, with its consistent theme of the qualitatively *more* deriving from the qualitatively *less*, so dominates our horizon that it is difficult to take seriously the opposite outlook which until five hundred years ago everyone took for granted. The second problem is of the opposite sort. The version of the Great Origins hypothesis that is most bandied about today puts that hypothesis in a bad light. I refer, of course, to Creationism, whose apostles have so muddied the waters with simplistic readings of the Scriptures, and scientific claims that are sometimes bogus, that it is next to impossible for the Great Origins thesis to gain a fair hearing.[2]

Let me take this second obstacle to the Great Origins thesis first. As the precise way to characterize the opposite of the Darwinian thesis I have chosen the phrase "the less from the more" for its generality and abstractness. As Adam and the animals were less than God, a literalist biblical account of how we got here fits the Great Origins hypothesis, but it is far from the only one that does so. All that the thesis requires is that we derive from Something that is superior to ourselves by every measure of worth we know. These transcendent objects include the ultimates of the great religious traditions — Allah, God, Brahman, Śūnyatā, the Tao, the Great Spirit — as well as philosophical ultimates, provided that they exceed human beings in intrinsic worth. Clearly included, for example, is the Neoplatonic One from which beings proceed by emanation rather than creation, and the Whiteheadian God whose primordial and consequent natures conspire to work upon the world their everlasting lure. I hope this latitude in the Great Origins thesis will keep it from being dismissed as Creationism.

The other bar to the Great Origins thesis, the poverty of the metaphysical imagination, is more difficult to deal with. Scientists who by virtue of their sensitivity are equally humanists are rhapsodic in hymning the grandeur of the universe. Einstein referred to its "radiant beauty which our dull faculties can comprehend only in their most primitive forms."[3] What is lacking is anything resembling Aristotle's Prime Mover, a first and final cause which in its very essence is luminously conscious and good. And if one does not sense the decisive difference these attributes make to a world view, this is the atrophy of which I speak.

How does one revive an ailing organ? Art might help if it were not itself at sea metaphysically; Walker Percy says that writers help us to understand the plight he cited but have no remedy to offer.[4] The energy that enters life through the Great Origins hypothesis does not derive solely from the heightened self-image that results from the discovery of royal pedigree. It also derives from the fact that there is in the Great Origins thesis no answer to the question of human origins that does not include the answer to the origin of everything. Here humankind and world conspire. They issue from a single source, and as that source is good beyond all conceiv-

ing, it is impossible that its offspring not be kin. In a single stroke
the self/world divide, laid wide by Descartes' mind/matter disjunc-
tion and the slash between primary and secondary qualities, is
mended.

In favoring small origins, Darwinism challenges the Great
Origins thesis. I shall argue that the evidence for Darwinism fails,
but that demonstration is needed only if Darwinism and the Great
Origins thesis are incompatible. Are they? Yes.

2. Darwinism and the Great Origins hypothesis are incompatible.

Darwinism and the Great Origins doctrine cannot be squared.
This needs to be argued, for it runs counter to the current drift
of mainline theology which sees Darwin as assimilatable. Vatican
II instructs the faithful to combine modern scientific theories with
Christian doctrine. It is widely held that evolutionary theory poses
no contradiction to Catholic belief. Except for fundamentalists,
Protestants concur, but scientists seem to feel that they are being
co-opted. Darwin saw his discovery as strongly resistant to admixture with belief in God, while Jacques Monod goes further. "The
mechanism of evolution as now understood," he tells us, "rules out
any claim that there are final causes, or purposes being realized.
[This] disposes of any philosophy or religion that believes in cosmic . . . purpose."[5] Realizing that this conclusion could be colored
by Monod's personal philosophy, I turn to the entry on "Evolution"
in The New Encyclopaedia Britannica for a statement that might
reflect, as well as any, consensus in the field. It tells me that "Darwin showed that evolution's cause, natural selection, was automatic
with no room for divine guidance or design."[6]

Which side is right? The question is complex, for a whole
swarm of issues is involved, including the way two important intellectual currents and the institutions they represent are competing for the mind of our age. I spent fifteen years at the Massachusetts Institute of Technology without seeing what a few paragraphs
in E. F. Schumacher's Guide for the Perplexed showed me clearly.
There is not one science. There are two, which Schumacher dubs
descriptive and instructional.[7]

Descriptive science is as old as the human race. Pivoting as
it does on careful observation and the organization of data thus
derived, no society could have survived without a touch of it,

though the quantity can vary enormously. When in the seventeenth century John Ray took the first steps toward creating a suitable system of classifying species in the plant world, he provided a good example of this first kind of science, as did Carolus Linnaeus whose naming of life forms in orderly classification established a context in which botanical studies could take place in a sustained fashion. Descriptive science is not confined to the study of nature; it is a part of every cognitive discipline. Even today in continental Europe, words for science tend to have this descriptive ring. *Wissenschaft* is an example. On the Continent, history is a science.

In the English-speaking world it is not, the reason being that here the word has come to denote modern science which turns on science in Schumacher's instructional mode. Instructional science takes the form: Do *X*, and *Y* will follow. In the formal, conceptual sphere we have geometry, mathematics, and logic, where we can issue instructions that work and thereby establish proof. Equally in the empirical, material world: our hands can manipulate objects, so again we can issue instructions as to what manipulations will achieve which ends and again establish proof. An important insight comes to view. Only through instructional science, which is to say, only in what we can ourselves do, can we truly explain and prove.

Applied to evolutionary theory, this distinction gives us descriptive evolution which tries to tell us *what* happened in life's ascent, and instructional evolution which takes up from there to explain *how* and *why* it happened. The ideal of descriptive evolution would be a complete cinematographic record of what has occurred in life's sojourn on this planet. We might think of it as a videotape which, accelerated enormously, PBS could run as a mind-boggling spectacular. It should be a silent film, in keeping with the eerie silence of the fossil record from which it would be primarily derived. Darwinism, on the other hand, is instructional evolution.

Descriptive evolution is essentially the fossil record. Fossils found in the earth's crust show that there have been changes in the constitution of plants and animals, and with the help of radioactive and potassium-argon dating these have been placed in historical sequence. Drawing primarily on this data, descriptive evolution weaves a story the chief features of which are: (a) that higher, more complex forms of life appeared later than simpler ones (much later); (b) that all organisms after the initial self-replicating protein molecule(s) issued from parents; and (c) that all species of life on earth can be traced back through their pedigrees to the simplest forms in which life initially appeared. Darwin contributed to descriptive evolution as just summarized, but his importance lies in his proposal for how it all happened: through natural selection working on chance mutations. It is this explanatory side of his work that I am calling Darwinism in this essay.

It is at once apparent that descriptive evolution is more compatible with the Great Origins hypothesis than is Darwinism, for, being silent on the question of causes, it leaves room for the possibility that God scripted and directs the entire production; if the heavens declare the glory of God, why not the fossil record? If we ponder the matter, though, we can see that psychologically, if not logically, descriptive evolution veils God's glory considerably.

Descriptive evolution works psychologically against the Great Origins concept. For on the one hand, though it brackets the question of *how* the more derives from the less, it nonetheless depicts it as so deriving. And it presents changes as occurring so gradually that nothing extraordinary seems to happen; miracle is reduced to microscopic, incremental accretions. Because these two features of descriptive evolution run psychologically counter to the Great Origins thesis, it is useful to remind ourselves that even descriptive evolution is not indubitable. Materially there are more anomalies, not to mention wide gaps, in the fossil record than the public recognizes, while formally the entire scenario rests on a postulate, uniformitarianism, which holds that the laws of nature do not change. Charles Lyell fixed this postulate into place in the 1830s with his three-volume *Principles of Geology*. As a geologist put it to me recently, "It's impossible to prove uniformitarianism; it's just that you can't be a geologist without it. We now know as Lyell did not that natural processes change — rates of erosion, for example. But natural laws must remain constant or geology isn't a science."

To his children's question, "Who made us, God or evolution?" a British theologian, Don Cupitt, found himself answering, "Both"; which answer, as we saw, is the one that most theologians are giving today. On reflection, though, Cupitt tells us, he concluded that his answer was "diplomatic, orthodox, and shallow."[8] For Darwinism does not purport to describe the instrumentalities through which God works. It is the scientific account for how we and other creatures got here, and as such it must, on pain of begging the question, proceed without recourse to anything remotely resembling divine intention or design. Monod has it exactly right when he writes: "The cornerstone of scientific method is . . . the *systematic* denial that 'true' knowledge can be got at by interpreting phenomena in terms of final causes — that is to say, of 'purpose.'"[9] It is important to see exactly what is being said here. As purposes and final causes entail realities that are greater than ourselves, Monod's dictum translates into saying that Small Origins accounts of how we got here are the only accounts that instructional science — on this point Darwinism — will allow. Darwinism qualifies as being scientific because its working principles are strictly nonteleological: natural selection is purely mechanical, and the mutations on which it works arrive solely by chance. But by the same token, if Darwinism is accepted as true, the Great Origins hypothesis is replaced by the Small Origins one.

3. In the face of its Great Origins rival, Darwinism fails.

I am not the first to call the claims for Darwinism into question, of course. A recent issue of *Environment* tells us that Darwin's ideas

> have long been under successful attack not just by religious fundamentalists or "scientific creationists" but by many biologists and such popularizers as the late Arthur Koestler . . . and Norman Macbeth. That this will be news to most educated laypersons and to many biologists is simply an example of cultural lag and the ability of dogmas to dominate not only religion but science as well.[10]

Macbeth's *Darwin Retried* (and in its author's eyes found wanting) has been out for over a decade now.[11] Asked on the November 1, 1981, PBS *Nova* program what his qualifications were for writing on a scientific subject, Macbeth answered that as a professional lawyer he considered himself an expert on evidence, and that it was in their handling of evidence that he faulted Darwin's defenders. More recently Jeremy Rifkin has published his *Algeny*, the central chapter of which is titled "The Darwinian Sunset." "Our children will not think of the world in a Darwinian way," he writes. "Darwin's theory of evolution will be remembered in centuries to come as a cosmological bridge between two world epochs."[12]

These are all lay verdicts, however, so we should go on to what the biologists themselves are saying. It came as a surprise to find that Darwinism has never gained much of a hearing in western Europe; *The New Encyclopaedia Britannica* notes that "natural selection is . . . not widely . . . recognized in western continental Europe" as evolution's cause.[13] Pierre Grassé for thirty years occupied the chair for evolution at the Sorbonne and edited the twenty-eight volume *Encyclopedia of Zoology*. In his *Evolution of Living Forms*, Grassé has this to say:

> The explanatory doctrines of biological evolution do not stand up to an objective, in-depth criticism. They prove to be either in conflict with reality or else incapable of solving the major problems involved. . . . Through use and abuse of hidden postulates, of bold, often ill-founded extrapolations, a pseudoscience has been created. It is taking root in the very heart of biology and is leading astray many biochemists and biologists, who sincerely believe that the accuracy of fundamental concepts has been demonstrated, which is not the case.[14]

Edwin Conklin, late professor of biology at Princeton, writes, "Religious devotion . . . is probably the reason why severe methodological criticism employed in other departments of biology has not yet been brought to bear on evolutionary speculation."[15] And in making the distinction between descriptive and explanatory evolution David Raup of the University of Chicago writes: "The record . . . pretty clearly demonstrates that evolution has occurred if we define evolution simply as change; but it does not tell us how this change took place, and that's really the question."[16]

A. THE FOSSIL RECORD

The only evidence that we have concerning the past history of life on our planet is found in fossils embedded in rock formations. Darwin admitted that in his day they did little to support his theory. "Geology . . . does not reveal . . . finely graded organic change," he wrote, "and this, perhaps, is the most obvious and gravest objection which can be urged against [my] theory."[17] He trusted, of course, that time would fill in the gaps, but how little it has done so Raup again attests. "We are now about 120 years after Darwin . . . and, ironically, we have even fewer examples of evolutionary transition than we had in Darwin's time," inasmuch as many that were thought to be valid are now known not to be.[18] Concerning links between species, an eerie silence prevails. "Evolution requires intermediate forms between species," says David Kitts, professor of geology at the University of Oklahoma, "and paleontology does not provide them."[19] The punctuated equilibrium theory — eons of invariance punctuated by quick (perhaps five- to fifty-thousand-year) spurts in isolated ecological niches — has emerged to account for the fact that, as Stephen Gould says, "phyletic gradualism [which would have left evidences of transitional links] is never seen in the rocks."[20] But does that theory amount to more than justification for continuing to believe in transitional forms when we have no traces of them?

B. POPULATION BREEDING

The breeding of domestic plants and animals which had begun in England in the 1760s had by Darwin's day produced famous breeds of Leicestershire sheep and Dishley cattle. Darwin was immensely impressed with this art and adopted it as a metaphor for his theory, not knowing that in the end it would work against him. For though mutations can effect changes within species (microevolution), with respect to species as wholes they insure stability rather than change. Species-continuity is insured by a constant barrage of subtle variations that allow the species to adapt if the environment should change; concomitantly, species-change (macroevolution) is blocked by the law of reversion to the mean. Beyond a certain point deviations become unstable and, instead of cresting into new species, die out. In a typical experiment that began with fruit flies that averaged thirty-six bristles, it was possible to raise the number to fifty-six or lower it to twenty-five, but beyond those numbers the lines became sterile and expired. As Luther Burbank noted early on, "there is a pull toward the mean which keeps all living things within some more or less fixed limitations."[21] Loren Eiseley is not the only one to have noted the unhappy consequences for Darwinian theory when he writes, "There is great irony in this situation, for more than almost any other single factor, domestic breeding has been used as an argument for evolution."[22]

C. NATURAL SELECTION

Darwin saw natural selection as his central discovery; he believed that he had found in it the engine of change that had brought higher forms of life into being. But problems have arisen.

If the fittest survive, why don't the less fit disappear? Gertrude Himmelfarb asks. If the hive bee's efficiency in containing a maximum of honey with a minimum of wax gives it a Darwinian edge, why are bumbling, inefficient bumble bees still around?[23]

Natural selection makes no room for long-range considerations; every new trait has to be immediately useful or it is discarded. How then are we to account for the emergence of complex organs or limbs which are made up of myriads of parts that would have had to have developed independently of one another through thousands of generations during which they had no utility? Stephen Gould reduces the problem to its simplest proportions when he asks, "What good is half a jaw or half a wing?"[24]

If novel faculties emerge because of their adaptive edge, why are some of them overqualified for that purpose, as Darwin and Wallace both conceded the human brain to be? Gould takes such points seriously, saying that it is time to free ourselves "from the need to interpret all our basic skills as adaptations for specific purposes."[25]

As no definition of fitness other than survival has been (or can be) proposed, the reasoning on this topic is circular. "Natural selection . . . amounts to the statement that the individuals which leave the most offspring are those which leave the most offspring. It is a tautology."[26] "The survivors, having survived, are thence judged to be the fittest."[27]

Finally, Darwin thought that natural selection accounts for the creativity in evolution — how life forms that are clearly higher emerged. Stephen Gould does not see that it does.[28]

D. EMBRYOLOGY AND VESTIGIAL ORGANS.

I was taught that the human embryo in the course of its development in the womb rehearses the entire evolutionary sequence — in Ernst Haeckel's catchy slogan, "ontogeny recapitulates phylogeny." Our useless tailbones, for their part, were cited as vestigial remains of the tails our ancestors had swung from. When I mentioned these matters in presenting an early draft of this paper, a biologist expressed surprise at my bringing them up. "We haven't taught those things in years," he said. It turns out that what I had been taught were incipient gills in the embryo are not gills at all, and that the coccygeal vertebrae — tailbone is a clear misnomer — are in no wise vestigial. Without the muscles they support, our pelvic organs would drop out.

E. BIOGENESIS

Darwin occupied himself only with the living world, but his followers extended his theory to explain how life originated from nonlife. In the early 1950s it was thought that experiments performed by Stanley Miller and Harold Urey had shown this to be possible, but it is now recognized, first, that the atmospheric conditions in which life arose were probably prohibitively different from those in the scientists' laboratory, and second, that the kind of amino acids that they produced — racemates — are not the kind that can support life.

F. MATHEMATICAL IMPROBABILITY

It used to be thought that geological time was immense enough to allow almost anything to happen, and so it is if we are thinking of isolated events like the number nineteen turning up on a roulette wheel precisely when it is needed. Now, though, attention has turned to the extent to which innumerable precise components must converge, each making its appearance exactly on schedule. This is more like the number twenty-three coming up on all the tables at Monte Carlo simultaneously, followed by the numbers twenty-four, twenty-five, twenty-six, and so on, still all appearing simultaneously. For things like this to happen, even four billion years is insufficient. Again a personal anecdote can make the point. At yet another presentation of this paper in progress it happened that the president of the International Association for Mathematical Biology was in the audience. He did not enter into the discussion, but at its close he came forward and identified himself. Then, very quietly, he said, "There wasn't enough time." It is for this reason that Fred Hoyle, Francis Crick, and others are turning to outer space, deeming it more probable that our planet was "seeded" with life from elsewhere than that it developed here.

"What is not in doubt," says Stephen Gould, "is the fact of evolution," or what I have called descriptive evolution. "But as to its mechanism [here called Darwinism], there is observational evidence for natural selection [true, but outside of microevolution?], but it could be false that it [that is, Darwinism in its distinctive claim] is as strong a determinant of evolution as we think."[29] More recent statements in which Gould associated adaptationism with Voltaire's joke—"Why do people have noses? To support their glasses!"—suggest that his own confidence in it is waning. *The New York Times Magazine* reported that "this forty-two-year-old paleontologist is putting himself more and more at odds with orthodox Darwinism,"[30] but the alternatives he is toying with—constraints imposed by developmental trends and anatomical architecture—are at this stage little more than conjectures.

The point of this critique of Darwinism has been to show how little (in the way of hard evidence) has been allowed to eclipse so much (the Great Origins principle). This is the more so when to the paucity of firm empirical evidence we add intuitive considerations which can only be listed.

—Max Muller, according to Nirad Chaudhuri's book *Scholar Extraordinary*, wrote to Darwin saying that he found it quite possible to believe that the human physique has evolved from simpler bodies, but the idea that human language emerged from grunts and brays struck him as out of the question.

—Can something emerge from nothing? Can a stream rise higher than its source? When I ask my students these questions they almost inevitably answer no. Yet William Bartley, the biographer and foremost interpreter of Karl Popper, tells us that the foundation of Popper's philosophy is the claim that something can come from nothing. What are we to make of these opposite answers? My personal reading of the matter is that Popper, having steeped his life in the philosophy of science, saw clearly the fundamental point. Only if we grant science the counterintuitive, something-from-nothing assumption can we look to it to explain anything above the material plane.

—The going word for that something-from-nothing legerdemain is *emergence,* and in countering reductionism by insisting that higher forms have ontological components that were not in their precursors, it looks in the right direction. But as an explanation for those novel components it is worthless; it recognizes their arrival while doing nothing to explain it. There would be nothing wrong with this if it did not presume to explain it, which it does by riding analogies that are spurious. The standard one is the liquidity of water which emerges from the convergence of two gases, hydrogen and oxygen. This, though, overlooks the fact that apart from the way water looks and feels to us (which introduces an issue the analogy finesses, namely, the emergence of sentience and awareness) its liquidity is simply a different arrangement of molecules in motion, or primary qualities only. Nothing new in kind has appeared at all. The same old primary qualities have merely been reshuffled.

Conclusion

Is it impertinent for someone untrained in science to tamper with a theory as technical as evolution has become? Who owns this issue?

It has been my contention that more than technicalities are involved. My basic question has been whether we should believe that Darwinism explains how we got here, and my negative answer is predicated on the claim that beliefs take shape on an unrestricted horizon which in this case includes considerations in addition to ones that are paleobiological.

It brings to mind the story of the ill-fated sky diver who, plummeting toward earth in a parachute that refuses to open, passes a hot-air balloonist whose blow torch won't shut off. "Know anything about parachutes?" he shouts, to which the balloonist counters, "No, but what about you? Know anything about gas stoves?" Whitehead predicted that, more than by any other factor, the future will be shaped by the way the two most powerful forces in history — science and religion — settle into relation with each other. That relationship has been my root concern. Though I have openly registered my perception that the Darwinian parachute has not opened very far, I know no more about such devices than the next person. I do know something about gas stoves, here representing convictions that can make the spirit soar. It is as Walker Percy says. Plummeting through sidereal time, we moderns under poor acoustical conditions shout across the expanses that divide our special-ties, "Know anything about this? About that?"

The speaker who has the best grasp of both is the one who most merits our attention.

NOTES

1. Marshall Sahlins, *Culture and Practical Reason* (Chicago: University of Chicago Press, 1976), p. 17.

2. I find myself in an awkward position here, for though I wish to extricate the Great Origins thesis from the Creationists' clutches, in ways they have my respect. Their deep commitment to one version of the Great Origins doctrine has made them more vigilant than other theologians in spotting places where Darwinism rides on faith rather than fact.

An important chapter in the sociology of knowledge is being written; one in which establishment forces as represented by the university, the American Civil Liberties Union, and mainline churches will not, in the eyes of history, emerge as heroes. I touch on these issues in Huston Smith, "Scientism in Sole Command," *Christianity and Crisis*, 21 January 1982; and in Huston Smith, "Evolution and Evolutionism," *The Christian Century*, 7–14 July 1982.

3. Albert Einstein, *Living Philosophies* (New York: Simon & Schuster, 1931), pp. 6–7.

4. See also Saul Bellow's 1976 Nobel Laureate Address: "The intelligent public is waiting to hear from art what it does not hear from theology, philosophy, and social theory, and what it cannot hear from pure science: a broader, fuller, more coherent, more comprehensive account of what we human beings are, who we are, and what this life is for. If writers do not come into the center it will not be because the center is preempted. It is not."

5. The conclusion of Jacques Monod, *Chance and Necessity* (New York: Vintage Books, 1972), as summarized in Don Cupitt, *Worlds of Science and Religion* (New York: Hawthorne Books, 1976), p. 12.

6. *The New Encyclopaedia Britannica*, s.v. "Evolution."

7. E. F. Schumacher, *Guide for the Perplexed* (New York: Harper & Row, 1976), pp. 100–10.

8. Cupitt, *Worlds of Science and Religion*, p. 1.

9. Monod, *Chance and Necessity*, p. 21, emphasis his.

10. Victor Ferkiss, review of *Algeny* by Jeremy Rifkin, *Environment* 25 (July–August 1983): 44.

11. Norman Macbeth, *Darwin Retried* (Boston: Gambit, 1971).

12. Jeremy Rifkin, *Algeny* (New York: Viking Press, 1983), p. 130.

13. *The New Encyclopaedia Britannica*, s.v. "Evolution."

14. Pierre Grassé, *Evolution of Living Forms* (New York: Academic Press, 1977), pp. 202, 206.

15. Edwin Conklin, *Man Real and Ideal* (New York: Scribner's, 1943), p. 52.

16. David Raup, "Conflicts between Darwin and Paleontology," *Field Museum of Natural History Bulletin* 50 (1979):24.

17. Charles Darwin, *The Origin of Species* (London: J. M. Dent, 1971), p. 239.

18. Raup, "Conflicts between Darwin and Paleontology," p. 26.

19. David Kitts, "Paleontology and Evolutionary Theory," *Evolution* 28 (1974):467. Darwinists must produce a family tree, a pedigree, Norman Macbeth observed on the *Nova* program earlier referred to, "and I regret to say that after 120 years they haven't produced a single solid phylogeny."

20. Stephen Jay Gould, with Niles Eldredge, "Punctuated Equilibria," *Paleobiology* 3 (1977):115.

21. Luther Burbank, quoted in Macbeth, *Darwin Retried*, p. 35.

22. Loren Eiseley, quoted in Macbeth, *Darwin Retried*, p. 36.

23. Gertrude Himmelfarb, *Darwin and the Darwinian Revolution* (New York: W. W. Norton, 1959), pp. 341–42.

24. Stephen Jay Gould, "The Return of Hopeful Monsters," *Natural History* 86 (June–July 1977):24.

25. Stephen Jay Gould, "The Evolutionary Biology of Constraint," *Daedalus* 29 (1980):46.

26. C. H. Waddington, *The Strategy of Genes* (London: Allen & Unwin, 1957), pp. 64–65.

27. Himmelfarb, *Darwin and the Darwinian Revolution*, p. 316.

28. *Unitarian-Universalist World*, 2 February 1982.

29. Ibid.

30. James Gleick, "Stephen Jay Gould: Breaking Tradition with Darwin," *New York Times Magazine*, 20 November 1983, p. 50.

Homo Homini Deus Est:
Feuerbach's Religious Materialism

MARX W. WARTOFSKY

> Religion is from the outset con-
> sciousness of the transcendental
> arising from actually existing forces.
> This more popularly.[1] — *Karl Marx*

Introduction

I DO NOT PROPOSE to give any detailed reconstruction of Feuerbach's philosophy of religion, or of his distinctive and problematic conception of species-being (*Gattungswesen*), or of his equally
problematic materialism. Rather, I would like to raise a question
not about Feuerbach, but by way of Feuerbach, namely: "Is
there a viable materialist conception of religion?"

This is a less simple question than it appears to be. Plainly,
there are materialist conceptions of religion, from Epicurus
through Marx and Engels, which explain religion as a function of
material human needs, and of the material conditions of human
life which give rise to these needs. The question is: Are such theories viable or adequate to explain the phenomenon of religious belief? A viable conception of religion is one which doesn't simply
explain religion away, but rather explains its origins, its distinctive cultural and historical forms, its persistence in various institutional contexts, its changes and development, its continuing
and present existence in the modes of belief and action of individuals. The question of whether there is a viable materialist con-

134

ception of religion is therefore a question of whether any of the presumptively materialist theories meet these requirements. What would it take for a materialist theory of religion to do so adequately?

The focus on Feuerbach is prompted by the fact that he gives the first and most fully elaborated materialist explanation of religion in modern times, in a way which attempts to preserve the reality of the phenomenon, and not merely to discount it. The burden of my title is the kernel of Feuerbach's thesis: "*Homo Homini Deus Est*" ("man is a God to man"). Feuerbach proposes that religious consciousness, revealed in its "true essence," is the human recognition of the human as divine, as the highest value, and as bearing within itself the grounds of infinity and perfection. That Feuerbach sees these divine qualities in the actuality of human existence, in the materiality of human need, feeling, and consciousness, and in the sociality of the human form of life is the intent of my characterization of Feuerbach's view as "religious materialism." But Feuerbach's theory fails. The failure is, nevertheless, important. For it opens up the possibility of an adequate theory in the most serious way and also anticipates the most serious difficulties that an adequate theory would have to resolve. Indeed, it is the critique of Feuerbach which seems to me to be the path to salvation — at least to theoretical or philosophical salvation. In Engels's play of words on Feuerbach's name, *Feuerbach* is the "fiery brook" which was the "purgatory" through which German post-Hegelian thought had to pass. This "fiery brook" still serves as the purgatory through which our own conceptions of religion have to pass, if they are to transcend the limits of the past.

In this paper, therefore, I propose to do several things: (1) To pose the general form of the problem that a materialist theory of religion has to solve — namely, the problem of transcendence. (2) To sketch Feuerbach's formulation of the problem, first negatively, in the form of Feuerbach's critique of theology, then positively, in terms of what he took to be a humanist resolution of the contradiction in theology. (3) To consider why Feuerbach's theory may be called a "religious materialism." Here I will question what is "materialist" about this materialism, and whether any materialism, properly so-called, can be characterized as "religious," or whether this is simply a *contradictio in adjecto*. (4) To sketch the philosophical and theological alternatives in the traditional conceptions of transcendence, and to explore whether a materialist theory of transcendence is possible. (5) To present the Feuerbachian and Marxian views of transcendence which, it seems to me, begin to formulate the concept in a materialist way. Here, I hope to show that dialectic — the Hegelian dialectic, in its transformations by Feuerbach and Marx — provides the clue to a materialist theory of transcendence, first, as a dialectic of consciousness, and then, as a dialectic of praxis.

What will have happened, by this time, to the notion of materialism is perhaps the crucial question of this paper, and also a crucial question to me, personally, for it concerns the wider question of how Marxism is to be understood, and whether it is viable. It should be clear, from this introduction, that I take the question of transcendence to be the conceptual heart of the matter, and that I take it, therefore, to be central to the characterization of religion. Whether or not there can be a viable materialist conception of religion hinges on this point. There can be, only if there is a viable materialist theory of transcendence.

Transcendence: a first approach

The reason that I approach the question of transcendence by way of Feuerbach is that he offers a striking and radical reformulation of the traditional theological problem. The traditional problem concerns the relation of God to the world, and it arises from Christian theology both as a general question of religious consciousness, and in a specific historical setting.

First, as a general question: no conception of religion can be viable if it doesn't deal with the present, with the concrete realities of present human life, in both their sordid and glorious details. At the same time, no conception of religion is viable if it doesn't deal with what transcends the present, with what is grasped as beyond the actual and the particular. The problem for traditional theology (and metaphysics) was how these apparently incompatible, if not indeed contradictory desiderata could be held together. The Christian mystery, the center of Christian faith, lay in the identification of these opposing requirements: of the present moment with eternity; of life here and now with everlasting life; of human finitude, suffering, and sin with infinite being, joy, and redemption. The Incarnation of the divine served Christianity (as it did pre-Christian religions) as the living metaphor, the concrete embodiment of this apparent contradiction. Christ was human, a living, suffering, dying individual; and was also God incarnate. The infinite and eternal God was identical with the finite and temporal human individual.

Feuerbach saw, in this paradox of faith, the very essence of Christianity. But he saw it as a rational contradiction only on the interpretation demanded by theology—namely, that God was nonhuman, superhuman, wholly other. In *The Essence of Christianity*, Feuerbach argued that this theological insistence upon the separateness of the human from the divine is in reality—nontheologically or anthropologically—nothing but the separation of the individual human being from his or her own species-nature; and that religious consciousness resides in the awareness of both the species-nature of the individual, and of the separation of the individual from this species-nature. Thus, he writes that his task is "to show that the opposition of the divine and the human is nothing but the opposition between human essence and the human individual."[2]

However, the traditional theological problem of transcendence also arose in a particular historical setting. And to that dimension, Feuerbach pays scant attention. The question is: Why did Christian theology formulate the notion of divine transcendence as it did? The burden of Christian theology in its early phases—whatever its sources in Greek or Jewish thought (or in their Philonic amalgam)—was to counter pagan identification of God (or of the gods) with nature (with natural objects or phenomena) or with any given human or ethnic character of a local sort. The task of theology was, both theoretically and practically, to counter idolatry. God, who creates the world, must stand beyond the world. God must be in some sense wholly other, precisely in not being limited to the conditions of finitude and transiency which are the sources of human need, suffering, and death. God is ultimately different, and this ultimate difference constitutes transcendence.

The difficulty which traditional Christian theology posed for itself in this formulation of transcendence is that this self-same transcendent God had also to see, to touch, to succor, to care for, to provide, to judge, to show mercy, to recognize, to hear, to understand, to heal — not in some realm beyond the world of finite, concrete, and daily human existence, but just in that very world itself. The transcendent God had also to suffer and die, to be born of woman, to bleed, to cry, to eat and drink. The infinite had to become, not symbolically, but actually, existentially finite. To worship Christ as a symbol of the Godhead would have been to substitute one idolatry for another. Symbols are not gods. So belief in God had to be belief not through Christ but in Christ.

Theology was then caught between the demands for a transcendent deity, distinct from the gods of the idolaters, and the demands for an immanent, embodied, incarnate deity, accessible to believers. Where theology posited the Incarnation as a mystery of faith, Feuerbach took theology to be the embodiment of a contradiction, precisely in that this theology sought to assert both rationally exclusive demands in a rational way. He argued that the belief of believers is not contradictory, for belief is not a matter of reason, but of feeling, of felt need. Belief is the activity of the practical imagination to supply what is needed in the imagination to realize the demands of feeling. It is, in effect, not yet rational because it is not a matter of asserting propositions. It is prelogical, the work of the heart. It becomes contradictory and rationally insupportable when it is transformed into rational terms, subject to the dictates of logic. Theology, Feuerbach argued, is the perversion of belief. The theory of transcendence, as in the rational theory of incarnation, is outright contradiction. It asserts mutually exclusive propositions. So runs, in brief, Feuerbach's critique of traditional Christian theories of transcendence.

And yet, Feuerbach himself had a theory of transcendence. How can that be? If Feuerbach were to have such a theory, by his own strictures, and on the grounds of his own critique, then in it the transcendent could not be conceived to be wholly other and yet identical with that from which it is wholly other. Yet, insofar as the divine — for Feuerbach's transcendent is the divine, and nothing less — is fully immanent, identical with the human and the worldly, in what conceivable sense could the divine be transcendent at all? The trick is to ground the transcendent in the human, but in such a way that it is human beings who, by their very nature, create the transcendent in the course of their characteristic activity. Thus Feuerbach's solution to the traditional problem is not to offer an alternative to the solutions already posed, all of which he rejects as self-contradictory, in that systematic critique of theology which comprises his major work, *The Essence of Christianity*. Rather, his solution is to radically reformulate the problem itself. He does this by taking it as a genetic question: How does the transcendent originate? How do human beings, finite flesh-and-blood creatures, individuals, arrive at such a consciousness, and what, in effect, is it a consciousness of? What is its object?

For Feuerbach, the object of religious belief exists, and not merely as a fiction of the imagination. Rather its exists in a full-blooded, ontological way, no less so than does the believer. In fact, the object of belief in the transcendent is oneself, the believer! Religious consciousness is nothing but human self-consciousness, whose object is the human itself.

Feuerbach's move, then, is to take the human as a consciousness of self which is at the same time a consciousness of an other like oneself. "Self-consciousness exists . . . by the fact that it exists for another self-consciousness; that is to say, it *is* only by being acknowledged or 'recognized'." This rough paraphrase is not Feuerbach, of course, but, recognizably, Hegel, in *The Phenomenology of Mind*.[3] Feuerbach takes Hegel's formulation as a basis, and elaborates it to mean that consciousness of oneself as a human being requires the recognition of oneself as a species-being. The condition for human individuality, as human, is the bond of consciousness in which the I knows itself to be an I only in relation to a Thou. The community of *I*'s and *Thou*'s, the human community or species-being, is therefore constituted in this essential mutuality of recognition itself. The being which the individual consciousness takes as the object of such human recognition is thus as much *I* as *Thou*, as much other as self, as much community as individual.

Now for Feuerbach, this species-being is the living, material community of human beings, and therefore an embodied or concrete universal. It is this species-being which is the object of consciousness of the transcendent. But there's the rub. For the individual is existentially finite, and a finite consciousness. Yet such a human individual's consciousness, even of this finitude, is a recognition of one's own finitude only with respect to, and by contrast to, the existence of others like oneself. One recognizes oneself to be human only in recognition of one's common humanity, one's human "essence," to use Feuerbach's term. And the representation of this human essence, this species-nature, is a recognition of that which lies beyond, transcends the limits of one's own individual finitude. The human consciousness is, in Feuerbach's view, this double awareness of one's separate and finite individuality and one's common, universal, or shared nature.

Insofar as the human being recognizes the separation of the self from others, one aspect of one's essential humanity is realized: one's own distinctiveness, existential uniqueness, the "I." Insofar as one recognizes one's universal, shared, or mutual nature with others, in the relation of I and Thou — since only individuals exist — another aspect of one's essential humanity is realized. But it is this otherness, this species-nature transcending the separate "I," which becomes the object of the consciousness of transcendence. Taken as symbolic "other," this Being becomes invested with characteristics no individual Thou can possess, but which expresses the potentiality of the community of *I*'s or *Thou*'s. It transcends the limits of any individual's existence or capacities. This abstracted "other" is then taken to be a transcendent entity; in short, a God. But in reality, this "God" is only the hypostatized community of individuals, misidentified with its symbolic representation in consciousness. Human dependence on other human beings becomes identified with human dependence on this "Other," beyond the limits of individual finite human existence. This "Other" becomes deified as that Being which stands over and against the concrete individual existence of *I*'s and *Thou*'s.

One step more. This new Being, this image of communal existence, becomes *God*. But Feuerbach says, if we recognize the genesis and nature of this God as "nothing but" the alienated form of human-self-consciousness, then we recognize what this "God" in truth is: "*Homo Homini Deus Est*" ("man is a God to man"). From this, there follow all the Feuerbachian aphorisms: "Theology is esoteric anthropology," and others.

The transcendent, as an object, has on the one hand been identified with the mystified, mistakenly hypostatized representation of the community of human beings, but has now, on the other hand, been demystified, recognized in its concrete existence as the flesh-and-blood community of human individuals itself. It is not the case, therefore, that an individual human being, as such, is or can be God; but only that God, as transcendent Being, is in living fact the community.

However, if the human is the divine, then the divine would seem to be a being of consciousness only, and not a material being, for species-being, the awareness of oneself in the relation to the other, is an intentional constitution of the community, in the act of mutually recognizing self-consciousnesses. In what sense can one say that Feuerbach goes any further than Hegel, in *The Phenomenology*? Is Feuerbach's humanism anything more than an identification of Hegel's *Idea* with human self-consciousness? If Feuerbach's view is to be understood as a materialist conception of religion, wherein lies its materialism?

Religious Materialism

If *Homo Homini Deus Est*, then Feuerbach's materialism must lie in his conception of the human being, or the person. His materialist conception of religion (if indeed he has one) must construe the object of religious belief as a material being, and the praxis of religion as a material praxis. However, there are two ways to interpret this requirement of materialism. The first is to argue that the object of religion is the material human being and that therefore religion is about this material being, but that religious consciousness concerns this being not in its concrete existence in the world, but only as an object in consciousness. Thus, the praxis of religion is belief, and belief, as an activity of consciousness, is not a material praxis but rather a mental praxis. Or (to be fully fair to Feuerbach, in this interpretation), belief is a praxis not simply of thought or of intellect or of reason, but rather of feeling. It is a matter of expression of a conscious need or want or wish, by a thinking-feeling-willing being; but the expression of this feeling or desire is in the imagination. The arena of this praxis of belief is therefore the imagination, and the activity of the imagination is not itself a material but a mental activity. Therefore, though the object of religion is material human existence, the praxis of religion is not a material praxis, but rather a reflection in the imagination *of* the material praxis or life-activity of the species.

The second interpretation of the requirement of a materialist conception of religion is that both its object and the activity of the subject as a religious consciousness are material. On this view, the praxis of belief would itself have to be construed as a material praxis. Belief would not simply be a matter of feeling or desire reflected upon in the imagination, but indeed, practical belief. The object of belief would still be an object of the imagination, but the imagination would no longer be an activity of merely inward or mental reflection, or even a matter of external representation of the object of belief. Rather, the representation itself would serve as a model for its embodiment in the world. It would reveal itself not only as purpose, or end of action, but would become actualized in that very activity. Such belief, then, is the activity of practical objectification, material praxis. It would not only interpret the world, it would also change it, in accordance with the imagination of what such a change would bring about.

Such an interpretation of the requirement for a materialist conception of religion raises two questions: (1) Why should such an object of belief as the human being, as species-being, be regarded as "material"? What is "materialist" in this reading of "material human existence," especially if we are talking not alone of individuals, but of their social species-being, their universality? What is, in short, a material universal? Is it no more than the Hegelian concrete universal? And if it is more, what do "concrete" and "material" signify here? (2) Why should such a materialism, however it is construed, be characterized as "religious"? Why not say, instead, that the "religious" has in fact been left behind, once the transcendent is no longer an imaginary or hypostatized entity of thought, but becomes instead the very activity of transcending the limits of the present in practical activity?

Feuerbach answers these questions in a variety of ways, and I cannot here offer more than a brief sketch of his thought. I can also say that his resolution of these questions remains tentative, problematic, and inadequate. But he does raise the problems, and raises them in such a way that the nineteenth century and a good part of the twentieth are taken up, both intellectually and practically, with the problems which Feuerbach proposes, and with a critique of his inadequacy.

First, what does Feuerbach mean by "material" or "materialism"? Certainly not the mechanist materialism of eighteenth-century natural science, or natural philosophy. He is concerned with material nature — the physicochemical stuff that is the condition of human existence. But materialism in terms of Feuerbach's humanism is focused on material needs. Thus, in his grossest version of such a "materialism" of organic nature, he repeats, with Moleschott, the adage with which he has unfortunately become identified: *"Der Mensch ist was er isst"* ("man is what he eats").

But the main focus of Feuerbach's materialism is his theory of *Sinnlichkeit*, ("sensateness" or "sensibility"), which is an interesting but confused empiricism in which the human sense organs themselves are the primary mode of our activity and our knowledge. *Sinnlichkeit* has also the connotation not only of sensationism, in the traditional epistemological sense, but also of the affective, intentional mode of our activity, in the awareness of needs and desires. In Feuerbach's case, this awareness is interpreted fundamentally as an awareness of two sorts of needs, which are closely related: the material need for bodily sustenance, from which there originates our feelings of dependence upon nature; and the social need for other people, interpreted not only as sexual need, but as a need for others in affirming and realizing our social or communicative nature. From this need there originates the feeling of dependence upon others not only for our bodily existence, but also for our spiritual existence, as self-conscious agents. Out of this need, of course, comes the awareness of ourselves as species-beings. *Sinnlichkeit*—both sense-awareness and also awareness of our dependency on nature and on other human beings — then functions, for Feuerbach, as the direct source of our ontological conviction that the world beyond us, both the natural and the human world, exists. Insofar as transcendence means the recognition of the not-myself, which at the same time has its being-for-us in relation to our sensibility, then this *Sinnlichkeit* is, for Feuerbach, the means of our self-transcendence.

Yet what are we to make of the sense of the term *religious* in Feuerbach? True, he writes: "My philosopy is — *no* philosophy; my religion is — *no* religion." Yet he is the philosopher of religion *par excellence*. He wants to save religion from its alienated, mystified form, reveal it to be the very arena of human self-recognition in thoroughly this-worldly terms. He wants to deny to religion that which makes it a fetter on the human mind. He wants to reveal the "secret of religion," namely, the divinity of the human as the thoroughly human understanding of its own nature. He writes that the true atheist is not the one who denies that God exists, but the one who denies the existence of the predicates of God — love, justice, mercy. These are divine predicates, but the object of which they are predicated is the human. Feuerbach, in effect, wants us all to become true believers, but not believers in the image of human essence, which is God; rather, believers in the existing reality of which this is the image, which is the human. In this sense, religion is, in Marx's phrase, "the consciousness of the transcendental arising from actually existing forces."[4] Feuerbach's materialism, insofar as he understood "actually existing forces," was certainly not Marx's, or Engels's. It was the materialism of social existence, but not yet of this social existence conceived in its determinate political, economic, historical forms, or modes of action. Thus Marx could write that Hegel, in *The Philosophy of Right*, was far in advance of Feuerbach's understanding of society or of concrete social beings.

Yet Feuerbach's materialism is a religious materialism in a sense which goes beyond the characterization of religion as simply the consciousness of species-being as the transcendent object of belief. It is religious in that it gives full recognition to the affective life, to the qualities of commitment, care, need, hope which make of human desire something infinitely different from animal need-awareness or animal gregariousness. With Hegel, Feuerbach says, "The animals have no religion." That is because the object of the animal's awareness cannot be the species. One may argue, against this, that species-recognition in animals does exist; that it is innate or instinctive; or even that it is acquired; and that it exhibits itself in maternal care, in mating, in gregariousness; and that it may be explained in terms of natural selection, by the adaptive advantages which distinctive species-recognition affords to species-survival in animals. But Feuerbach is pre-Darwinian, in this respect. Also, he is acutely aware of the difference that speech, language, representation, make in distinguishing animal from human consciousness. It is the capacity to envision the universal and the transcendent as an object of imagination which allows for intentional human agency, especially in respect to the future. It is this capacity which marks off human from animal life. Marx was to propose a historical materialism, in which this conscious intentionality became the hallmark of creative human praxis. It was praxis undertaken to satisfy conscious purposes and needs, thus a praxis in which human existence, and its material conditions, could be raised to the level of a conscious object which guided activity and gave rise to rationality. Marx's sketch, here, is largely unfulfilled as yet. But it presages a notion of historical transcendence based in the very features of human social praxis.

In Feuerbach's account of the nature of belief, there remains a rich source for the fuller realization of a theory of such praxis, emphasizing its subjective, felt, or affective dimensions, as well as the distinctively human, rational dimensions. These dimensions may not, properly speaking, be "religious," but they represent what remains the province of religion, and has not yet been adequately realized in the theories of social, political, or economic praxis. In this sense, Feuerbach's religious materialism, in all of its inadequacies, poses contemporary problems for any materialist theory, including historical materialism, which may then have to reappraise its foundations radically in order to be able to account systematically and viably for this fundamental aspect of human belief and human activity.

Transcendence: a second approach

Feuerbach's religious materialism thus provides an approach to a materialist theory of transcendence on two grounds.

First, he proposes (within the limits of his humanist materialism) a materialist interpretation of the transcendent object of religion — of God — as the embodied, living human community or species-being. Second, he proposes, or suggests, a materialist interpretation of the method by which religious consciousness achieves its recognition of the transcendent object, namely, by the activity or the praxis of belief, or faith (*Glauben*). But now it is necessary to take a second look at the concept of transcendence, this time not so much in terms of the problem that theology poses for religious consciousness, but in terms of the philosophical or metaphysical formulations of the problem.

The standard theories of transcendence in metaphysical thought, as well as in theology proper — at least in the rationalizing theologies that Feuerbach attacks as "speculative" — posit the transcendent either as a rational presupposition, or as the independently existing reality to be discovered by thought, or as a sheer convention of language or thought. Or else, they immerse the transcendent indistinguishably so that it is mystically and mysteriously identical with what it transcends. It is mind, thought, penetrating the veil of sensibility, that uncovers the universal, that transcends particularity, that overcomes the transiency and disconnectedness of things, that grasps what lies behind, beneath, beyond, and either discovers or invents the conceptual order of things.

Well, this is, of course, a method. But it is only adumbrated in the traditional views. Its elaboration as an explicit process — indeed, one may say, its discovery as a method — is due to Hegel. Since the issue is transcendence, I will focus on only one aspect, but, to my mind, the crucial one in this method. The method is dialectic. But what is it a method of? It is precisely the method of overcoming particularity, finitude, the disconnectedness of things. What Hegel takes it to be is the very nature and process of consciousness, of thought itself. Whatever Hegel's debt to Kant, to Fichte, and others, he alone develops rigorously and systematically the step-by-step account of how thought passes from the immediate here-now, to what is other, to the not-self, to the relation of subject to object. The method, simply, is difference, or negation. *I* am distinct from the *not-me; now* is different from *then; here* from there; the bud from its flower — homely distinctions to be sure. And if only these, if simply difference alone, then not yet dialectic; rather, what Hegel calls abstract negation. *Omni deter-minatio est negatio* ("every determination is a negation"). So what? To be a *this* is not to be a *that*. But mere difference is not yet the relation between *this* and *that*, how *this* bears on *that*, how *thisness* depends on *thatness*. It is the relation of the present moment to what lies beyond it, of the finite individual to what is external to that individual, that marks for Hegel the passage of thought from dumb and brute immediacy to synthesis, meaning, understanding, thinking. In this way, thought, establishing the relation of the object of thought to itself, makes its own what lies before it as its object. The sheer otherness of its object becomes appropriated. In the Hegelian jargon, this otherness is overcome, transcended, negated, *aufgehoben*, raised up, so to speak, into a content of thought, into its own content.

Nothing can be an object for thought, in Hegel's terms, without at the same time having become such an object. Thus the total or abstract — that is, disconnected — externality of what lies beyond this activity of thought becomes an object for thought only on condition of this appropriation.

The mysteries and horrors of the Hegelian dialectic are well-enough publicized to have scared off two to three whole genera-tions of Anglo-American philosophers. But its point is relatively clear, after all, if we take it in homely fashion. We get beyond our-selves and our present moment by activity upon what lies ready to hand. The wider we cast the net of our activity, the more we con-nect this with that, in a widening circle of relations. The sense of the process as a whole points to the totality of all the relations we would discover and appropriate, were we to continue the process to its infinite limits. It is this *notion of totality* which we grasp heuristically as the very object of the process of thought. We do not grasp the totality in its actuality, however. (This would be the fabled Identity of Knowing and Being which marks dialectical philosophy from Plato to Hegel.)

So, with Hegel, we have got ourselves a transcendent object of sorts, here. But, in effect, we have turned the transcendent ob-ject into no more than an object of consciousness, to be appropri-ated by thought and in thought.

Here is where Feuerbach's critique of Hegel begins, and

with it, his critique of speculative philosophy as a whole. Earlier, Feuerbach had explored the relation of thought to belief. His argument was that speculative philosophy had either ignored or subordinated belief or faith to thought, or had, in good dualistic fashion, simply excluded it from the system of reason. In talking about Descartes as a philosopher and as a Catholic, Feuerbach says that Descartes held his reason and his faith apart. He writes, "Descartes himself excluded belief from the domain of thought; he accepted his belief in an unconditional way, without thought or criticism or inquiry, as it was handed down to him."[5] At this stage (in 1838), Feuerbach's humanist theory of religion was fully rationalistic. What the religious belief in God really comes to is the recognition, by human beings, of the divinity of their own thinking consciousness, as constituting their human essence. "So bifurcated is man," he writes, "that he affirms — or at least imagines he can affirm — in belief what he directly denies in reason! A split in man, a contradiction which will remain . . . so long as religion is not recognized as man's own true essence, as identical with his reason."[6] In Hegel, philosophical awareness comes to the fore; belief remains reason's dependent. It is, at best, consciousness's representation to itself of its own rational essence in the form encumbered by the imagination, by sensuality, by sense-imagery, by anthropomorphic personality. The philosopher's God, by contrast, is stripped of all these sensory, imaginative, and personal embodiments.

But, Feuerbach complains (against his own earlier views as well, since this had been the thesis of his Hegelian dissertation [1828]), this identity of reason and human essence, or species-being, is a mere thought-unity, not the real unity of living, flesh-and-blood human beings. That real unity grows, instead, out of the demands of feeling, of need, of the recognition of the other *not* as an object of abstracted thought or reason, but as an object of love, of need, of feeling-dependency, of sensibility — in short, as an object and as the content of *Sinnlichkeit*. Now, to be fair to Hegel (especially to the Hegel of the *Jena Realphilosophie*), he too had generated the intentionality of thought, of consciousness, from desire, from felt need (*Begierde*).[7] But, Hegel argued there, the satisfaction of desire, of need, in the practical appropriation of its objects in consumption, leaves no trace in consciousness. It is animal desire, which vanishes without a trace, or is transcended in the incorporation of the objects — for example, food — which satisfy it. Human beings create the satisfactions of their needs in embodied, external form, by labor, by the use of tools — so says Hegel in the early writings — and thus they objectify this desire in the external forms of those relatively permanent, not immediately consumed means that are created in order to carry out the activity of satisfying desire. Here the object of consciousness is tied directly to feeling, to need; and insofar as belief posits, in the imagination, the image, the projection or representation of what would satisfy it, belief itself — not simply as representation, but as intention bound to the fulfillment of a represented need — is thus concretely bound to activity, to practical realization of needs.[8]

Feuerbach's critique of Hegel (which overlooks this earlier theory of practical activity) is that Hegel sees the activity of satisfaction as mere thought activity. The Hegelian dialectic, therefore, is characterized by Feuerbach as a monologue of thought with itself; whereas what is needed is a dialogue of thought with feeling, with belief, with sensibility, with the empirically felt or sensed other of thought. Feuerbach proposes, therefore, that the method of transcendence — not of imaginary, ideal transcendence in consciousness or in thought but of real transcendence, in "real" life, that is, in feeling, needy, practical life — that this method of real transcendence lies in belief, faith, the transformation of the imagined community of thought into a real community of living, feeling beings. Thus Feuerbach sees the method of transcendence, by which finite individuals overcome their isolation and recognize themselves as species-beings in the act of fellow-feeling, in love. This truth, says Feuerbach, is represented in the faith of believers in its imaginative and mystified form: "God is love." The human self-consciousness which had its realization in thinking the other, in Hegel and in the early Feuerbach, here gives way to a self-consciousness which achieves itself in feeling.

Feuerbach writes: "Man becomes self-conscious in terms of his object: the consciousness of the object is the self-consciousness of man."[9] But the object of love is the other as human, the Thou, which responds to our feeling with feeling. The dialectic here becomes a dialectic of feeling, in the communion of shared and reciprocal feeling. The condition for the transcendence of individual finitude is community, and this community is a community of feeling. This transcendent object, taken as the object of feeling, is by virtue of that alone a religious object, according to Feuerbach. God is, in effect, the externalized representation of this fellow-feeling. And feeling transforms its object from an object of mere dispassionate perception into an object which is related to the practical, the wished for, the satisfying—in short, the good. Endowed by feeling with value, the object of belief, as against the object of mere speculation or thought, becomes an other which is appropriated by belief.

, Feuerbach provides a method of transcendence in his theory of belief. But it remains a praxis of belief, not yet a material praxis, not yet the concrete activity of transcending the present. In this sense, Feuerbach falls behind Hegel in two fundamental respects: he fails to recognize the domain of the political and the economic as the concrete domain of practical human activity. He recognizes these aspects only abstractly, whereas Hegel, in *The Philosophy of Right* (especially in the section on "The System of Needs") and elsewhere, raises this domain to theoretical importance at least. Feuerbach also fails to recognize the historicity of human self-transcendence. True, like his master, Hegel, Feuerbach is also a master of the history of ideas and the history of religion. But historical praxis as real transformation and transcendence of the present lies beyond Feuerbach's ken.

Yet, the praxis of belief provides a method which points toward a materialist theory of transcendence. It is no secret that Marx's critique and appropriation of Feuerbach focus precisely on Feuerbach's notion of "material," practical, concrete, sensuous existence, and that Marx faults Feuerbach's notion of the human as not yet concrete or differentiated enough. That Feuerbach's thinking-feeling-willing creature of needs, who is at once an I and an I-Thou, is still too abstract a being, is the burden of Marx's *Theses on Feuerbach* and his longer critique and discussion in *The German Ideology*. The nub of his criticism is that a resolution in consciousness—even in practical, believing "religious" consciousness which posits real human need as its object—is not enough.

It is just this ahistoricism which Marx criticized in classical political economy. And insofar as Feuerbach conceives of species-being as an ahistorical essence — whose development simply consists in the progress of its self-revelation in consciousness, but whose object of consciousness, species-being, remains a fixed and unchanging being — Feuerbach, too, falls under the interdiction of ahistoricism. To be fair, Feuerbach does have a strong sense of natural development, anticipating a theory of the natural evolution of the human species.[10] And indeed, he sometimes suggests just the notion of historical self-creation of the species by its own activities which is so central to Marx's thought. Thus, Feuerbach writes:

> Man cannot be derived from nature! True! But man as he directly emerged from nature was only a natural being, not a man. Man is a product of man, of culture and history. There are even plants and animals that have changed so much under human care that they (the original forms) are no longer found in nature. Would you then take recourse to a *Deus ex machina* to account for their origin?[11]

Programmatically, and in temperament, Feuerbach is open to the conception of human self-transcendence by historical practice, not only in consciousness or belief, but in modes of material and social existence. But it is not given to Feuerbach to develop this conception. Engels, in his critique, attempts to explain the limitations of Feuerbach's views in the context of the development of the natural sciences of his time, not yet imbued with the notions of process and evolution which were shortly to develop. Engels also adduces Feuerbach's divorce from active political life and intellectual exchange, in the long years of his rural existence in Brucksberg, as reason for his failure to comprehend the historical, political, and economic processes at work in Germany.[12] Still, Feuerbach's theory makes of religious belief the very ground for material transcendence, once it is realized what the role is which such belief — demystified, self-conscious as to its object, the human — plays in shaping the nature of practical activity itself.

Seeing the present historically permits one to appropriate the past as more than merely temporal beforeness. The brute pastness of the past, its inexistence, is transformed from abstract negation as time, to determinate or concrete negation as *aufhebung*, as what has become embodied, incorporated in the present. Thus history makes the past our past, and it is our past that provides the determinate conditions for present activity. What is this recognition in the present of the creative possibilities of human achievement, of the species-capacities for perfectibility, but belief? Belief, faith, is thus not the misdirected anticipation of what is superhumanly possible, but the anticipation of what is humanly possible. The mere projection in the imagination of possibilities as objects of contemplation is thus not true belief, or faith, but passive, regretful, and impotent reflection. True belief is active belief, the belief whose object is seen as the realizable future, made by human effort and action. Such belief, therefore, entails not only idly imagining future possibilities but regarding them as possible on the grounds of the present itself. But the present, here, is not an object of reflection, or of the passive, contemplative consciousness. Just as history is appropriated as value, made one's own as heritage, so too is the present comprehended as the realm of creative activity which ever transforms it, and makes of time a measure of activity, of change.

Belief, here, becomes commitment, care for the future, anticipation of what is to come in the mood of positive expectation. In short, it is hope. Hope, as active belief, animates purpose, and provides the normative element in teleological work and action. Purposes, needs, wants are posited not only as abstract goals, but as felt, value-laden ends, or, as Feuerbach would say, objects of the heart.

Such transcendence of the present, and of the limits of finite individuality, as an anticipation of a future realizable by social, communal practice — if not in one life, then in the ongoing transcendent life of the species — is as material as it can be, because it is the practical transformation of the present by human activity: technological, social, political, and ideational. It is no mere interpretation of the world, but that interpretation of it which leads to changing it. But such change, such revolutionary praxis has as its animating spirit a vision of human possibilities which sees the divine as within the grasp of our own creative activity, and as the object of our hope. Such a theory of belief, as a materialist theory, exceeds the bounds of contemporary materialism, which has as yet no consistent theory of hope, or of this sort of recognition of the transcendent. But the transcendent, thus conceived, is within the realm of human possibility. And a theory of hope as active, practical, efficacious belief in such human possibilities, is needed.

NOTES

1. Karl Marx and Friedrich Engels, *The German Ideology*, 3rd rev. ed. (Moscow: Progress Publishers, 1976), p. 102.

2. Ludwig Feuerbach, *Sämtliche Werke*, ed. W. Bolin and F. Jodl, 10 vols. (Stuttgart: Fromann Verlag Günther Holzboog, 1903–1911), 6:17.

3. G. W. F. Hegel, *The Phenomenology of Mind*, trans. J. B. Baillie (New York: Macmillan, 1931), p. 229.

4. Marx and Engels, *German Ideology*, p. 102.

5. Feuerbach, *Sämtliche Werke*, 4:287–90, n. 39.

6. Ibid., 4:175.

7. G. W. F. Hegel, *Jenenser Realphilosophie II, Die Vorlesungen von 1805–1806*, ed. G. Lasson (Leipzig: Felix Meiner, 1931), 20:194f., 213–17.

8. Ibid.

9. Feuerbach, *Sämtliche Werke*, 6:6.

10. Ibid., 10:19–20, 26–27; 8:161–65. See also my discussion of this in Marx W. Wartofsky, *Feuerbach* (London: Cambridge University Press, 1977), pp. 397–401.

11. Feuerbach, *Sämtliche Werke*, 10:237.

12. Friedrich Engels, *Ludwig Feuerbach and the Outcome of Classical German Philosophy*, in Karl Marx, *Selected Works*, 2 vols. (New York: International Publishers, 1936), 1:439–40, 450.

Commitment in a Pluralistic World
GEORGE E. RUPP

I

WE LIVE IN AN ERA when the traditional foundations for faith are severely shaken. In a sense the Protestant principle has triumphed. No individual or insitution has unquestioned authority.

In an extension of this Protestant principle beyond what the Reformers themsevles envisioned, the authority of the Bible itself has not gone unquestioned. Impressive numbers of people may still insist that they accept the Bible as the inerrant authority for their faith. Similarly, significant numbers of the faithful declare their submission to the teaching authority of the Church — to the Magisterium and to the Pope when he speaks *ex cathedra*. But the need to interpret and adapt authoritative pronouncements in their everyday application characterizes the behavior of even those who subscribe to inerrant authority in principle. Think of fundamentalist interpretations of the Sermon on the Mount that somehow still support American superpatriotism. Or consider birth control among devout Roman Catholics. In short, no authority remains unquestioned in practice.

The situation is analogous to that of true believers in the political realm. In recent years there has been no shortage of declarations of support for the United States Constitution as virtually sacrosanct. And yet every position on the political spectrum has its recommendations for improvement. In some instances, the proposed amendment is quite self-consciously advanced to rectify limitations in the time-bound and partial vision of the framers of the Constitution. The Equal Rights Amendment is a case in point. In other instances the change is presented as consistent with the intention of the framers of the Constitution; so the amendment is offered as a more specific application designed to address new issues and to counter intervening misinterpretations of fundamental rights. The proposal for a constitutional amendment to ban state support for abortions illustrates this pattern. But in each case, the effect is to propose amendment in what is a foundational authority of American political life.

Because we discount the excesses of political rhetoric, we are not overly surprised at the proposing of constitutional amendments. We know that there have been more than a few formal amendments and that there will be more over the years. But in our religious communities there is no similarly formalized procedure for amending the pronouncements of our foundational authorities. Nor is there a formally established record of those amendments over time. As a result, change in our religious traditions strikes us less as a process of orderly amendment and more as a shaking of the very foundations of faith.

II

Changes in belief and practice have occurred in the course of the history of all religious communities — even the most tenaciously conservative ones. But our sense of a shaking of the foundations of faith has an edge to it that distinguishes our situation from much of the past. The reason is that we are crossing the threshold into a new era in the history of human religious life. What characterizes this new era is an increasingly general recognition of our individual and corporate role in fashioning the religious worlds, the symbolic universes, in which we live.

Awareness of this role is not unprecedented. Exceptional individuals — both critics of religion and initiates in its mysteries — have for millennia insisted on this dynamic contribution of the human imagination to religious traditions. An intriguing Western example is the quite self-conscious recasting of Greek mythology in the late drama of Euripides. And in the East, both elaborate symbolic inventiveness and vigorous iconoclasm are evident among initiates in, for example, tantric or Zen Buddhism.

What is new in our situation is that not only exceptional individuals but rather also the prevailing culture as a whole is coming to recognize our collective role in fashioning religious symbols. The threshold into this new era is admittedly wide. In the West, we have been in the process of crossing it for at least several centuries. But the shift from the insight of exceptional individuals to a cultural ethos of general recognition is nonetheless a profoundly challenging transition for religious communities.

The challenge may be formulated quite simply: Are religious communities viable in this new situation of increased self-consciousness? Can religious communities survive in this situation? Religious communities provide symbolic universes for those of us who are their members: rituals, injunctions, images, and ideas through which we interpret our experience and which in turn shape that experience. The question is whether or not we can continue to live within such a symbolic universe once we recognize its status as a creation of collective human insight and imagination.

I do not think we have enough information about this question. We are in effect living out our various answers. For several centuries in the West, the presumption has been that the recognition of religious symbols as human artifacts requires a rejection of those symbols. But we have also come to see that we unavoidably live within one or another symbolic universe. Thus a rejection of religious symbols does not in itself settle the issue of what values we commit ourselves to and what meanings we affirm. That issue remains solidly grounded in all of our living no matter how severely the traditional foundations for faith are shaken.

III

Religious communities have for millennia been moving toward the periphery of society — or at the least toward a diffusion throughout the social structure. In the institutionally least complex cultures about which we have data, there is no differentiation of a religious group from the society as a whole. Instead, the tribe is a single political-economic-religious entity. In more complex societies, religious institutions typically are differentiated from political and economic ones. The priest and the king are no longer the same person. In our own tradition, in which this differentiation has become sharpest and most self-conscious, there is a church distinguished from the state. But separation of church and state as two more or less unified spheres mutually balancing and correcting each other is not the final stage in this line of development. Instead, as the process of differentiation continues, the dichotomy of state and church yields to a series of regions or dimensions of society that mutually influence each other: not only the political and the religious, but also the economic, the educational, the legal, the artistic, and so on.

The result of this process of differentiation is a sense of movement of religious communities toward the periphery of the social system. Religious life is not inescapably integral to our social existence, as in tribal culture. Nor is a unified religious community institutionalized as one of two central authorities that structure the social system, as in medieval Europe, for example. Instead, religious communities are among those voluntary associations to which we may belong as we struggle to orient our lives, to appraise competing value systems, and to commit ourselves to the causes that seem most compelling.

Viewed from the perspective of traditional religious authority, our situation is, then, doubly dubious: individuals are more and more aware of their role in shaping religious traditions, and religious communities are increasingly marginal in the social system as a whole. The two developments reinforce each other. The result is that our religious life is beset with the same dispirited individualism that plagues so much of contemporary society. Even those of us who affirm religious values as crucial to our identities may do so apart from any commitment to a self-consciously religious community. We Americans have a two-hundred-year tradition here: in the words of Thomas Paine, "My mind is my church"; or, as Thomas Jefferson put it, "I am a sect myself." A religious dimension to the culture available directly to individuals displaces religious institutions. Here, as elsewhere in our society, individualism threatens to run amok.

An effective response in this situation must engage the issues focused in modern Western individualism. This need is a religious imperative: central to the religious life is the struggle against our idolatrous glorification of the self. But the need to address the issue of unchecked individualism also follows from considerations of social psychology and the sociology of knowledge. Thomas Paine and Thomas Jefferson to the contrary notwithstanding, every person is not and cannot be his or her own church.

In part because religious communities are no longer centrally and unquestionably authoritative in contemporary society, we do have an increased awareness of our role in shaping the symbolic universes in which we live. But we do not simply invent our symbols. Instead, we participate in changing traditions and therefore bear responsibility for the ongoing development of the symbolic resources available through those traditions. In some cases, it may be most responsible simply to reject a tradition. Even then we are not, however, moving out of every symbolic universe. Nor are we creating an entirely new one. Instead we are engaged in a process of critical appropriation through which we assess and often reinterpret the symbols available to us.

To focus this general description of what I am calling critical appropriation, I want to sketch two contemporary illustrations of the dynamics involved. The first is the impact of feminism on contemporary religious life and thought. And the second is the religious and ethical challenge of limits to growth in our biosphere.

IV

The impact of feminism has made us painfully aware of how deeply patriarchal are the symbolic forms and institutional patterns of Jewish and Christian traditions. In the most virulent expression of this sexism, women are simply barred from positions of authority in the liturgical and administrative life of the community. But even when this extreme is rejected, there remains the sexism that pervades the language and imagery of our churches and synagogues. Those of us who have tried to locate biblical texts or liturgies or hymns that do not have sexually exclusive language know how pervasive is this sexism in virtually every aspect of our religious traditions.

For significant numbers of contemporary Christians and Jews, this pervasive presence of sexist language and imagery is simply unacceptable. It is unacceptable in the straightforward sense that it interferes with the very act of worship. Instead of being incorporated into a vital community that transcends the individual, we experience exclusion that vitiates any sense of a common and inclusive body.

This contemporary state of affairs is very much a product of historical development. For thousands of years participants in biblical traditions have been able to celebrate their common life without being conscious of the sexism that pervades those traditions. That third person singular masculine pronouns and nouns like *man* and *mankind* are intended as inclusive in reference was for our forebears a grammatical point that did not violate their conscious experience. Similarly, references to God as masculine were not perceived to be dignifying male as distinguished from female experience. But that is no longer the case for increasing numbers of women and men. In sum, authoritative traditions have come into direct conflict with our contemporary awareness of the role of gender in the symbolization and institutionalization of religious life.

In theory, we can envision three ideal typical responses to this situation. One is to insist on the inviolability of the authoritative traditions and therefore to reject the claims of contemporary awareness as illegitimate human self-exaltation. A second is to reject completely the pretensions of the tradition and to affirm the new awareness as alone having true authority — as exercising genuine power in our common life. The third response is to recognize that neither authoritative traditions nor contemporary awareness can be rejected completely and that, therefore, there is no alternative except to attempt to do justice to the power of both.

As this formulation suggests, the three theoretical responses in practice are points on a single spectrum. Even the most conservative traditions change over time; and even the most unqualified commitment to radically novel insight or awareness draws on the resources of the past. Responses to a specific issue may fall at multiple points on the spectrum. But none of them can fail to take a position with reference to both poles. To adapt an aphorism from Kant: exaltation of current awareness apart from the symbolic resources of the past is empty; fidelity to tradition without attention to contemporary experience is blind.

Specifically on the issues focused in contemporary feminism, a full spectrum of responses is represented. It ranges from modest renovation among those who want to continue to dwell in the house of traditional authority, through efforts at more systemic transformation, to emphatic rejection of Christian and Jewish traditions in their entirety. But in each case, there is the recognition of the need for at least some changes and there is also, despite protestations to the contrary, very substantial continuity. Commitment "beyond God the Father" is still heavily dependent on theological and philosophical images and ideas fundamentally shaped in Western patriarchal traditions.

In exemplifying the process of critical appropriation through which we assess and often reinterpret the symbols available to us, the feminist movement also illustrates the complex relationship between Western individualism and the increased self-consciousness about commitment today. In a sense, the movement in its contemporary form is itself a powerful expression of just this individualism. After centuries of accepting and affirming identities that subordinated their individuality to the prerogatives of others, women have insisted that they, too, must be able to do their own thing. At the same time, the feminist movement has had the greatest impact when it provides a community in which this new individuality is nourished and sustained. The broader culture can and does offer various stimuli to individuals, especially through the mass media. But this general cultural awareness is certainly not as effective in enabling change as is a community of shared commitment in support of that change.

In this respect also, the feminist movement exemplifies the general issues involved in contemporary commitment. Talk of assessing alternatives and reinterpreting traditional symbolism unavoidably sounds highly individualistic. But that process of critical appraisal in turn shapes our living most effectively when we participate in a community that shares our commitment. Through this active collaboration, both the symbolic resources of the tradition and the participants are changed.

V

Like the impact of feminism, the challenge of limits to growth in our biosphere has implications for both the symbolization and the institutionalization of our common life. In short, this challenge also affects both our ideas and our actions.

It is, I think, helpful to attempt to gain some historical perspective in viewing the impact on religious life of this sense of limits to growth. Most of the traditional forms of the great world religions generate their power through appeal to an order of reality that is the ultimate destiny of the human and in comparison to which this historical existence is radically deficient or even hopelessly corrupt. In much Christian piety, this realm is heaven over against earth or the liberating vision of God over against enslavement to the world. For the Theravāda Buddhist, this destiny is the attainment of the other shore, of nirvana over against *saṁsāra*; for the Pure Land Buddhist, it is rebirth in the western paradise of Amida. For virtually all Hindus, the goal of the religious life is the attainment of *mokṣa*: deliverance from the round of birth and death that constitutes ordinary historical life.

In popular piety, deliverance to this other realm — heaven, nirvana, the Pure Land, union with the ultimate through release from recurrent births — is often portrayed as the destiny of the faithful or disciplined or devoted individual. In the various religious traditions there are, however, also resources for interpreting this deliverance in less individualistic terms. Liberation from Egypt that leads to settlement in the promised land is a dramatic instance of corporate and this-worldly deliverance in biblical faith. So too are certain Mahāyāna Buddhist tendencies — for example, the vow of the *bodhisattva* to save all sentient beings rather than attain deliverance alone. But the predominant pattern is that such corporate or inclusive transformation is projected into the future or into an apocalyptic end time or is realized apart from all ordinary historical processes. In the end there is a transforming resurrection of all humankind. Or in a final vindication of divine power, the kingdom of God is established in utter discontinuity with the dynamics of human historical development. Or through rigorous spiritual discipline, enlightenment is attained and all of reality is seen to be Buddha-nature — even though to ordinary human vision it is unchanged. Or through renunciation of worldly involvements, the transtemporal identity of the self with the ultimate is realized in a single all-comprehending whole. In sum, even though in such instances the goal of the religious life is envisioned as a reality that transcends the individual, its realization is still viewed as discontinuous with ordinary historical life.

To this pattern of traditional religion in both its individual and universal forms, the post-Enlightenment West has posited a direct and quite simple alternative: human progress. The goal of human life is not envisioned as discontinuous with history. Instead human history itself is presumed to be progressing inexorably into, or at least is thought to be developing toward, even greater fulfillment. Like the pattern of traditional religion, this alternative is expressed in both individualistic and corporate forms, as is illustrated in the numerous versions of bourgeois individualism and Marxism. But in all of the variations, transformation discontinuous with ordinary life is replaced with hope for the future of human development. The vision of heaven above is translated into aspirations for the earth below.

Although it has been severely shaken by the cataclysms of our century, this presumption of continuing progress is still central to the cultural ethos of much of the West even today. It is a salient feature in the ideology of both laissez-faire capitalism and Marxism. It certainly has shaped the rhetoric and programs of parties at all points on the political spectrum. In alliance with traditional tendencies to ethical perfectionism and spiritual discipline, commitment to progress has also found expression in religious and philanthropic communities, as dedication to human welfare has become a goal significant in its own right rather than a temporary means to transtemporal salvation for both the donor and the recipient.

Because the presumption of progress has been central to so many post-Enlightenment cultural traditions, it unavoidably informs our current discussions of limits to growth in the biosphere. Indeed, those discussions become traumatic precisely because the very idea of limits to growth seems to contradict the tenet of indefinitely extended progress which is still central to much of our culture.

At first glance, threats to the ideology of progress might appear to signal a revival of what I have called the pattern of traditional religion. After all, the attractiveness of traditionally valued forms of religious development is only enhanced with the recognition that indefinite material progress cannot be sustained. Striving toward ethical improvement and disciplined spiritual attainment does not depend on the exploitation of limited resources. From this perspective, only the illegitimate secularized versions of religion that focus on this-worldly welfare are shown to be untenable. Traditional religion, in contrast, is vindicated through its refusal to compromise with secular culture in its preoccupation with material progress.

Despite the so-called moral majority and the resurgence of conservative religion, the situation is not that simple. The preoccupation of the post-Enlightenment West with progress is not simply an aberration. Nor does the impending collapse of that preoccupation signal a return to the simple truths of traditional religion. We are all children of the Enlightenment who cannot simply return to the comforting dualisms of traditional religion. Instead, for most of us, too, visions of heaven have come to represent hopes for our common life here on earth. To use Buddhist imagery, the land of Amida Buddha is our historical life transformed and purified.

In short, as it has been for the proponents of progress, the place for us is here; but in contrast to the future orientation of the proponents of progress, the time must be now. There must be a transformation in the personal, social, and cultural dynamics of our common life in history. But that transformation cannot be envisioned as only a future realization of all the ideals and aspirations that motivate present action. Instead, we must participate now in the corporate reality to which the symbols of religious traditions testify — in Christian imagery, the reality of spirit, the kingdom or commonwealth of God, the divine-human body of which we are all members.

For those of us who cannot return to the dualisms of traditional religion, there is a special urgency and also a sense of tragedy in our appropriation of such symbols of human destiny. This double sense of urgency and tragedy is with reference not only to the individual but also to humanity as a whole — indeed to all of life as we know it. Many of us cannot affirm individual survival of death in some other realm. As a result, we place a special premium on the contributions we are enabled to make and the satisfactions we are allowed to enjoy in all the dimensions of our daily living. A similar sense of tragedy and urgency seems to envelop our corporate existence. That is, there appears to be a final limit to the viability of the earth as an ecosystem capable of supporting life as we know it. So our corporate life also is lived in the face of a final death that accentuates the need to realize value here and now.

In this context of limits to growth in our biosphere and even a final term to the viability of our ecosystem, to affirm that we are all members of one body has definite implications for action. Any such affirmation calls for measures to redress the enormously uneven distribution of wealth that makes a mockery of all talk about an inclusive human community. And the fact that available resources are limited serves to accentuate the indefensibility of dramatically inequitable distribution. The easy answers of the recent past become less and less plausible: proportionately the same slices of an ever larger socio-economic pie may have some attractions even to those with small pieces; but if the pie cannot increase in size indefinitely or even for very long, then the alternative of reslicing it becomes compelling.

In sum, in the context of limits to growth, our appropriation of such religious images as the spiritual community, the kingdom or commonwealth of God, and the divine-human body of which we are all members entails a commitment to radical programs of redistribution rather than the easy gradualism that assumes indefinitely extended socio-economic growth. As we move increasingly to an integrated planetary culture, we must, therefore, press for policies that protect and further the interests of the third world. Similarly, as our society recognizes the long-term untenability of affluence driven through such devices as planned obsolescence and investment in superfluous armaments, we must struggle toward institutional patterns that reinforce simplicity and frugality rather than unnecessary production and consumption. Only through this double movement toward reduced consumption and redistribution of wealth can we be faithful to affirmations of inclusive community.

VI

The need for redistribution of resources in the context of limits to growth is not as directly a personal challenge as are the issues at the heart of the feminist critique. Yet both challenges call for a fundamental change in personal, social, and cultural patterns that must begin as particular communities actualize new or reaffirmed values in their common life. In both cases, there is a general cultural awareness of the need for this change. But also in both cases, the call for change is most effective when there is a community of shared commitment in support of that change.

A critical question focused through the examples of the feminist movement and the limits to growth in our biosphere is where this community of mutual support is to be located. More specifically, can it be located within religious communities?

This question brings us full circle to the issues involved in the collapse of traditional authorities. Not only the traditional foundations for faith but also other authorities are shaken. Yet the reverberations of the collapse seem especially pronounced in the case of religious communities. Religious life has so powerfully shaped human identities at least in part because it has engaged the deepest levels of the self at the earliest and perhaps the most formative stages of development. For precisely that reason, increased self-consciousness about our individual and corporate role in fashioning our symbolic universes constitutes a particularly acute threat in this case.

In the wake of the collapse of traditional authorities, religious communities will survive only if they conduct genuine power to their members — only if they provide a context in which individuals are delivered from their self-preoccupations for commitment to more inclusive causes. To this end, the rituals, injunctions, images, and ideas of particular communities must be represented effectively so that they both interpret the full range of contemporary experience and in turn shape that experience in ways that elicit affirmation.

This need is not just the expression of an abstract intellectual interest. Instead, it directly affects our living in all of its empirical concreteness. To refer again to the two illustrations I sketched, the issues focused in the feminist challenge to religious imagery and institutions affect not only our ideas but also our most fundamental individual and corporate identities. Similarly, our increased awareness of limits to growth in our biosphere affects every dimension of our living. Consequently, interpretations of contemporary experience through reference to traditional images and ideas must in turn shape our lives in ways that we affirm. In the case of the feminist challenge, we must realize the potential in biblical and other religious traditions for supporting inclusive communities that enhance the female as well as the male dimensions of the human. And in the instance of limits to growth, we must come to affirm our situation as finite moments integral to an order of being and value that is dynamic and has the capacity to be inclusive and just. In sum, for religious communities to survive, there must be an emotionally powerful and intellectually satisfying expression of post-conventional faith that is adequate to the full range of our developing experience.

The need to relate traditional symbols to the dynamics of contemporary life is certainly not a new imperative for religious communities. But our greater self-consciousness about this process of appropriation has both a threatening and a promising aspect. Our new awareness can inhibit or even block the energy generated through religious commitment. We can become self-conscious in the debilitating sense of looking only at ourselves and exaggerating our role as individual arbiters or even manipulators of traditional symbols. But recognition of the role of human insight and imagination in the fashioning of our religious worlds can also be liberating. It can release both our critical and our creative capacities as we seek to act out of a corporate vision that we are committed to making our own. Because we recognize our responsibility for this process, we must identify those places in the tradition that do not adequately interpret and acceptably shape our experience. We must enlarge those places so that they can accommodate all that we affirm. Only this inclusive commitment can be at one and the same time faithful to the past, adequate for orienting us in the present, and promising in projecting us and our world into the future.

Can Virtue Be Taught?
A Feminist Reconsiders

ELIZABETH KAMARCK MINNICH

Surely it is time for the true grace of women
Emerging, in their lives' colors, from the rooms, from the harvests,
From the delicate prisons, to speak their promises.
The spirit's dreaming delight and the fluid senses'
Involvement in the world. . . .

Coming close to the source of belief, these have created
Resistance, the flowering fire of memory. . . .
Muriel Rukeyser, from "Letter to the Front," Part X[1]

FRAMING THE QUESTION

I WOULD KNOW, or think I did, whether virtue can be taught had
I a philosophical position specifying what sort of thing it is that
we wish to teach. I could respond had I a theory of pedagogy fram-
ing for me what teaching is, what it can and cannot do. Had I
such grounding, I not only could but confidently would proceed
directly to an answer: my work, then, would be to convince others
that I am right, that I have achieved that desired philosophical
creation, an Impregnable Argument. However, not only do I not
have a theory of virtue that suffices, nor a completed theory of
pedagogy, but I am not convinced that it is safe for me to respond
directly to the question precisely because it is one of the oldest and
most fundamental within the dominant Western tradition. The
vast amount of thought given to it affords me the opposite of aid
or comfort: it is precisely in such areas that we most need to be
careful. If we do not approach such culturally central topics with
all our feminist-critical senses awake, we are liable to be led down
well-trodden paths, which, however clear and distinct and elegant

and proper, remain within the maze of a world of meanings defined in male terms claiming to be universal. Some may indeed be universal, but we will not know that until/unless we submit them to critique. Our tools of thought — to change the metaphor to recognize also method — having been developed through the centuries in which "man" was imperially proclaimed actively to "embrace" women, to subsume us by right, by logic, by "nature," need to be carefully examined lest they betray us once again.

A feminist stance is informed, then, by a spirit of *resistance.* "Feminist ethics is born in women's refusals to endure with grace the arrogance, indifference, hostility, and damage of oppressively sexist environments. It is fueled by bonds among women, forged in experiments to create better environments now and for the future, and tried by commitments to overcome damage already done."[2] It is also informed by *respect* for the lives and experiences of those whose wisdom has not been consulted: "Ethics benefits from reflection upon our own experience, upon choices we have actually faced,"[3] where "our" is remembered to include the extraordinarily diverse people who have for so long been forced into the singularity of the Woman who is Man's Other.

We are, then, required to face the basic problems posed by an effort to comprehend that which and those who have been predefined in ways we do not accept. "Comprehension," as Hannah Arendt knew, "does not mean denying the outrageous, deducing the unprecedented from precedents, or explaining phenomena by such analogies and generalities that the impact of reality and the shock of experience are no longer felt. . . . Comprehension means the unpremeditated, attentive facing up to, and resisting of, reality — whatever it may be."[4]

Thus, feminist critique of dominant modes of thought and their related systems and forms of life moves and helps us to learn to think ourselves free, to think more freely, recognizing but also resisting reality. Such work is also now, as it always has been, carried forward for the sake of loving creative vision, a radical stance: "The feminist religious revolution thus promises to be more radical and far reaching than liberation theologies. It goes behind the symbolic universe that has been constructed by patriarchal civilization, both in its religious and in its modern secular forms. It reaches forward to an alternative that can heal the splits between 'masculine' and 'feminine', between mind and body, between males and females as gender groups, between society and nature, and between races and classes."[5]

Feminist critique, as I invoke it here, is, then, an expression of a commitment to a resistant, respectful, reflexive, critical, creative approach that asks us to look behind, or below, received knowledge and dominant traditions in an effort to locate whether, when, where, how modes and methods of thought, deriving from old exclusions and devaluations, may continue to skew our ability to think on all levels.

Such critique is required of us today because of the historical creation and enduring effects of the system of male dominance called patriarchy. It is possible as well as required because we are embodied creatures of place and time who are capable of thinking about and beyond any given construction of meaning and truth. I believe, then, that we move toward some understanding of what we will choose *virtue* to mean as we think about how we need to think about it in the first place. That is, we enact some notions of what *virtue* means and how we might teach it by how and with whom we approach the question itself.

CONTEXTUALIZING

We are creatures as well as creators of history, of language, of culture; we are meaning-making creatures, born as such into a world that we take into ourselves from the moment we are born. To resist reality in the name of comprehension involves preparing to confront the meanings and systems that are most deeply entrenched.

At the beginning of the master narrative of the dominant Western tradition, as Nicholas Lobkowicz reminds us, "When the Greeks opposed to each other *theoria* and *praxis* . . . what they had in mind was a distinction between various kinds or walks of life—a distinction which permitted them to tackle the kind of question of yore it was customary to ask at the Delphic oracles: Who is the most pious, the most happy, the wisest, the best man?"[6] "The Greeks"—meaning, of course, the few males who had the leisure to consider such questions—then prescribed the sorts of virtues, understood as excellences of kind, characterizing lives to be led only by some "kinds" of people: "the 'citizen's virtue'— that is, his being capable of participating in government — would not belong to every citizen; only those released from necessary and menial occupations, have the leisure required for governing."[7]

We must notice now that the citizen's virtue, like the virtues of any life then considered worthy of "a free man," is premised on the exclusion and devaluation of those forced to serve him, to "free" him from all that sustains us in being. We cannot simply say, "That was then; this is now. There is no point in dwelling on the prejudices of a past age, or imposing on them our values." To rush past the context is to ignore that what was actually said about "man" is fundamentally implicated with a gender hierarchy that hides as it marginalizes and devalues one half of humankind, along with male slaves and those who worked with their hands— and with them, the virtues of labor, both productive and reproductive. Functioning here are the historical injustices we are still struggling to set right, and those remain with us as both practices and modes of thought.

UNTANGLING OLD KNOTS

We see in Lobkowicz's study of "the Greeks" their and his *faulty generalization*, from a few men to humankind and from a few Greeks to "the Greeks"; *circular reasoning*, defining virtue by reference to those few men's lives, and then justifying their being the only ones allowed to live those lives by referring to the virtues ascribed to them; and *mystified concepts*, such as that of virtue that obscures its exclusion of women from the possibility of achieving it, leaving women subject to a separate and distinctly unequal notion of womanly virtue that is not human virtue. Thus, we end up with *partial systems of knowledge*[8] as of belief and morality that perpetuate as they derive from, and return to justify, entangled gender and class hierarchies of "kinds" of humans.

We need, then, to watch for where and how *invidiously hierarchical definitions* of "man" and "his" virtues are worked into the ways we think about humans and our virtues at all levels, and all the time, lest we perpetuate them. The past, as has been said, is not only not dead; it isn't even past.

Still with us are also *oppositional definitions* which not only distinguish male from female but oppose them in a way that divides us at the same time it holds us together as mutually defining through our opposition: "the opposite sex." "Virtue" derives from the Latin *virtus*, "manliness, valor, worth, etc., from *vir*, man," and means "the possession or display of manly qualities; manly excellence, courage, valor."[9] By such definitions there cannot be a "virtuous" woman, except as that "unnatural" creature, a "manly woman." She does not thereby become human, as Man is, but aberrant, neither a proper woman nor a natural human. As Mary Wollstonecraft put it, "If there be but one criterion of morals, but one archetype for man, women appear to be suspended by destiny . . . ; they . . . must not aim at respect, lest they should be hunted out of society as masculine."[10]

For women, virtue has been defined quite differently, as we all know. A "good woman" is one who successfully enacts her gender role, which is distinguished sharply from that of man, and is fundamentally based, as a man's virtue is not, on sexuality. A good woman is not sexually "loose," out of the control of a man to whom she belongs. For the meaning of virtue for woman, see "chastity, sexual purity, esp. on the part of women. Of easy virtue: see Easy. . . ."[11] This is, of course, both a gendered oppositional definition, by which females cannot have/display human virtue because we cannot properly be "manly," and a sexualized definition that supports the hierarchy by requiring "sexual purity" of women as it is not required of men.

This is, *mutatis mutandis*, a theme of the relations between women and men we see around the world. Any definition of Woman that defines her/us primarily as a sexual/reproductive being leads to the reduction of our humanity. It locks us all into that terrible dance of repulsion and yearning, of unequal mutual dependency, that is so familiar between men and women and that poisons the highly sexualized relations of white and black, colonist and native, civilized and primitive—"us" and "them."

Such entangled, mutually constitutive, naturalized oppositions play against the *Man/Nature division* in any of its forms. They all place males—to varying degrees, depending on how "civilized" and "rational" their "kind" is held to be—against, rather than mutually within, a Mother Nature that both sustains and is felt to threaten to engulf him. Thus Man/civilization/rationality is not only distinguished from but radically separated from Woman/the primitive/the sexual/emotive.

This is dualistic and divisive; it is also dangerously because faultily abstract. Man, taken to be the defining kind of human, is alienated, dissociated, not only from women and from Nature and from "lesser" men, but from those aspects of himself that he in fact shares with them. That is, since all the qualities and activities and modes of life of the lesser people are also always human, Man, in distinguishing himself from them/us, splits himself from himself as well. The privilege explained and justified by the old division between thought and action, mind and body, has many costs. As Stanley Cavell observed, "The requirement for purity imposed by philosophy now looks like a wish to leave me out, I mean each of us, the self, with its arbitrary needs and unruly desires."[12]

Thinking about our thinking as a result of his searing experiences in war, the philosopher J. Glenn Gray noted:

> The dissociation of man as individual and as species from the limitless backgrounds of his being is another quality which constitutes the monstrous character of contemporary civilization. . . . Thoughtlessly we conceive nature as external environment. Thinking, and presumably remembering, too, is supposed to be "non-natural." But that which sustains us in being is surely as much these nonmaterial activities of thinking, remembering, creating as digesting, breathing and locomotion, and the like."[13]

Even Glenn Gray, trapped by the faultily universalized and purified "man," oddly does not note, as we must in a spirit true to his work, that "the dissociation of man . . . from the limitless backgrounds of his being," from all "that which sustains us in being," is profoundly related to the early and persistent dissociation of a few privileged males from the lives of all those who took care of the necessities of life from which virtuous men were freed by the labor of defined-as-lesser Others. We have all paid the price of such dissociation. It does indeed run through the "monstrous character of contemporary civilization." It defines a virtuous human as manly, masterful, in control, and in opposition to others. Those others have been identified with Nature, while Man has been supposed to rise above nature through dominance, in order to be free.

ACTION

The question of freedom reminds us that successful critique of concepts and systems of thought does not of itself change social, cultural, economic, political systems that have realized those concepts and systems. Revealing the errors and curiosities on which constructions of gender as of class and race have been based does not change the fact that such tragic nonsense is implicated in almost all present systems of thought as in daily life. Thus, moral inquiry must be critical, resistant, respectful, reflexive, and responsible to action.

Here it is critical to note the complementarity of philosophical-political strands of critique from feminist scholars, Third World people, environmentalists, pacifists, proponents of multiculturalism. No matter where we begin critique of the dominant tradition we arrive at similar observations. When a few define themselves as the inclusive term — the norm and the ideal — there is nowhere for the rest of us to go except out of the central category, and down the scale of worth. Thus is injustice, and the violence that attends it, established and justified. Thus do we become divided against each other and ourselves, trapped in sterile combat. It is difficult, then, to conceive of *human* virtue.

TRANSFORMATIONS

Let me, then, explore a few of the ways we are attempting to think ourselves free of the old and still present invidious hierarchies of thought, of method, of action.

Recentering

Those who have been most marginalized and oppressed have turned to their own lives of struggle and resistance, fury and love. They have put at the center that which was marginalized, divided, repressed.

Seeing knowledge as grounded in experience, theorists such as Nancy Hartsock, Sara Ruddick, and Hilary Rose argue that the activities assigned to women, understood through the categories of feminist theory, provide a starting point for developing claims to knowledge that are potentially more comprehensive and less distorted than those of privileged men. They believe that women's sensuous, relational, and contextual perspective allows them to understand aspects of nature and social life not available to those men who are cut off from such activities. Thus women's experiences provide a basis for developing an alternative epistemology that unifies manual, mental, and emotional activity.[14]

Such recentering is not singular. We do not move from Man to an equally mystified, abstract, dissociated Woman. We struggle to remain in conversation with many women as well as to speak of our own experiences so that we do not once again suffer the loss of multiple realities. As Patricia Hill Collins notes in her effort to explore an epistemology developed from Black women's experiences: "First, Black women's political and economic status provides them with a distinctive set of experiences that offers a different view of material reality than that available to other groups. The unpaid and paid work that Black women perform, the types of communities in which they live, and the kinds of relationships they have with others suggest that African-American women, as a group, experience a different world than those who are not Black and not female. Second, these experiences stimulate a distinctive Black female consciousness concerning that material reality."[15]

Pushing us not only through the barriers between kinds of women, but through those between the conscious and the repressed, Ruth Ginzberg, learning and thinking with Audre Lorde, notes that Lorde "identifies the erotic as 'a considered source of power and information within (women's) lives' that 'rises from our deepest and nonrational knowledge'. The erotic, she claims, provides 'the power which comes from sharing deeply any pursuit with another person,' as well as 'the open and fearless understanding of . . . [the] capacity for joy'. . . . This," says Ginzberg, "is a political claim, not a claim about hedonism or 'rights' to pleasure. . . . [Lorde] sees the erotic as an epistemic force that tempers the individualistic sense of self; it is the source of both power and information, which encourages resistance to atomism and unchecked individualism and which leads to understanding. . . ." And she concludes, "I suggest that there is a conception of moral philosophy emerging from the writings of Audre Lorde and other lesbian feminist theorists that is based in the very acts of surviving. . . ."[16]

Reconfiguring

Such efforts to bring that which was denied and hidden fully into consciousness, culture, and thought undo the dangerous dissociations we have been noting. They erupt them from within, not by turning old hierarchies upside down, or collapsing ego into id, but by reconfiguring what was always there. With *more* now relating us, we must learn to make distinctions that are not divisions; to think far less crudely about *sameness* and *difference* in order to escape the old pattern of mutually created oppositions. As Agnes Heller puts it, thinking about the relations of sameness and difference reconceived in relation to "the good life" as public life: "Although the good life of each and every person is unique, it is simultaneously shared by the members of a community, a group, a society; however . . . all these shared ways of life, are again unique: they cannot be ranked and compared."[17] We need to be able to think not of difference and sameness across the old hierarchical lines, but of uniqueness that is discernible and has meaning precisely because of our human commonality.

But because we persist in respecting the experiences of those we have now put at the center, we do not fall back into understanding uniqueness or commonality in ways that erase either actual individuals or particular communities. We are precisely not trying to locate the good life in abstraction from real and possible lives led by those whose existence is constantly at risk. "Survival . . . is central to any conceptualization in which the summum bonum (if there is such a thing) is not taken to be something that transcends physically, psychologically, and socially embedded life but rather that is taken to be just exactly that. The sketch that emerges is that of an immanent rather than a transcendent philosophical theory, in which survival is not transcended but embraced."[18] We are seeking to reconfigure, not to reinscribe in and for different bodies, the good life of the "free man," and thus we no longer flee but attempt to comprehend the wisdom of human life in its intimate relations to necessity.

Revaluing

We are thus revaluing the lives prescribed for women in different groups, at different times, in different cultures. This, of course, is a research project as well as a conceptual task. The qualities of women as of Woman are evidently prescribed in all sorts of ways in philosophies, religions, political theories, economic systems, in codes of mores, manners, and morals. If we would locate a fuller array of the virtues discerned and prescribed for humans of all sorts, we can do so by remembering and revaluing what it has meant to be a woman. This is the sort of work Mary Daly, Katie Cannon, Patricia Hill Collins, Carol Gilligan, Sara Ruddick, and Nell Noddings, among others, have been doing. What was both prescribed for women and scorned in relation to the falsely generalized or even universalized Man is reevaluated.

Thus, among other coexisting and complementary efforts, we begin work on an "ethics of care," in which the "maternal" (Ruddick), the "caring" (Gilligan), the "feminine" (Noddings) are recast from the qualities "naturally" to be expected from females, to become suggestive of virtues to be attained by humans. We undo the dissociation of Man from all that sustains us, all of us, in being. We reconsider notions of justice that exclude care, and struggle to rethink care as it interrelates with justice, drawing, as Ruddick does, on experiences within the family, and as Hill Collins does, on the paid and unpaid work Black women perform.

Redefining

Once having begun such philosophical and empirical work, we find that revaluing is much more than an effort at addition. It requires more basic transformation of our theorizing, as of our action. While "manly" strength is considered central to a citizen or a leader's virtue, gentleness and compassion remain problems, signs of weakness, marks of the devalued effeminate. While power is defined as the ability to make people do as one wills, we continue to conflate power with domination. The military remains the epitome of masculinity, and pacifism can only be scorned as effeminate. It is no accident that the effort to revalue "feminine" virtue has led to rethinking pacifism, nor that it has led other feminist thinkers to create "ecofeminism."

We redefine culturally central terms, concepts, frames of meaning and hence of action. As Sara Ruddick writes,

> A feminist maternal politics of peace: peacemakers create a communal suspicion of violence, a climate in which peace is desired, a way of living in which it is possible to learn and to practice nonviolent resistance and strategies of reconciliation. This description of peacemaking is a description of mothering. Mothers take their work seriously and create a women's politics of resistance. Feminists sustain that politics, devising strategies, celebrating strength, resisting violence and contempt. Together mothers, feminists, and women in resistance are members of an "imaginative collective" . . . (which) subverts the mythical division between men and women, private care and public defense, that hobbles both maternal and peacemaking endeavors. As men become mothers and mothers invent public resistance to violence, mothering and peacemaking become a single, womanly-manly work — a feminist, maternal politics of peace.[19]

With the redefinition of "maternal" to become a human term, our move to recenter with the marginal within the material reconfigures the old transcendent/immanent division as well. We need not choose between the life of the mind, the spirit, and the body. "Man is mortal" must yield to the recollection that humankind is also always *natal*.[20]

J. Glenn Gray understood the violence of forgetting such foundational human connections. He related "dissociation" to "living godlessly," a product of that "remoteness from reality" that Hegel diagnoses as the "fury of abstraction." Notions of virtue that are built on and require splitting off aspects of humanness that are then projected onto Others over whom some few men are justified in exercising dominion reveal that "fury." The passions of the masculine mind, uncontrolled by the realities of human embodiedness within real human natural and historical contexts, are more dangerous than those of the body uncontrolled by reason because reason is, unlike body, limitless.

REASON

We ask how any thought relates to body. As Maxine Sheets-Johnstone notes, "The consequence of leaving the body behind is unexplained concepts, that is, concepts that are simply taken for granted with no thought as to how they might have originated . . . (which) not only perpetuates the errors of a partial and in consequence biased metaphysics (but) also creates conceptual problems in the very real sense of assuming concepts to arise *sui generis.*"[21] We are attempting to undo such bizarre dissociations of thoughts from thinking, and of thinking from the embodied natal/mortal, reproductive/productive, meaning-created and creating particular person who thinks as, of, and beyond what and who she or he is.

Thus, having undertaken to begin revaluing the virtues of dissociated/alienated Man's Others, we uncover again the need to transform, and not merely add to, Man's virtues. As Alison Jaggar notes, "Typically, although again not invariably, the rational has been contrasted with the emotional, and this contrasted pair then has often been linked with other dichotomies. Not only has reason been contrasted with emotion, but it has also been associated with the mental, the cultural, the universal, the public, and the male, whereas emotion has been associated with the irrational, the physical, the natural, the particular, the private, and, of course, the female."[22] There are now many studies of reason, often focused especially on science and the Enlightenment dream, that discern hidden but potent biases on many levels. Such critiques come also from nonfeminist scientists. As Abraham Pais wrote, in a study of the great physicist Niels Bohr, "the best we can say" about nature, according to Bohr, "is always partial and incomplete; only by entertaining multiple and mutually limiting points of view, building up a composite picture, can we approach the real richness of the world. (Bohr) called this important idea 'complementarity' and applied it not only to explain why matter sometimes acts like a particle and sometimes like a wave, *but also to rebuke Nazi claims of cultural superiority. . . .*"[23] (emphasis added)

These critiques underline the fact that the claims we make for reason *have effects* in, even as they also reflect, the world. If we would rethink reason, the defining virtue of Man from Aristotle on, we must do with it what we have done elsewhere. We must critique it to uncover its biases, its definitional and operational implications with foundational invidious divisions and dissociations. We do this in order also more creatively to explore its functioning in all the modes written out of its "proper" sphere as characterizing lesser humans. We then find that what John Dewey called "the quest for certainty" is, as he argued, closely related to Man's quest for dominion over others, and over the earth. Bohr's idea of "complementarity" provides an intriguing alternative model that is consonant with Dewey's move to transactional analysis, Gilligan's ethics of care, Ruddick's drawing on and drawing together of maternal and pacifist thinking, Noddings' revaluation of the virtues of femininity, and J. Glenn Gray's plea for the undoing of abstract thinking that perpetuates dissociation from all that sustains humans in being.

NEW WAYS

A picture, a collage, a weave of many strands old and new begins to emerge, suggesting a way of thinking that is resistant, respectful, reflexive, and critical. It refuses dualistic and/or invidiously hierarchical divisions that cannot be breached in favor of distinctions within wholeness. It emphasizes transactional mutuality over oppositional relations. It explores connection, complementarity, relationality within the matrix of experience where we are called to practice both care and justice. And it struggles to retrieve and revalue all aspects of the meaning of being human, from the bodily to the rational to the transcendent, in the name of our fullest unique and common potential. Such a vision has always threaded its way through the dominant tradition, never disappearing entirely, often emerging into full view. Nevertheless it needs to be rediscovered and reconfigured so that it can be freed of the startling lapses from its own intellectual and moral coherence it has suffered because of the depth and range of always divisive gender constructs that have entangled with the other primary divisions of humans into "kinds."

There are models. Working herself free of old ways by immersing herself in them to find the Ariadne's thread, listening for

guidance to "the orphic voice," the philosopher, poet, and novelist
Elizabeth Sewell discerns in poetry a method, a logic, that does
not suffer from the "fury of abstraction":

> It is not a matter for specialists, but for people. . . . The
> method, the postlogic, is a way of using mind and body to
> build up dynamic structures (never fixed or abstract patterns)
> by which the human organism sets itself in relation to the
> universe and allows each side to interpret the other. The mind's
> relation to its structure or myth is inclusive and reflexive. It
> is not detached; the working mind is part of the dynamic of
> the system, and is united, by its forms, with whatever in the
> universe it is inquiring into. The process of making the inter-
> pretive myth is carried out in language, and the structure of
> its language in its dynamic with the mind both conditions
> and is conditioned by the mutual interpretation. The body
> is an essential part of the method. The method bears a close
> relation to sex and fertility. Love is a necessary part of its
> working. . . . It lies to everyone's hand and we have to return
> to it, not as a vague ornament of life but as one of the great
> living disciplines of the mind, friendly to all other disciplines,
> and offering them and accepting from them new resources
> of power.[24]

We can see some fruits of Sewell's teaching in the collabora-
tive work of Sande and Larry Churchill, philosophers who are
her students as well as being involved with both the dominant
tradition and feminist critique. Here, they prepare to think about
ethics brought into creative tension with the realities of clinical
practices:

> Human ethical activity is complex and multi-faceted. It in-
> cludes deciding and acting, reflection and contemplation, sus-
> taining habits over time, nurturing character, and many other
> kinds of activity. It is part logic, part acts of will, part turn-
> ing of emotional sensibilities, part feats of imagination. Be-
> cause ethics embraces such diverse kinds of activity, ethical
> theories need to be diverse and multifaceted as well. Yet this
> is frequently not the case. . . . We invite you to think of the
> approach to ethical theory we will undertake in this essay not

as a linear and progressive rational argument which makes additive and cumulative points for the purpose of unifying or totalizing a theory. Rather we think of our approach as a collage. . . . The emphasis is on showing how images are interdependent and gain their meanings from the whole, rather than being serially or chronologically anchored.[25]

The Churchill critique, like that of Elizabeth Sewell and others, has also led them to accept the challenge to create which that critique carries with it. They know the intellectual, political, and ethical importance of changing methods of thought, and recognize that such a method often entails shifting our shaping metaphors. Just how imaginatively stimulating such shifts can be is vividly displayed by Cornel West, who envisions "new world bricoleurs with improvisational and flexible sensibilities that sidestep mere opportunism and mindless eclecticism; persons from all countries, cultures, genders, sexual orientations, ages and regions with protean identities who avoid ethnic chauvinism and faceless universalism; intellectual and political freedom fighters with partisan passion, international perspectives, and, thank God, a sense of humor . . . with intellectual rigor, existential dignity, moral vision, political courage, and soulful style.[26]

Inspired by this evocation of a virtuoso of humanity, we return to an old question: How is one to realize well all that one might be? How is one to help others do so as well? There are no prescriptions, although there are methods of thought and practice as there are inspiring models to be found everywhere, among us all. For the moment, it is no small thing to recognize that how and where and with whom we *begin* will make the difference in our own undertaking of the old quest. We begin again with the inspiration of the great African-American educator Anna Julia Cooper, who wrote in 1892:

It is not the intelligent woman vs. the ignorant woman, nor the white woman vs. the black, the brown, and the red,—it is not even the cause of woman vs. man. Nay, 'tis woman's strongest vindication for speaking that *the world needs to hear her voice.* . . . The world has had to limp along with the wobbling gait and the one-sided hesitancy of a man with one eye. Suddenly the bandage is removed from the other eye and the whole body is filled with light. It sees a circle where before it saw a segment. The darkened eye restored, every member rejoices with it.[27]

NOTES

1. Muriel Rukeyser, "Letter to the Front," from *Out of Silence* (Evanston, Ill.: TriQuarterly Books, 1992). © William L. Rukeyser.

2. Claudia Card, ed., *Feminist Ethics* (Lawrence: University Press of Kansas, 1991), p. 4.

3. Ibid.

4. Hannah Arendt, *The Origins of Totalitarianism* (Cleveland: World Publishing Co./Meridian Book, 1966), p. viii.

5. Rosemary Radford Ruether, *Women-Church: Theology and Practice* (San Francisco: Harper & Row, 1985), p. 3.

6. Nicholas Lobkowicz, *Theory and Practice: History of a Concept from Aristotle to Marx* (Notre Dame, Ind.: University of Notre Dame Press, 1967), p. 3.

7. Ibid., p. 20.

8. For discussion of these conceptual errors throughout the dominant tradition, see my *Transforming Knowledge* (Philadelphia: Temple University Press, 1990).

9. *The Oxford English Dictionary* (Oxford: Oxford University Press, 1978), p. 239.

10. Mary Wollstonecraft, *A Vindication of the Rights of Woman* (New York: W. W. Norton & Co., 1967), p. 69.

11. *The Oxford English Dictionary* (Oxford: Oxford University Press, 1978), p. 238.

12. Stanley Cavell, *Conditions Handsome and Unhandsome* (Chicago: University of Chicago Press, 1990), p. 77.

13. J. Glenn Gray, *The Warriors: Reflections on Men in Battle* (New York: Harper & Row/Harper Colophon Books, 1970), p. xix.

14. Nancy Tuana, *Woman and the History of Philosophy* (New York: Paragon House/Paragon Issues in Philosophy, 1992), p. 116.

15. Quoted in ibid., p. 117.

16. Ruth Ginzberg, "Philosophy Is Not a Luxury," in *Feminist Ethics*, ed. Card, pp. 131–32.

17. Agnes Heller, *Beyond Justice* (Oxford: Basil Blackwell, 1991), p. 324.

18. Ginzberg, "Philosophy is Not a Luxury," p. 132.

19. Sara Ruddick, *Maternal Thinking Toward a Politics of Peace* (Boston: Beacon Press, 1989), p. 244.

20. Cf. Hannah Arendt, *The Human Condition* (Chicago: University of Chicago Press, 1970).

21. Maxine Sheets-Johnstone, *The Roots of Thinking* (Philadelphia: Temple University Press, 1990), p. 289.

22. Alison M. Jaggar, "Love and Knowledge: Emotion in Feminist Epistemology," in *Gender/Body/Knowledge: Feminist Reconstructions of Being and Knowing,* ed. Alison M. Jaggar and Susan R. Bordo (New Brunswick: Rutgers University Press, 1989), p. 145.

23. Richard Rhodes, review of *Niel Bohr's Times: In Physics, Philosophy and Polity* by Abraham Pais, *New York Times Book Review,* 26 January 1992.

24. Elizabeth Sewell, *The Orphic Voice: Poetry and Natural History* (New Haven, Conn.: Yale University Press, 1960), pp. 404–5.

25. Sande and Larry Churchill, "Reason, Narrative and Rhetoric: A Theoretical Collage for the Clinical Encounter," in *Theological Analyses of the Clinical Encounter,* ed. Gerald McKenny and Jonathan Sande (Kluwer Academic Pubs., forthcoming).

26. Cornel West, in *Out There: Marginalization and Contemporary Culture,* ed. Ferguson, Gever, Minh-ha, West (Boston: Massachusetts Institute of Technology Press, 1990), p. 36.

27. Anna Julia Cooper, *A Voice From the South* (New York: Oxford University Press, 1988), pp. 121–23.

Can Virtue Be Taught in a School? Ivan Illich and Mohandas Gandhi on Deschooling Society

LEROY S. ROUNER

THE QUESTION "CAN VIRTUE BE TAUGHT?" is the subject of Plato's *Protagoras*. I will sketch Socrates' approach to the problem in that dialogue, and then compare and contrast Ivan Illich and Mohandas Gandhi, both of whom are critics of modern schools. Socrates has little to say about cultural context, and nothing at all to say about academic institutions, since there were none in his day. Illich and Gandhi, on the other hand, both focus on the urban, industrial context of institutionalized education. And since our question is not whether virtue can be learned but whether it can be taught, I have some observations about the different models of teaching offered by Socrates, Illich, and Gandhi, and some tentative conclusions about the kind of teaching we need today.

The *Protagoras* begins with Socrates' being awakened before dawn by his excited young friend Hippocrates who announces that Protagoras has just come to town. He pleads with Socrates to arrange for him to become Protagoras' pupil. Like most well-to-do young men in the Athens of his day, Hippocrates yearned to be able to speak well, in order to make his mark in the Assembly, the center of power and prestige. Since speaking well required thinking well, rhetoric was regularly associated with wisdom.

Protagoras was a Sophist, one of a number of itinerant sages who took on the sons of the aristocracy as temporary pupils, and became wealthy in the process. Since education had not yet been institutionalized, these Sophists were the educational establishment. Studying with them was better than getting into Harvard. It was as though Henry Kissinger, or John Kenneth Galbraith, came to stay for a couple of months at the home of some wealthy business person with intellectual aspirations, and agreed to take on a few well-heeled local lads as pupils in a short course on meaning, truth, and success.

Socrates, of course, was an anti-establishment *enfant terrible*. He disliked the sophists for charging fees for teaching (he called it intellectual prostitution), and he disagreed with Protagoras profoundly because Protagoras was a relativist and believed that morals were shaped by various communities. Protagoras argued that "man is the measure of all things." Socrates, on the other hand, was an intellectual purist and a bit of a fundamentalist. He believed in absolutes. He argued tirelessly that, if there are plural virtues, like courage and temperance, then there must be a singular, absolute, normative reality called *virtue* in which the various virtues participate, and hence gain meaning and reality. The *Protagoras* does not deal with the metaphysical question about the nature of virtue, or how we come to have this knowledge. Later, in the *Meno*, Plato proposes his theory of reincarnation, arguing that we already know what virtue really is from a previous life, and that this knowledge has been obscured by common opinion and traditions of all sorts. So Socratic dialectic is largely deconstructive. It pulls away this veil of false assurance, leaves us naked with our ignorance, and thus readies us for a "synoptic insight" into the true nature of virtue. Here lies the connection between Socrates and Gandhi, who was much influenced by the Hindu nondualistic philosophy of Sankara. Sankara's doctrine of the world as *māyā* or "illusion" has much in common with Socrates' view that common opinion (*doxa*) is misleading when it comes to questions about the ultimate nature of things.

Without this transcendent understanding of virtue, Socrates argued, there was no point in trying to teach people specific virtues, like courage or temperance. They wouldn't get it, because one can't understand why courage is a virtue if one doesn't first understand what the word *virtue* means. Students will have a preliminary understanding of what the term *courage* represents, but it won't help them to *be* courageous, because they won't have any way to understand the reality of virtue in which the concept of courage is grounded. As my teacher John Herman Randall used to say, "They will get the words right, but miss the tune." They will be able to "talk a good game" but not play it. The head knows, but not the heart.

From Socrates' point of view, the purpose of teaching someone about courage was not just so that they could give an adequate definition of it, and defend that definition in debate, although the dialogues sometimes make it seem that way. That goal trivializes the purposes of education by aestheticizing or intellectualizing them. The purpose of teaching someone about courage is to make them courageous. The purpose of education is not to tinker with people's minds, or gild their tongues. Socrates, for all his lofty idealism and ingenious dialectic, is essentially down to earth. He reminds me of some of my friends in rural New Hampshire, where I live. They would say: "Is all this talk about courage gonna make you brave? And if it don't, it's all about nothin', ain't it?" Socrates would have agreed.

Socrates fascinates modern philosophers because he is both an analytical philosopher and an idealist. His dialectical method evolves a philosophy out of the analysis of language. But he also believes in the determinative reality of absolute ideas. And he was much beloved of the existentialist, Søren Kierkegaard, not only because he was such an individual, but because his ultimate focus was always personal, immediate, practical, and lifegiving. His transcendent ideals were not abstractions; they were those necessary structures of meaning which alone make a genuinely human life possible. So, when the young Hippocrates first comes to Socrates as a potential pupil of Protagoras, Socrates does not ask him whether Protagoras' instruction will get him into law school, or guarantee a six-figure income. He asks, "What will he make of you?" That question, I suggest, is as close to the bone as the philosophy of education gets.

The current curriculum debate tends to miss this point because the critical question after four years of college is not primarily information, but transformation. The test is less how much students know, of whatever cultural tradition, because they are going to forget most of that content in five years. The test is who a student has become in that process. In other words, "What have they made of you?"

It is this existential tension which keeps the debate going between Socrates and Protagoras, because the ultimate issue for both of them is not the analytical problem of definition, or the abstract question of ideals, both of which might have been readily resolved. The ultimate issue is a philosophy-of-life question. How can I understand who I am and what I do in a way that is coherent, and makes sense to me, and therefore has some integrity? In other words, how can I live a good life? Socrates is looking for a "synoptic intuition" into the transcendental reality which actually enables life decisions. Knowledge of this kind would be inherently transformative. If we *really* knew what virtue meant, we would *be* good.

This is where most of us get stuck, because Socrates seems too "idealistic." You and I usually know what we ought to do, but we usually don't do it, because we don't want to. Our wills are in conflict with our intellect. And modern theories of knowledge support our skepticism about Socrates' argument from a different direction, because they tend to focus on "clear and distinct" ideas as the necessary conceptual material for proper reasoning. Our idea of an idea is therefore more like a coin or a bucket than a cloud. But the ground issues of ethics — love, virtue, loyalty, and the like — are never clear and distinct. They are not hard coins, or measurable buckets. They are always cloudy. They are mysteries.

So the question can be recast: How can one know a mystery? Can mysteries be taught? For Socrates, the deepest dimension of knowledge joins heart and mind, will and understanding. The problem is not whether *ethics* can be taught. Ethics is not a mystery; it is an intellectual structure of moral principles. Ethics *per se* is only the tuneless prescription of social oughts.

Virtue is a song. One has to get the tune right in order to know virtue. Can the soul sing? And if not, how can the soul be taught to sing? So virtue is a mystery, a song, a transforming vision. Can anyone really teach that? And how do we get it, if in fact we do? Socrates finally suggested that it was a gift from the gods, which is probably right. But that didn't negate the importance for him of the educational process, the dialectical exploration of what words mean, how ideals are viable, and what actually works for us in the real world. At the very least these were a necessary prolegomenon to the vision. They constructed the most reliable platform from which to view the transformative insight. That was what dialectic was all about. Socrates, professing ignorance, sought to be a midwife of ideas in others. The truth was there, buried under a lot of intellectual confusion in their souls. Socrates relentlessly asked all the awkward questions which would clarify this confusion.

But there is a dimension to the problem which Plato never engaged, and that is cultural context. *Our* question is about teaching virtue *in context*. Is the modern school a viable context for teaching virtue? Both Illich and Gandhi answer "No."

Illich's *DeSchooling Society* is part of a larger critique of modern institutions generally, which included industry, medical practice, and so forth. In regard to schools: "The pupil is . . . schooled to confuse teaching with learning, grade advancement with education, a diploma with competence, and fluency with the ability to say something new. His imagination is 'schooled' to accept service in place of value. Medical treatment is mistaken for health care, social work for the improvement of community life, police protection for safety, military poise for national security, the rat race for productive work."[1] In other words, Illich is opposed to all the major institutions of modern life, and schools are here a paradigm case of that opposition.

Schools, he argues, blur the distinction between process and substance. They persuade you that process is meaningful, that "going through" school produces something substantial which, in fact, it does not. He argues, rather, that modern institutionalization (of education, health care, social welfare, crime protection, national security) "inevitably leads to physical pollution, social polarization and psychological impotence."[2]

Further, we have assumed that "school" and "teaching" are necessary for learning. Illich argues, to the contrary, that most of what we need to know we learn outside "school" and that we are taught, not by paid professional instructors, but by others in our culture who have learned their particular skill outside school. School appropriates "the money, men and good will available for education and in addition discourages other institutions from assuming educational tasks. Work, leisure, politics, city living, and even family life depend on schools for the habits and knowledge they presuppose, instead of becoming themselves the means of education."[3]

Illich's argument is that if we were serious about education we would take advantage of the educative opportunities of community life. We didn't learn how to speak our mother tongue in school. Dad taught us how to drive a car, and Mom taught us how to cook, or maybe vice-versa, but the point is that these fundamental skills are all learned informally, outside institutions.

Illich is persuaded that our problem is rooted in the invention of childhood by the middle class in industrial societies. Childhood was unknown to most historical periods, and is still unknown today outside industrial societies. "Before our century neither the poor nor the rich knew of children's dress, children's games, or the child's immunity from the law. Childhood belonged to the bourgeoisie. The worker's child, the peasant's child and the nobleman's child all dressed the way their fathers dressed, played the way their fathers played, and were hanged by the neck as were their fathers."[4]

Even today, Illich notes, "In the Andes you till the soil once you have become 'useful'. Before that you watch the sheep."[5] Further, he is persuaded that, given the choice, most people would pass on childhood. "Neither Stephen Daedalus nor Alexander Portnoy enjoyed childhood, and neither, I suspect, did many of us like to be treated as children."[6]

A major criticism of schooling is the role of the teacher. Illich argues that "we have all learned most of what we know outside school. . . . We learn to speak, to think, to love, to feel, to play, to curse, to politick, and to work without interference from a teacher."[7] And teachers, in Illich's view, impede education beause they are cast in the roles of *custodian, preacher, and therapist*. The teacher as custodian is an orchestrator, guiding the pupil through labyrinthine rituals, like qualifying examinations, which Illich finds unproductive. The teacher as moralist "substitutes for parents, God, or the state. He indoctrinates the pupil about what is right or wrong, not only in school but also in society at large. He stands *in loco parentis* for each one and thus ensures that all feel themselves children of the same state."[8]

The teacher as therapist is perhaps the most dangerous model for Illich. The teacher "feels authorized to delve into the personal life of his pupil in order to help him grow as a person. When this function is exercised by a custodian and preacher, it usually means that he persuades his pupil to submit to a domestication of his vision of truth and his sense of what is right."[9]

Illich sounds radical but is, I think, a conservative, calling for less government, more freedom, and letting the good times roll. He is essentially an optimist. He thinks people are good and will learn from life experience what they need to know. We don't really need schools. Like Socrates he is a deconstructionist, albeit a modern one. Get rid of those structures which impede genuine learning, he argues, and things will take care of themselves. There are lots of people out there ready to teach us what we need to know. In this he is not unlike Protagoras, who argued not only that virtue can be taught, but that there are lots of folk out there teaching it — parents, kindergarten teachers, police officers, and others.

Illich is, however, primarily concerned with what his colleague Paolo Friere called "the pedagogy of the oppressed," emphasizing that universal education in schools is hopelessly expensive. If the poor are to be educated it will have to be outside school, in the family, the work place, and in communities of common concern. But for all his criticism of "schools," he is an academic intellectual. He works in a "think tank." Granted it is in Cuernavaca, Mexico, rather than in Stanford or Cambridge, but the intellectual ethos is much the same.

Gandhi, on the other hand, was a practitioner. From the early years in South Africa to the time of his death he was engaged in a social reform movement. He was educated in schools, both in India and England, and was profoundly influenced by a few writers like Tolstoy and Ruskin. He was also deeply influenced by traditional elements of Hindu life and thought, but his key ideas were largely generated from his life experience. Even when he seemed to be borrowing from tradition, as with his emphasis on nonviolence or *ahiṃsā* as a way of life, he was, in fact, reinventing these ideas in order to meet the needs of his own social reform movement.

Ahiṃsā, for example, had always been a principle of personal piety in Indian culture. To kill was to infect one's soul with bad *karma* and thus impede the process of *moksha*, salvific freedom from the bonds of illusion and particularity in this world. Gandhi, however, presented *ahiṃsā* as a social principle, a way of dealing with one's neighbors, whether friends or enemies. And in the course of his long life of social activism, he almost persuaded a whole nation that this was what their tradition had always meant by *ahiṃsā*. Gandhi's program of social reform involved political freedom from British colonial rule. Politics, however, was, for him, the means to a renewal of Indian society. British colonialism was detrimental to India, he believed, not primarily because it robbed India of its right to self-government (which tended to be Nehru's view) but because it corrupted the Indian spirit through the values and institutions of modernity.

Like Illich, he was opposed to urbanization and industrialization because they corrupted the good life. And like Hannah Arendt, he believed that individuals found their creative potential best fulfilled in the type of small community found in the Greek *polis* or the traditional Indian village.

And, of course, it was not hard to criticize the British educational establishment in India. The British were not concerned with an imaginative teaching of virtue; they were primarily interested in training. They needed clerks to serve in the lower echelons of colonial administration, and they needed people who spoke their cultural language. So the curriculum required Shakespeare and the metaphysical poets of people whose English was minimal at best. Rote learning thus became the order of the day, and produced a generation of people who could only hope to get the words right, and had no idea of what the tune might possibly be.

Gandhi's philosophy of education was much like Illich's in that it was opposed to this impersonal and culturally alien educational establishment, which had robbed his countrymen and countrywomen of their cultural self-confidence and spiritual power. He said, "It does not make men of us. It does not enable us to do our duty."[10]

Gandhi believed that "true education is something different. Man is made of three constituents, the body, mind and spirit. Of them, the spirit is the one permanent element in man. The body and the mind function on account of it. Hence we can call that education which reveals the qualities of spirit."[11] He goes on: "The knowledge that is being imparted today may possibly develop the mind a little, but certainly does not develop the body or spirit. I have a doubt about the development of the mind too, because it does not mean that the mind has developed if we have filled it with a lot of information."[12]

He concludes: "Education, character and religion should be regarded as convertible terms. There is no true education that does not tend to produce character, and there is no true religion which does not determine character. Education should contemplate the whole life. Mere memorizing and book learning is not education. I have no faith in the so-called system of education which produces men of learning without the backbone of character."[13]

Gandhi's role as educator took its departure from the classical Hindu model of the relation between the *guru*, the spiritual teacher, and the *adhikarin*, the qualified student. This involved continuing, intense interaction between teacher and student in all the details of daily living, until the genius, or insight, or divine reality within the guru was inexplicably transferred to the student. The student suddenly grasped a "synoptic insight" into truth.

Gandhi's project was to establish this traditional interaction between guru and student on a huge scale, which was India itself. Gandhi was the guru, and the whole of India was the student. The project's microcosm was the life of the ashram, the intimate personal community in which Gandhi lived. But the macrocosm was India. Gandhi made himself a constant presence in the life of the nation, through political action, and especially through his writing. He wrote endlessly, inconsistently, specifically about a whole host of problems. And the extent to which he regarded his own life as an experimental instrument for the transformation of a nation is vividly illustrated by his sexual experiments.

Gandhi was persuaded that colonialism had robbed Indian men of their manhood. They had been made submissive through military conquest and political control, but they had been robbed of their spiritual power through the colonialist's celebration of male sexuality as generative, having families and children and being heads of large households. This is more profound than a criticism of pornography, for example. It is a criticism of what we would call natural male sexuality. Gandhi held a traditional Hindu view that male semen is a source of inner spiritual power, and that the loss of semen was a loss of power. Therefore the practice of *Brahmacharya*, the love of Brahma, included sexual chastity, not as a means of ascetic denial, but as a means of empowerment. Semen moved through the spinal column, throughout the body, making possible those heroic feats for which yogis have long been known: the endurance of heat and cold, the ability to live creatively with only a few hours sleep a night, and freedom from depression or mood changes. Gandhi experienced all of these. He hoped for a new generation of genuinely strong men who had appropriated these powers for themselves, and were ready to use them in the service of the New India.

Gandhi used himself as an experimental project in how one's inner spirituality could be empowered by sexual discipline. And this was not just white-knuckle abstention. He wandered naked around the ashram, to make this a natural thing. Eventually he even slept naked with two naked young women, testing himself and them with the possibility of transcending what my mother used to call "bad thoughts."

But at least once Gandhi's experiment failed. He awoke with an outward and visible sign of what, for him, was an inward and spiritual disgrace. Since he had already made his experiment public, he wrote an article in *Young India* about this personal failure and, by implication, what it meant for the future of the nation. This *is* a little bizarre, and Gandhi may well have dehumanized himself in the service of spiritual renewal in the New India. But it shows how far he was willing to go in making himself an educational tool for the transformation of the Indian character. He was custodian, preacher and therapist for the whole nation, and the *nation* was his school. He wanted people to change radically, and he was ready to use himself as a transforming vehicle for that change.

What, then, can we use from these two radical educational *enfants terribles?* Like Socrates, they are both anti-establishment, anti-institutional, and thus anti-modern. So, first of all, they give us historical perspective on where we are, and some new ideas on where we ought to be going.

In the Middle Ages, the great cultural forces in the West were the church and the university. In the modern world the great cultural forces are the state and the multinational corporation. Neil Rudenstine at Harvard has just called for a new alliance among the state, the corporation, and the university if the university in America is to maintain its role as a predominant institution. But the crisis in the university is precisely that the university has *become* a corporation, and therefore gradually lost the distinctive educational vocation that Socrates articulated so well in his question to Hippocrates: "What will he make of you?"

Both Illich and Gandhi criticize schools for creating a world of ideas and interests which are not directly related to our experience of ourselves and our world outside school. They are both Utopians. They want to dismantle our present educational institutions, on the grounds that they are too expensive, essentially unproductive, and therefore unnecessary. This dismantling might be a good thing, except for those of us who would be out of work, but that's not going to happen. Schools are not even likely to be reformed, because they are such effective means of social success in our society. My father, who had been a poor boy from the wrong side of the stockyards in Omaha, Nebraska, at the turn of the century, eventually went to Harvard, and he urged me to go to Harvard because it would make connections that would serve me for the rest of my life. And of course he was right. So Utopia is a lost cause. But Josiah Royce reminds us that lost causes today are often highly influential tomorrow. And even if they are not, they keep us focused on the purpose we serve. The fact that it never happens doesn't mean it wasn't right.

My lost cause is the hope for a growing group of people within the university who seek to *personalize* education, connecting the material of their discipline in various ways to the real life-world of students. We are left with three models of teaching for doing that. One is Socrates, the midwife of ideas, who professes to know nothing except a method whereby people may hopefully come to know their own ignorance. A second is Ivan Illich who is persuaded that true education comes from those functioning in our real culture, and not in the abstract and unnecessary institutions of schooling. These people already know what we really need to know. They are our parents, friends, co-workers, and the like. The third is Gandhi, who tried to make his own spirituality a transforming vision of virtue for India.

Illich doesn't think we need a special class of people called "teachers." Gandhi and Socrates, on the other hand, were both teachers in their own way, and both believed that the transformative insight into virtue is finally discovered by individuals in their own souls, rather than imposed by someone else from outside. So you can't "teach" virtue, but you can help people get to the place where they can learn it for themselves. They differ in their method of doing this, however. Socrates focused almost entirely on rational argument, and refused to play the role of the wise one. Gandhi played the role of the virtuous wise one to the hilt. For our present purposes, Socrates did not personalize his teaching enough, whereas Gandhi personalized it too much.

By personalization I do not mean that we should spend more time with our students, by having more office hours, open doors, inviting them home, and so forth. Nor does personalization mean that teachers should consciously try to be role models for their students. A certain amount of role modeling inevitably takes place. Insofar as this imitation is well chosen and establishes good habits in the imitator it is valuable. More than that, it is the way we all begin to learn to be good at anything. As Socrates said about learning "knacks" like cooking, one should find a good cook, and watch what they do, and then go practice.

That is really Illich's populist model of education. But Socrates knew something that Illich ignores and that is that *episteme*, real knowledge, has to be prepared for by what my teacher Ernest Hocking called "the hard work of thought." It is why Socrates said one has to have a process of dialectic first. In Illich's happy world, it all happens by itself if people just get out there and live. My view is that we have to work at it. And school is the workplace.

But Socrates lived in a world where rational argument was widely trusted; and we no longer live in that world. For most of our students, a rational proof for an ethical principle no longer "proves" much of anything. Socrates knew that rational proof needed myth in order to be persuasive, even in his culture. But the myth he appealed to was the myth of a common culture, whereas our students no longer have a common culture. Their myth needs to be brought home. The myths of our culture need to make connection with the inner myth of their individual lives. As the feminists have insisted, we all need a chance to tell our own story.

Gandhi is surely right that virtue is learned from those who are virtuous, and that we become virtuous by choosing our mentors well. But his is ultimately an authoritarian model. In the individualistic West, we eschew gurus because we fear spiritual totalitarianism. If virtue is a song, it is a song sung in one's own voice, and a major purpose of higher education is to help students in both arts and sciences find their own voice as artist or scientist. Like good parents, role models can initially enable this discovery, but they soon become barriers to it. If one's first novel sounds like Ernest Hemingway, that's all right; one is learning a craft. If a second novel sounds like Ernest Hemingway, the author is well on his or her way to becoming a bad writer.

The personalization of education means paying increased attention to the "inwardness" of both teachers and learners. "Inwardness" (Kierkegaard) is not a psychological category; it is a category of spirit. Spirit is not only what characterizes one most definitively as an individual. It is also an indication of what drives that character, that is, what one cares about most deeply. Spirit serves the mind at that moment when mind reaches beyond the dialectic of empirical experience to the "synoptic insight" concerning the nature of virtue itself. It is spirit which teaches the mind to sing, in its own voice.

It is hard for us to teach virtue because our educational process excludes the element of spirit in much of our study, thus divorcing the material of study from the lively care which students instinctively have for it. And if there is no vital connection between their real lives and the material they are studying, there is no possibility that they will be taught virtue.

The teaching of religion is a case in point. John Updike's novel *Roger's Version* includes an unfair but telling critique of Harvard Divinity School for teaching theology historically and sociologically. Students thus learn that this is interesting material. But, as in most religion departments in this country, what students learn is everything they ever wanted to know about a religion except why anyone would believe it. (The analogy in my field of philosophy is everything one ever wanted to know about a philosophy except whether it is true or not.) And eventually the material is no longer interesting; it is only curious. And it is readily forgotten, because it makes no connection with one's own religious experience, whether positive or negative.

I was asked to teach the Existentialism course in the Boston University Philosophy Department a couple of years ago. We made our way through the relevant material from Dostoevsky to Sartre. But then I read them a little book of my own about the death of my son, and for a term paper assignment I said, "Don't write *about* existentialism. You will learn what existentialism is about best by *being* an existentialist philosopher. Write an existential paper. I've told you my story; now you tell me yours. Write me something with a little blood on it."

I got papers about childhood sexual abuse, and alcoholism, and deaths in the family, and all manner of tragedies. I was stunned to know what most of them were going through while trying to do their academic business. And the papers were, for the most part, excellent: well-crafted, reflective exercises in existential philosophizing. They were so good I tried to get them published. I think that many of them wrote over their heads, but they seemed grateful for a place where their education made contact with their real lives.

Now an Existentialism course is obviously a unique example, since what I am proposing, in a way, is an existentializing of education, but that connection can be made fruitfully in many different contexts, and not simply in the liberal arts.

The dangers of personalizing education are legion. To focus on the spirit-informed mind could collapse education into therapy, or make school into church, and both of these would be disastrous. It could also make teacher-student relations dangerously intimate. But why do so many of our students at Boston University want to study with Elie Wiesel? Because he tells his story. And he makes his story connect with his students' stories, and the stories of others. And those students remember everything he says.

So the dangers of personalization may be legion, but they may also be overemphasized. We already have a built-in model for this kind of education in conservatories and schools for the arts, where "finding one's own voice" is what education is all about. Students there are saved from sentimentality and overpersonalization by the rigors of the discipline. But the focus remains on who the individual is becoming — an actor, a musician, an artist. Personal transformation is obviously at the heart of conservatory education. Perhaps less obviously, it is also what education in the liberal arts and sciences is all about. The critical question is still, "What will they make of you?"

NOTES

1. Ivan Illich, *DeSchooling Society* (New York: Harper & Row, 1971), p. 1.

2. Ibid.

3. Ibid., p. 8.

4. Ibid., p. 26.

5. Ibid., p. 27.

6. Ibid.

7. Ibid., p. 31.

8. Ibid.

9. Ibid.

10. Ramashray Roy, *Self and Society: A Study in Gandhian Thought* (New Delhi and Beverly Hills: Sage Publications in collaboration with United Nations University, Tokyo, 1984), p. 44.

11. Ibid., p. 45.

12. Ibid.

13. Ibid.

Psychoanalysis and the Self:
Toward a Spiritual Point of View
JOHN E. MACK

Not very long ago I had a dream
So bright and glowing it startled me
Into a great glow of transcendental joy.
The dream? Everything around me black as sin
I, walking toward some unknown goal,
My body virginal in youth and pure,
Naked, rosy and quite beautiful.
And from me emanated shining light;
While all about me I could dimly see
Small swarthy men with evil weaponry,
Arms thrust out to mutilate and kill,
Ready to slash through my integrity.
But as they came within my numinosity
They melted into darkness and were gone
And I walked on, untroubled and serene.

> Harriet Robey, aged 90, Freudian trained
> psychiatric social worker, "reared with-
> out belief in God." August, 1991

THE TITLE OF THIS PAPER relates to a 1959 article by David Rapaport and Merton Gill, entitled "The Points of View and Assumptions of Metapsychology."[1] Rapaport and Gill suggested that there are five fundamental points of view which inform psychoanalytic theory and practice and the psychodynamic psychotherapies that derive from psychoanalysis. These are (1) the dynamic point of view, which concerns the direction and magnitude of psychological forces; (2) the economic point of view, which has to do with the distribution and transformation of psychological or emotional energies; (3) the structural point of view, which describes the more or less permanent configurations of the psyche, or those which are slow to change; (4) the genetic point of view, which concerns propositions about psychological origins and individual development; and (5) the adaptive point of view, which demands that psychodynamic explanations take into consideration our relationship to the environment and questions of survival in the external world. I argue that depth psychology is now in need of a sixth, a spiritual, point of view in order to understand more fully the psyche and conditions of human life as we now experience them.

The above assumptions are based on too limited a view of the psyche and have been unable, therefore, to provide a basis for addressing many of the fundamental problems that we now confront in clinical, social, and political settings. Addictive disorders, child abuse and other forms of domestic violence, the variety of complex conditions brought together as personality disorders, the increased reliance on affect-muting psychotropic drugs and the turning away of many patients from traditional therapies to "holistic" or "alternative" treatment approaches (which themselves include spiritual elements), reflect profound unmet emotional hungers that psychoanalysts and other mental health professionals are finding difficult to understand and treat within established theoretical frameworks and therapeutic parameters. Contemporary self psychology, pioneered by Heinz Kohut and his followers,[2] reflects this basic dissatisfaction within the field. Psychologist Philip Cushman has applied the term "empty self" to sum up this contemporary sense that something is wrong or missing.[3] At the same time, out-of-control global crises of human origin, such as the rampant destruction of the living environment, the spread of ethno-national violence, and the proliferation of weapons of mass destruction, are forcing us to reexamine the nature of the psyche or self and our relationship to nature and one another, individually and collectively.

Spiritual matters are by nature subjective and complex. They are difficult to discuss within a scientific or empirical framework. But spiritual experience is so fundamental a dimension of the inner lives of human beings throughout the world, and the language of spirituality so universal a way of speaking, that the task is worth undertaking.

Spirituality is often associated with dramatic personal events, such as religious conversions,[4] and other peak "highs" or mystical experiences, which we tend to disparage. Yet as Barbara Marx Hubbard has written,

> What sexuality was to the Victorian Age, mystical experience is to ours. Almost everyone experiences it, but almost no one dares to speak about it. We have been dominated by a scientific, materialistic culture which has made us feel embarrassed about our natural spiritual natures. Yet we read that sixty percent of the American people have had mystical experiences. We are a nation of repressed mystics![5]

But most spiritual experiences are less dramatic and more subtle. They have in common the sense that there is another reality beyond that which is immediately manifest to our senses or reason. This reality is numinous, that is, mysterious and containing or filled with a power that is beyond comprehension, called "divine" when it seems to contain something of a wondrous nature or higher value beyond ourselves.

Also fundamental to religious experience and to an apprehension of the divine is the sense that the universe is not simply a chance creation or a random flux of matter and energy, but that there is some sort of design, or even intention. The nature or direction of this intentional design is, however, beyond our knowing. Paradoxically the way to get a little closer to knowing is to acknowledge our not knowing and the depths of mystery it embodies. When a sense of the divine becomes embodied in a single feature or a multiplicity of beings, people speak of God or gods. The spiritual world is also reflected in the myths that native people have created since before the beginnings of recorded history to set forth their experiences of the powers that reside in nature. Through myths the inner domain of human consciousness is connected to the surrounding world. Shamans are selected for their knowledge of and special access to the world beyond the manifest. The great powers of this world, often perceived in the spirits of animals, are used for healing purposes. Artists sometimes experience the process of their creativity as occurring beyond themselves, tapping into a source in nature from which they draw that is shaped by their efforts but exists in another realm.

Small children also have quite ready access to this spirit world — or have not yet had these experiences dismissed or reasoned away. I recently met with a three-year-old girl who told me of her "real" world, a world filled with animal and human figures commingled in a complex melange of elements from the hylotropic and holotropic realms. For her the foxes and bears of the mythic domains were as real as the day-to-day life with her parents and brother. Yet she was in no way psychotic; she was able to navigate admirably at school and at home and was considered by her teachers to be a model child.

Disturbing emotions, such as great fear and sadness as well as exaltation and joy, darkness as well as light, are associated with the spiritual realm, which may account for some of our resistance to opening ourselves to its reality. Psychoanalyst Hans Loewald has described clearly the way we distance ourselves from the depths of religious experience and the reason for this:

> Psychoanalysts tend to consider the idea of eternity, religious experiences connected with it, as well as the "timeless" experiences I described, in pragmatic fashion as useful and often necessary defenses, or as mental sanctuaries people must have to cope with the fear of death, castration, and with the trials, tribulations, and the transitoriness of human life. I do not doubt the truth of this view. But it is not the whole truth. I believe that "intimations of eternity" bring us in touch with levels of our being, forms of experiencing and of reality that themselves may be deeply disturbing, anxiety-provoking to the common-sense rationality of everyday life.[6]

Spiritual or religious experience calls forth the language of the sacred, words like *soul, spirit, transcendence, reverence,* and *faith.* Psychoanalysts and other dynamically oriented psychologists have tended to be uncomfortable with this language. Because the sense of merger or fusion with the mother in early infancy, recaptured in the therapeutic setting, has qualities much like the sense of oneness of mystical experiences, we have sometimes made the error of equating the two phenomena, reducing profound religious consciousness to infantilism or childish wish-fulfillment. Freud himself denied the reality of the spiritual domain in his own experience.[7] Recent writings on this subject have been much more sophisticated and open to the significance of these matters.[8]

Many of us in the West, who have been educated in both our families and our schools in the epistemologies of rationalism and empiricism, have found ourselves cut off from the realms of the sacred, whereas virtually all other peoples throughout history have experienced its presence and central importance in their lives. According to historian of religions Mircea Eliade, "*All* history is in some measure a fall of the sacred, a limitation and diminution."[9] The separation of self from nature and the divine, of which nature is a supreme manifestation,[10] may be one of the great negative achievements of Western civilization, one which we are now desperately striving to undo before it is too late. How and why we have done this to ourselves are questions which take us beyond the reach of this paper. The answers lie in the extreme development of reason and empiricism — of which technology is a derivative — for the purpose of controlling and dominating one another and all of nature, at the expense of feeling and the intuitive ways of knowing that might have helped us live in greater harmony with other peoples and the natural world.

What, then, would *be* a spiritual point of view? It would include the following elements:

1. An attitude of appreciation, or a sense of awe, toward the mysterious in nature, including our own natures, and toward all of creation, resisting the tendency to explain the motives behind spiritual experience or belief. In Eliade's words, "There is always a kernel that remains refractory to explanation, and this indefinable, irreducible element perhaps reveals the real situation of man in the cosmos."[11] Joseph Campbell in his interviews with Bill Moyers spoke of the tendency to reduce mystery. "The mystery has been reduced to a set of concepts and ideas," he said, "and emphasizing these concepts and ideas can short-circuit the transcendent, connoted experience. An intense experience of mystery is what one has to regard as the ultimate religious experience."[12]

2. Opening ourselves to the experience of the cosmos and of all beings in nature as sacred. This has little to do with idealization or the denial of hostility or aggression. It is, rather, about reverence or respect, an openness to the possibility of value that

is hidden from our perception. In Christian theology this attitude, when applied to human beings, is sometimes called "exaltation" or a sense of the exalted nature of humankind.[13]

3. The application of a cosmological as contrasted with a materialist perspective on reality. This means thinking and experiencing systematically and opening ourselves to the possibility that there is a design and, if not harmony, at least appropriate relations in nature, including human relationships.

4. A subjective sense of hesitation or doubt, especially in the clinical setting, appreciating that this does not reflect unassertiveness or obsessionalism but facilitates a deepening of the therapeutic dialogue. In the words of Christian theologian Glen Tinder, "hesitation expresses a consciousness of the mystery of being and dignity of every person."[14]

5. A distrust of all human-made institutions, even as we will, of necessity, participate in them. This includes psychoanalytic institutes and departments of psychiatry and other professional organizations as well as political entities, such as nations, and even churches. For institutions may be essential in carrying out basic societal functions, but by requiring of us an identification with their purposes, rules, and reward systems, they may obstruct our relation to the numinous or holotropic and to spiritual experience itself. Institutions may stand as vehicles for expressions of congealed power on the part of individuals and groups, and will, perhaps inevitably, find the self-empowering experience of contact with the divine as threatening or subversive. For spiritual experience by its very nature ties us to the primary power in nature; elevates the confidence of individuals in their own thoughts, emotions, and perceptions; and diminishes blind loyalty to any humanly built structures. Established churches and other institutions may, paradoxically, be especially distrustful of spiritual experience and direct contact with the divine, since their power and reason for existing derive from their role as intermediaries setting the conditions of appropriate congregation and worship, while interpreting the nature of the divinity.

6. In the clinical setting a spiritual point of view means the development of an attitude toward emotionally troubled patients or clients that is less medical or pathology-focused while

stressing, nevertheless, the healing function of the therapeutic enterprise and the relief of suffering. The distinction here is subtle, a matter of emphasis. It means stressing our connection with our patients, rather than the differences, the shared fate and common source of our mutual pain and experience of what it is to be human. Personal growth and empowerment, even "enlightenment," would receive relatively greater emphasis than conflict resolution or cure.[15] As in the case of community psychiatry when it became a formal discipline in the 1960s, many of us will realize that we have been including a spiritual point of view in the practice of our discipline all along. We just have not called it that.

Increasing numbers of clinical practitioners, including psychoanalysts or psychoanalytically-oriented psychotherapists, and their clients are following what in religious traditions had been called a "spiritual path." Many are returning to the formal religions of their families, sometimes interpreting them in new ways, or joining other churches or religious groups, in order to discover or rediscover the spiritual core of the self from which they feel they have become disconnected. Others find the beginnings of a spiritual opening in psychoanalysis itself, sometimes modified by its practitioners, or in more traditional psychotherapies. The popularity of alternative forms of psychotherapy which emphasize spiritual techniques and opening is related to the spiritual hunger discussed at the beginning of this paper. The burgeoning in the West of meditation practice, largely derived from Eastern religions, and of spiritual retreats, also reflects the spiritual awakening and transformation that is occurring in our society. Buddhist theory and practice, with its emphasis on mindfulness and upon living in harmony with nature, has been particularly attractive to American clinicians, some of whom combine psychotherapy with Buddhist spiritual methods. Psychedelic substances, such as LSD and psilocybin mushrooms, which have the capacity to undo the culturally programmed obstacles to spiritual experience, though largely still illegal in the United States, have been important agents of spiritual opening and transformation for many psychotherapists. Increasing numbers of voices within the mainstream of American society are arguing that these agents should be made legal, at least for those conducting responsible research, in order to understand human behavior or neuropsychological functioning.[16]

A spiritual point of view requires that we modify or extend our notions of the self. *Self* is a bridging concept, joining psychology with sociology, philosophy, and religion. When used in a religious context, it is sometimes spelled with a capital S to suggest a vast, sacred, and ineffable domain. In recent years the ways that self is thought of in psychology and in religion have come closer together. Within psychoanalytic psychology self has connoted something which, though abstract, is fairly literal and bounded, a structure not very different from ego, the property of discrete individuals. The total self is an aggregate of more or less cohesive self-representations, both a locus and a source of agency. Self in a spiritual sense is something more mysterious or mythic, a space or possibility, a ground of being or source connected with the divine. Self in this sense is not discrete or limited to an individual, but a kind of fluid potential through which one connects with other selves and all of reality. There is even talk now of an "eco self" to indicate a flowing connection of a person with nature. The self in a spiritual sense is the locus of wounding and pain but also of transcendence and transformation.

Although *self* must remain an abstraction, we need to posit some such notion to account for the subjective sense that we exist. Through self we connect with others and with all of nature, and in this sense self is both a social or communal and a somewhat mystical concept. Buddhist poet and monk Thich Nhat Hanh speaks of "interbeing" to express this related or intersubjective aspect of self, while psychoanalyst George Klein uses the awkward but descriptive phrase "we go" to capture the social or connecting subjectivity of self.[17]

This connecting self is associated with desire, especially the desire to merge or fuse with another, or, as in the case of mystical experience, longing for oneness with all of creation or with God. There is a paradox for the self in this merger, for its fulfillment requires the death of the self or ego (in the psychological, small *s* sense), but from this death experiences of rebirth emerge. The cycles of ego death and rebirth, both terrifying and sublime, lie at the root of primary spiritual experience and have their first psychological analog in the phases of the birth process which are alternately largely blissful and secure (intrauterine life), terrifying and overwhelming (the crushing experience of passage through the birth canal), and sublime and transcendent (delivery and emergence into the world).[18]

Erik Erikson in some of his later writings has focused on the significance of the sense of *I* in religious or spiritual experience.[19] For Erikson the sense of *I* is a spiritual notion in that it derives from a core of personality that lies deeper or beyond psychosocial identity. It is the "place" (language fails us here) where Self connects beyond itself to something greater, with the divine or transcendent, and human beings discover their oneness with being itself. It is from the sense of *I* that existential issues derive: questions of life, death, and rebirth, or what Erikson calls the psychology of "ultimate concern."[20] According to Erikson, the *I* is at the "Center," "where the light is."[21] From the sense of *I* we derive our deepest values and intentions. It is the experiential core of identity behind the internalizations that create the sense of self in its purely psychosocial connotation. This deepest "place" of self is also associated with a sense of ultimate stability (perhaps because through the sense of *I* we are, ultimately, connected with the divinity), cohesiveness, and wholeness. Conversely, the absence of a core sense of *I* or self is associated with fragmentation and personality disruption. The tension between fragmentation and wholeness is a fundamental dilemma of contemporary life, at least in Western countries, and thus has important therapeutic implications.

The explicit inclusion of a spiritual point of view has significant implications for the practice of psychoanalysis and psychodynamic psychotherapy, although many of the elements that I would designate as belonging in this category are already becoming part of the way therapists function in the clinical setting. A spiritual view implies an attitude toward the patient or client as a person of special value. Inequalities of power are built into the therapeutic setting — accommodation, for example, to the therapist's schedule or differences of accessibility — but they need to be acknowledged as part of the clinical reality and not analyzed simply as elements of resistance or transference distortion. The enabling or empowering dimensions of the therapeutic relationship would receive relatively more emphasis in the healing process as compared to interpretation and insight. The transforming power of

human connection, and of empathy and love, although always recognized as important in psychotherapy, would be more openly
recognized and developed.[22]

A greater openness and sharing of one's own experiences, as
appropriate, becomes a more accepted part of the therapeutic
work, including admitting mistakes or apologizing for difficulties
our own blindnesses or inadvertent actions may have caused or
aggravated. The attitude of not knowing, of mystery and uncertainty discussed above, would be applied to the work with clients.
Paradoxically this attitude is likely to bring forth greater awareness on the part of both client and therapist of hitherto unknown
dimensions of self. In addition to elements in the unconscious
warded off by specific defenses, this attitude of openness and not
knowing can create a greater awareness of those culturally imbibed
habits of thought — opinions, assumptions, and institutionally imposed ways of perceiving the world — that are unconscious by being so much a part of our daily lives (rather the way a fish might
be unaware of the water it swims in) but restrict our ability to
live and choose freely.

Wounds, loss, separation, grief, trauma, and emotional depri-
vations are the pathogenic forces of human life. Addressing the
lasting impact of these forces and events that have occurred at
various stages of a person's life is the bedrock of psychotherapeutic
work from all of the psychoanalytic points of view. Once again,
a spiritual point of view would bring a different emphasis. Established psychodynamic approaches tend to be concerned with the
resolution of conflict, the repair of hurts and trauma, and the
achievement of, or return to, a baseline of normal functioning.
A spiritual point of view stresses — paradoxically again — the transformative power of the affects associated with biographical wounds
and other disturbing historical experiences. The spiritual element
derives from the belief, which lies at the boundary between experience and faith, that each person possesses within him- or herself a potential for wholeness. This does not mean, of course, that
human beings do not have defects (especially biologically based
ones), limitations, and irreparable wounds. It is, rather, a point
of view which gradually establishes its validity through enabling
greater wholeness. When therapy is conducted through a spiritual point of view the language of the sacred may creep into one's

speech — words like *soul, divine, transcendent,* and *mystical* — as if no other way of speaking can quite capture the ineffable quality of this domain.

An emphasis on wholeness as a therapeutic objective carries with it the implication that some expression of social responsibility, or work for the larger human community, is part of a positive outcome. A commitment to the human future comes, inevitably, to be added to Freud's idea that a successful result in therapy is reflected in the ability to love and to work. This relates once again to our notion of self as connected with other selves, interrelated in an implicit web of ties that must, inevitably, expand our identifications beyond the boundaries of our families and ethnic groupings. The extraordinary success and healing power of AA and Twelve-Step work derives from this recognition of interconnectedness beyond the individual. The program of repair and community service that constitute the later steps of AA are directed at an expansion of spiritual growth. The twelfth step is introduced with, "Having had a spiritual awakening as a result of these steps, we tried to carry this message to alcoholics and to practice these principles in all our affairs."[23]

Another important dimension of the interconnectedness that lies at the heart of spiritual experience is the sense of continuity over time and the ties we feel to previous generations.[24] Native peoples place much more emphasis generally than we do in the West upon temporal continuity and planning for future generations. Psychiatrist Arthur Kornhaber has attributed the extraordinary strength of feeling between grandparents and grandchildren (and also great-grandparents and great-grandchildren) to the spiritual bond that connects us across generations. I have rarely seen such unmitigated joy as when my wife's mother at her eighty-fifth birthday party returned to the party after being called to the phone and announced with her arms thrown wide (a gesture none of us had seen her make for many years) and her eyes glistening, "I'm a great-grandmother."

Kornhaber tells the story of seven-year-old Annie, whom he had brought with several other elementary school children to visit a nursing home as part of an intergenerational program linking the two institutions. Annie went up to a seemingly lifeless old woman in a corner of the room, who, it turned out, had known her grandfather. In a few moments the woman was vitalized, transformed, "spirited." When Kornhaber asked Annie what she had done she replied, "Nothing at all, she just combed my hair." He concluded,

> This spiritual dimension of the self not only contains love, wonder, and joy but has the capacity to "illuminate" and "transform" the young and the old. Children seem to sense the spiritual qualities of older people and can transform what society generally sees as useless people into valuable elders. The child's view confers power and influence on the aged, who are often ignorant of their own influence. But when love is present, children are blind to the wrinkles that so often blind everyone else.[25]

Nonordinary or altered states of consciousness (largely unknown in the modern West, which has largely cut itself off from experience of the divine, but quite familiar to native peoples throughout the world) have extraordinary value in regaining spiritual power and recognition. These states can be achieved by methods which include hypnosis (abandoned by Freud with vast historical consequences for the therapeutic enterprise), meditation, mind-altering or "psychedelic" drugs used in the appropriate context, and psychoanalytically derived approaches which permit a suspension of linear consciousness and the emergence from the unconscious of elements of the holotropic or transpersonal realm.

Of particular value in this regard is the holotropic breathwork method developed by Stanislav and Christina Grof, which utilizes deep rapid breathing, evocative music, focal body work, and mandala drawing to gain access beyond the biographical level of experience to the perinatal period and the transpersonal realms, where feeling connection becomes possible with objects, creatures, and spirits that is not available to us in ordinary (hylotropic) states of consciousness. Thousands of therapists and their clients have found the Grof method to be a useful way to gain access to the healing power that lies in these deeper levels of the psyche. The holotropic breathwork method has a good deal in common with the traditional healing methods that shamans have used throughout the world, connecting their native "clients" with the transformative powers of animal spirits and other mythic forces that hold meaning in a particular culture. Perhaps the remarkable hold that our relationship with pets often has represents a vestige of the lost connection with the power of animal spirits in human life.

Most of the therapeutic methods that utilize nonordinary states of consciousness to access deeper realms of consciousness have in common an emphasis on the healing power of forces that are already present within the individual, a kind of inherent wisdom of the body/mind or soul. The therapist, healer, or spiritual healer in this context acts as a facilitator, a holder of the therapeutic ground, bringing forth what is already there but inaccessible to consciousness as the result of barriers erected by wounds or traumas from the past, or the restrictions of consciousness that are inherent in, or imposed by, Western society.

The threats on a global scale confronting us and much of the earth's life can be thought of as a spiritual crisis, for at its core it represents the separation of human beings from one another and of humankind from nature. The crisis is double-edged. On the one hand we must face massive destruction from wars in which technologically advanced weaponry, including nuclear devices, can cause death and suffering on a vast scale. At the same time we are experiencing a slower extinction of life through the erosion of the ecosystems that are themselves the life forms which support biologically more advanced organisms. What are the sources of these interrelated destructive processes, and how can we respond?

The global crisis derives from the techno-materialism of Western culture (and of those that imitate us in the search for power and a better life) which has now reached an extreme of destructiveness incompatible with the sustaining of life. The archetypal polarities of connection or closeness on the one hand and distancing and separation on the other are inherent dimensions of human nature. But the twin materialist quests for control of the earth's limited physical resources and for absolute security through the dominance of advanced weaponry have exaggerated these polarities to the extent that they have become a terminal threat to life.

Erik Erikson has called the extreme differentiation of one human group from another to the extent of denying the humanity of the other group "pseudospeciation."[26] Pseudospeciation reflects above all a kind of large group egotism, through which a people seeks to elevate its collective self-regard at the expense of another. Theologian Glen Tinder has described this process well.

Idealism in our time is commonly a form of collective pride. Human beings exalt themselves by exalting a group. Each one of course exalts the singular and separate self in some manner. In most people, however, personal pride needs reinforcement through a common ideal of emotion, such as nationalism. Hence the rise of collective pride. To exalt ourselves, we exalt a nation, a class, or even the whole of humanity in some particular manifestation like science. Such pride is alluring. It assumes grandiose and enthralling proportions yet it seems selfless, because not one person alone but a class or nation or some other collectivity is exalted. It can be at once more extreme and less offensive than personal pride.[27]

The polarizing and dichotomizing tendencies of the human mind become exaggerated in the context of hatred and fear. Ethno-national conflicts, with their complex histories of killing, loss, and grief, deepen these polarities in vicious cycles of destruction, rage, and distrust unless new leadership intervenes that can heal and transcend the conflicts. Traditional leaders are likely to accentuate the polarities by calls to just or holy wars in which the forces of good are perceived as attached exclusively to one's own cause and all negativity to the other's. The language of religion can be especially dangerous when placed in the service of these polarities, as it amplifies their emotional intensity by invoking the greater powers of the universe on behalf of the interests and conflicts of a particular group.

What is called for then is a means of discovering a wider human identity, not one that denies the polarities of nature and human feeling, but one that integrates them in a larger sense of purpose and connection. This shift would continue the process of spiritual transformation already taking place that is manifest now in the multitude of global initiatives that are striving to discover authentic international partnerships while respecting the uniqueness of ethno-national and cultural traditions. For individuals this process requires the discovery of a true core self of *I* through which we connect beyond ourselves to diverse *others*. This too is essentially a spiritual task. In Erikson's words, "Here an overweening conscience can find peace only by always believing that the budding 'I' harbors a truthfulness superior to that of all authorities because this truth is the covenant of the 'I' with God, the 'I' being more central and more persuasive than all parent images and moralities."[28] To achieve this evolution in practical terms will mean, at the least, a deliberate educational program aimed at teaching children, adolescents, and adults how to resist the threats, blandishments, and exhortations of traditional leaders who choose to play upon our polarizing tendencies, chiefly through manipulating the mass media, for the purpose of maintaining enmities and justifying the wars they create.

Lee Atwater when he was facing death found a "new spiritual presence" in his life:

> My illness helped me to see that what was missing in society is what was missing in me: a little heart, a lot of brotherhood. The '80s were about acquiring—acquiring wealth, power, prestige. I know. I acquired more wealth, power, and prestige than most. But you can acquire all you want and still feel empty. What power wouldn't I trade for a little more time with my family? What price wouldn't I pay for an evening with friends? It took a deadly illness to put me eye to eye with that truth, but it is a truth that the country, caught up in its ruthless ambitions and moral decay, can learn on my dime. I don't know who will lead us through the '90s, but they must be made to speak to this spiritual vacuum at the heart of American society, this tumor of the soul.[29]

Human beings grow when, in the confrontation with death, they are enabled to discover a new personal perspective, sacrificing their egoism before it is the body's time to die. This is what Eastern religions refer to as ego death. We are all, in literal terms, facing our own death. But what will be required of us, individually and collectively, for us to know the "spiritual vacuum" of our society? How can the transforming power of the confrontation with death on such a scale as we now confront on earth be experienced so that we may arrest the destruction we are creating for ourselves and much of our planet's life without having to reach, like Atwater, the point of no return? It seems to be a question worth asking, for the preservation of the planet is a fight worth fighting.

J. M. Coetzee in his novel about South African apartheid and its wounds, metaphorically titled *The Age of Iron* to describe an imperviousness to feeling and caring, gives these words to a dying white woman whose death is linked symbolically to the death of the culture:

> Such a good thing, life! Such a wonderful idea for God to have had! The best idea there had ever been. A gift, the most generous of all gifts, renewing itself endlessly through the generations.[30]

It is the responsibility of each of us to discover ourselves more fully, to become conscious of "Self," "Self-Conscious" in the larger sense that can ensure life will, indeed, be renewed through the generations.

NOTES

1. David Rapaport and Merton Gill, "The Points of View and Assumptions of Metapsychology," in *The Collected Papers of David Rapaport*, ed. Merton M. Gill (New York: Basic Books, 1977).

2. Heinz Kohut, *The Analysis of the Self*, Psychoanalytic Study of the Child, monograph no. 4 (New York: International Universities Press, 1971); Paul H. Ornstein, ed., *The Search for the Self: Selected Writings of Heinz Kohut 1950–1978* (New York: International Universities Press, 1978), vol. 1; Arnold Goldberg, ed., *Advances in Self Psychology* (New York: International Universities Press, 1980).

3. Philip Cushman, "Why the Self Is Empty," *American Psychologist* 45 (1990): 590–611.

4. Chana Ullman, *The Transformed Self: The Psychology of Religious Conversion* (New York: Plenum Press, 1989).

5. Barbara Marx Hubbard, *The Hunger of Eve* (Eastbound, Wash.: Island Pacific Northwest, 1989), pp. 179–80.

6. Hans W. Loewald, *Psychoanalysis and the History of the Individual* (New Haven and London, Conn.: Yale University Press, 1978), p. 69.

7. Sigmund Freud, "Civilization and Its Discontents," in *The Standard Edition of the Complete Psychological Works of Sigmund Freud*, ed. James Strachey (London: Hogarth Press, 1930), p. 65.

8. Ana-Maria Rizzuto, *The Birth of the Living God: A Psychoanalytic Study* (Chicago: University of Chicago Press, 1979); W. W. Meissner, *Psychoanalytic and Religious Experience* (New Haven, Conn.: Yale

University Press, 1984); Loewald, *Psychoanalysis*; Arthur Deikman, *The Observing Self: Mysticism and Psychiatry* (Boston: Beacon Press, 1982); Joseph H. Smith and Susan A. Handelman, eds., *Psychoanalysis and Religion* (Baltimore: Johns Hopkins University Press, 1990), vol. 2; K. Wilber, *Eye to Eye: The Quest for the New Paradigm* (Garden City, N.Y.: Anchor Books, 1983).

9. Mircea Eliade, *Shamanism: Archaic Techniques of Ecstasy*, Bollingen Series 76 (Princeton, N.J.: Princeton University Press, 1974), p. 19.

10. Thomas Berry, *The Dream of the Earth* (San Francisco: Sierra Club Books, 1990).

11. Eliade, *Shamanism*, p. 14.

12. Joseph Campbell (with Bill Moyers), *The Power of Myth* (New York: Doubleday, 1988), p. 209.

13. Glen Tinder, "Can We Be Good Without God?" *Atlantic*, December 1989, p. 78.

14. Ibid., p. 85.

15. John E. Mack, "Changing Models of Psychotherapy: From Psychological Conflict to Human Empowerment," Center for Psychological Studies in the Nuclear Age, Cambridge, Mass., 1990; John E. Mack, "Toward a Psychology for Our Time," in *Psychology and Social Responsibility*, ed. Sylvia Staub and Paula Green (forthcoming).

16. Winifred Gallagher, *American Health*, December 1990, pp. 60–67.

17. George S. Klein, *Psychoanalytic Theory: An Exploration of Essentials* (New York: International Universities Press, 1976).

18. Stanislav Grof, *Beyond the Brain* (New York: State University of New York Press, 1985).

19. Erik H. Erikson, "The Galilean Sayings and the Sense of 'I,'" *Yale Review* (Spring 1981): 321–62; Hetty Zock, *A Psychology of Ultimate Concern* (Amsterdam: Rodopi, 1990).

20. Zock, *A Psychology*.

21. Erikson, "Galilean Sayings."

22. Alfred Margulies, *The Empathetic Imagination* (New York: W. W. Norton & Co., 1989).

23. *Alcoholics Anonymous: Twelve Steps and Twelve Traditions* (New York: Alcoholics Anonymous World Services, 1977), p. 109.

24. Arthur Kornhaber, *Between Parents and Grandparents* (New York: St. Martin's Press, 1986).

25. Arthur Kornhaber, *Vital Connections: The Grandparenting Newsletter*, (Fall 1990), p. 2.

26. Erik H. Erikson, *Gandhi's Truth* (New York: W. W. Norton & Co., 1969).

27. Tinder, "Can We Be Good?" p. 78.

28. Erikson, *Gandhi's Truth*, pp. 117–18.

29. Lee Atwater and T. Brewster, "Lee Atwater's Last Campaign," *Life*, February 1991, p. 67.

30. J. M. Coetzee, *The Age of Iron* (New York: Random House, 1990), p. 109.

Happiness, Tranquillity, and Philosophy

CHARLES L. GRISWOLD, JR.

> The happiness of mankind, as well as of all other rational creatures, seems to have been the original purpose intended by the Author of nature, when he brought them into existence.
>
> —Adam Smith[1]

FEW QUESTIONS POSSESS as great an existential urgency, and general philosophical interest, as "what is happiness?" If happiness is not *the* ultimate end of our activities, as Aristotle argued, it is certainly *an* ultimate end. A life without happiness seems scarcely worth the having. The "pursuit of happiness," in Jefferson's Lockean phrase, seems thoroughly woven into all our projects and aspirations.

The topic nonetheless possesses several strange features. The first is that philosophers have had relatively little to say about it in spite of its enormous importance to human life. One would have thought it an indispensable topic for a Platonic dialogue; yet no Platonic dialogue is devoted to it. Aristotle and some of his Hellenistic descendants did, of course, write on the subject. But they are the exceptions that prove the rule. There exist some limited treatments by major Christian and medieval philosophers; one thinks of the remarks by Boethius in *The Consolation of Philosophy* and by Thomas in the *Summa Theologiae*. But no major medieval treatise devoted to the subject has come down to us. Descartes, Spinoza, Locke, Leibniz, Berkeley, Voltaire, Hutcheson, Hume, Burke, and Smith offer us remarks, but once again no extended treatment. Diderot ruminates on the subject, and in *Les Reveries du promeneur solitaire* Rousseau offers us something more like a meditation than an argument. Kant has relatively little to say about the nature of happiness, even though happiness plays a major role in the architectonic of his ethical system. For Hegel, too, the topic is of derivative interest.[2] Husserl, Heidegger, and Sartre have precious little to say; Nietzsche's remarks are scattered; surprisingly, there are no long treatments in Emerson, Thoreau, James, or Dewey. Among the classical utilitarians, only Sidgwick makes extensive remarks, but these scarcely amount to a comprehensive treatment of the subject.[3] We have Bertrand Russell's essay,[4] a few scattered remarks by Wittgenstein, nothing by Whitehead of note. There exist contemporary discussions and no doubt there are other pieces one might mention.[5] My point is that by and large the major philosophers in the Western tradition have not paid the topic a great deal of attention.[6]

This leads me to a second observation about this subject. Nonphilosophers seem generally to assume that there is an answer to the question "what is happiness?" Some claim to have found it and (perhaps for a fee) will tell you how to do the same. At the same time, there seems to be general agreement that happiness *is* a hard thing to "find," that is, to define and to attain. It is a strange situation; happiness is so much a part of us as to be unable to remain unknown; yet we cannot find it.

A third observation is that "happiness" is used in many ways. It can be spoken of as contentment, or tranquillity, or blessedness, or ecstasy, or as a mood, or as well-being, to name a few. One could speak of it in the long-term or in the short-term sense. We are not always clear about which sense we have in mind when we talk casually about our being "happy." Our vocabulary of happiness is not a fail-safe guide to the meaning of the term.

In identifying a sense of what happiness can mean, however, one must appeal to some intuition or opinion, and inevitably others will appeal to other intuitions and opinions.[7] We must, as Aristotle says, start with what is known to us in order to reach what is knowable in itself (*Nicomachean Ethics* 1.4.1095b2–7). But parts of what is known to us conflict with other parts.

This problem is implicit in prephilosophic ordinary intuitions. People often assume that happiness has a "you'll know it when you see it" quality. Yet people also recognize that they frequently see mistakenly; they will say "I thought he was so happy! I've known him for years! I can't believe he committed suicide!" Or again, people often associate the accumulation of wealth with happiness, and perhaps are motivated to accumulate wealth precisely because they think it will bring them great happiness. Yet moralists have always told us, and experience seems to confirm, that neither the pursuit of wealth nor success in that pursuit bring happiness.[8] So we must recognize that there are conflicts between prephilosophical intuitions about happiness. I see no way of avoiding this old methodological problem, though I do not infer that the problem is fatal to any effort to reach more than parochial conclusions.[9]

In approaching the notion of happiness, I have one particular sense of the term in mind, namely that in which we can speak of a person as generally "happy," as happy over the long term. In my long-range sense of "happiness," you could say you are happy even though at the moment of saying it you might not feel happy. We often feel happiness at this or that object; for example, I can be happy when I receive tenure. But this is different from the happiness that applies to a life as a whole and which thus arises from a certain way of leading a life. In choosing to reflect on happiness in this more comprehensive sense, I am following Aristotle's lead. You recall his remark that "one swallow does not make a spring, nor does one sunny day; similarly, one day or a short time does not make a man blessed (*makarion*) and happy (*eudaimon*)."[10] Kant too, for all of his differences with Aristotle, speaks of "happiness" in this long-range sense (see note 6 above). I thus mean to distinguish happiness from joy, ecstasy, a romantic transcending bliss, and the like. Happiness, in the sense I am discussing it, is not a mood. These may perhaps be referred to legitimately by our word "happiness," but I am interested in discussing this other sense of the term, because it is precisely this sense which people seem most to have in mind when engaged in the pursuit of happiness.

"Happiness" has both subjective and objective qualities; it is both an experience and a notion, and neither of these two dimensions should be ignored. Calling such and such the conditions of happiness is to have a view of this rather than that experience of which these are the conditions. At the same time, first-person reports of one's experience can be mistaken. As I reflect on what I mean when I say my life is or is not happy, I see that I have judgments in mind about myself, the world, what is satisfying now and over the long term, what is worth pursuing and avoiding, and so forth. I could be mistaken in assessing any of these things.

I shall argue that the experience of happiness is best understood, *ab initio*, in terms of tranquillity. At the same time, I shall suggest that we cannot be happy unless we rightly assess the conditions of our happiness. I shall attempt to elucidate what happiness is by distinguishing it from what I shall call "contentment," and shall explore further the connection between happiness and assessment or reflection. One needs a right understanding of happiness in order to be happy. Then I will attempt to understand the relationship between happiness and a particular kind of reflection, namely, philosophy. Like Epictetus, I think it crucial to explain why a Socrates can be happy even when faced with execution, and the explanation involves the relation between philosophy and happiness. I shall argue that the sort of account Epictetus gives of this remarkable phenomenon is, however, incomplete at best.

My argument resembles that of ancient ethical theories in that it connects happiness with virtue (or excellence of character), virtue with reflection, and reflection with philosophy. I am also incorporating the more modern view that happiness should be described as, in part, a feeling or experience of a certain sort.

Needless to say, there are many other issues that a comprehensive treatment of the subject would have to cover, including a discussion of what constitutes a well-ordered life. I cannot here offer any such comprehensive treatment. In the course of my rough sketch of this subtly textured landscape, I have adhered to Aristotle's injunction that one should expect only so much precision as the subject matter allows, and I trust the reader will do the same.

I. HAPPINESS AND TRANQUILLITY

> Happiness consists in tranquillity and enjoyment. Without tranquillity there can be no enjoyment; and where there is perfect tranquillity there is scarce any thing which is not capable of amusing.
>
> —Adam Smith[11]

Happiness is best characterized in terms of tranquillity. So understood it captures the connection between happiness and being at rest. Happiness is more like rest than motion, in two senses. First, in the sense of lacking significant discord; it is peaceful, at a deep level. Second, it is more like coming to a stop rather than like a process of moving towards a goal. Happiness resembles an end state, a completion or fulfillment, rather than a condition of lacking and overcoming of lack.[12] For this reason, happiness and contentment seem alike, and later I will say more about the difference between the two. When one says "I have lived happily" or "I am deeply happy" one means, among other things, that one does not experience significant internal discord, and that fundamentally one occupies a spiritual place from which one does not desire to move. One is not, at a deep level, anxious; basically, one is properly oriented, and one's fundamental stance towards the world is complete, at rest. I am sketching, as a starting point, this sort of view of the experience of happiness.

"Tranquillity" usually translates the Greek term *ataraxia*, a term that is the natural competitor to *eudaimonia*, which is the one that Plato and Aristotle use. The latter is normally translated, with trepidation, as "happiness," and less often as "blessedness"; *ataraxia* is also difficult to translate, and "tranquillity" is something of an approximation. "Imperturbability" also captures something of its sense.

The word *ataraxia* does not occur in Plato and Aristotle. It is to be found in important passages in Sextus Empiricus, Epictetus, Marcus Aurelius, and Epicurus, among others. The alpha privative is not, of course, captured by "tranquillity," and this is one way in which the translation is imperfect.[13] In its verbal form, with or without the alpha privative, the word goes back to Homer. There it is used of horses, among other things; a horse struck by an arrow "disturbed" (ἐτάραξε) the chariot and other horses (*Iliad* 8.86); "Taraxippus" ("Disturber of Horses") spooked race courses. In a number of writers the verb can refer to mental or physical personal disturbance, or to the "disturbance" of a polis, that is, the upsetting of civic discord, since stirring up trouble, agitating, distracting, leads to loss of *ataraxia* in the community. One can "disturb" a thing, as when one stirs up a body of water; a mud-slinger or muck-raker can "disturb" an individual or community; one can "disturb" in the sense of meddle, upset; an army or navy that is thrown into confusion is thus described by Thucydides. At 4.96.3 Thucydides uses the verb in describing a battle in which Athenians mistakenly kill one another as a result of their general confusion and disorientation.

In general, then, peacefulness and calmness (ἡσυχία) are akin to *ataraxia*. Understood as *ataraxia*, happiness is a state of mind, or better, a state of soul. In speaking of *eudaimonia*, Epictetus explicitly equates it with *ataraxia*, with freedom and absence of passions (*apatheia*).[14] It is rather like a state of peacefulness, being in control, inner harmony, calm, rest; as opposed to a state of war, desiring that which is out of one's control to obtain, internal discord, disturbance, motion, perturbation. But I do not want to endorse this Stoic view in its entirety, not just because similar views about happiness as *ataraxia* are to be found in the Sceptics and Epicureans, but also because there are problems with it. Let me elucidate the direction of my argument by means of several passages from Hobbes.

In Part I of Hobbes' *Leviathan*, we read: "*Continuall successe* in obtaining those things which a man from time to time desireth, that is to say, continuall prospering, is that men call FELICITY; I mean the Felicity of this life. For there is no such thing as perpetuall Tranquillity of mind, while we live here; because Life it selfe is but Motion, and can never be without Desire, nor without Feare, no more than without Sense."[15] Further on in the book Hobbes takes up the same theme. After declaring that there is no such thing as a summum bonum, contrary to the "books of the old Morall Philosophers," he states: "felicity is a continuall progresse of the desire, from one object to another; the attaining of the former, being still but the way to the later. . . . And therefore the voluntary actions, and inclinations of all men, tend, not only to the procuring, but also to the assuring of a contented life. . . . I put for a generall inclination of all mankind, a perpetuall and restlesse desire of Power after power, that ceaseth onely in Death."[16] Life is, in other words, continually in motion because ceaselessly driven by desire, anxiety, and fear, and fundamentally, the fear of violent death. Human life is fundamentally disturbance, disquiet, or ταραχή. From this anxiety or motion Hobbes explains a wide range of human phenomena, from competition to conscience, to ambition to curiosity to eloquence.

If life were like this, in motion and anxious, then we surely would not call it happy; we would not possess what Hobbes calls "perpetuall Tranquillity of mind." Hobbes seems right in associating contentment with the movement from one satisfaction to the next; it seems intrinsically unstable even though it seeks stability. The operative contrast in Hobbes' picture, then, is between "felicity"—or what we might, taking our cue from his own words, better call repeated "contentment"—and tranquillity over time. Felicity is inseparably interwoven with anxiety, whereas tranquillity is not. We can accept that some lives, that of the tyrant for example, lack even felicity; Xenophon's *Hiero* provides a wonderful discussion to that effect, and helps us understand why the notion of the "happy tyrant" is oxymoronic.

Hobbes' parallel distinctions between felicity and tranquillity, motion and rest, desiring and completion, seem basically right. But we need not accept the view that happiness has been completely described in this manner, or that it is impossible in this life.

On this view, the enemy of tranquillity is anxiety. I have in mind not so much anxiety about this or that event, but rather a general anxiety about things being out of kilter, not stable, not holding, potentially dissolving.[17] When Hobbes talks about the fear people have that their competitors might gain enough power to threaten them, he is getting at the latter, though he remains within the sphere of the political. That nagging doubt, or even the quiet dread of . . . of what? Perhaps it is something like dread that the foundations on which we built our life are not yet finished, or may crumble, or never were well laid. Perhaps (we think silently to ourselves) my life has been a waste, amounted to nothing. What have I become? What will become of me? Was this a praiseworthy life? Even worse, the soul may whisper to itself: "I don't know, things are so difficult to discern clearly, I seem surrounded by grayness and beyond that by darkness, everything is so . . . indefinite, formless." When questions such as these eat away your soul, anxiety or ταραχή has won out over happiness (cf. Adam Smith, TMS 6.2.3.2., p. 235).

Ataraxia captures what one might call the affective, subjective dimension of happiness. And that feeling or experience or state of mind is, speaking in broad terms once again, something like a sense of basic tranquillity, restfulness, peacefulness.

The association of happiness with tranquillity is a very old one, and seems to me to articulate one fundamental view of the matter. A competing view follows Aristotle in associating happiness with activity (*energeia*). The debate between Stoics and Aristotelians, in other words, articulates basic alternatives. Aristotelians define happiness as activity of the soul in accordance with excellence (*arete*). There is a place, if a problematic one, for "external goods" in this picture; happiness is not just the exercise of virtue. This is what one might call an objectivist definition of happiness, and it has several obvious advantages. It provides us with a means of assessing claims to happiness and of explaining how people can be mistaken in thinking they are happy. It links up happiness with ethics and with how one leads one's life as a whole. It provides a basis for distinguishing between happiness and contentment.

Putting aside problems of making sense of the notions of soul, natural function, and excellence, and the famous difficulty of reconciling practical and theoretical virtue, however, this definition does not link up clearly with the experience of happiness.[18] Aristotle says that excellence (*arete*) is not a *pathos* (*Nicomachean Ethics* 2.5.1105b27), and never says that happiness is a feeling (a *pathos*).[19] Since happiness is *energeia*, its activity would seem at odds with the passivity connoted by the term *pathos*. And as an activity in accordance with virtues that by definition are not feelings, it would be strange if happiness were understood by him as a feeling or emotion. His word for happiness (*eudaimonia*), and his association of happiness with human flourishing, lead him to think of happiness as a condition of self rather than an experience.

But, surely, the happy life is something someone actually experiences. Could the proper functioning of soul be compatible with a life of unsettled anxiety? Could one be happy in Aristotle's sense but not be aware that one is happy? About the closest Aristotle gets to a sustained discussion of the experience is in the analysis of pleasure in Book I, 8, of pleasure and friendship in Book IX, 9 (he notes for example that friends help the good man become aware of his own existence as something good), and of pleasure and theoretical virtue in Book X of the *Ethics*. He does grant that a life of misery and pain (such as that of Priam) cannot be happy. Yet this remains distant from some view of what it feels like to be happy. Aristotle's reticence on the subject leaves open the objection that he has analyzed not happiness so much as the conditions for being ethical, and further that one could be ethical in his sense but, affectively speaking, be unhappy.[20] It is hard to see how Aristotle would link up tranquillity with activity of the soul in accordance with virtue, especially because that activity indisputably requires, on his account, moral virtue. Can the tumultuous life of the courageous statesman or soldier be happy in the sense of "tranquil," on Aristotle's view?

And there is a second difficulty with the Aristotelian view of happiness. He views happiness as activity, not simply in the actualization of potentiality but in specific actions; the telos consists in actions or activities (*Nicomachean Ethics* 1.7.1098b15–20). Happiness is being at work in accordance with excellence. For Aristotle it cannot be characterized as *kinesis* because *energeia* is not a movement from a beginning point to some telos: it is the actualization of that telos.

Kinesis ceases when it reaches its telos; *energeia* does not. Yet *eudaimonia* is not simply lack of movement either; it is the kind of spiritual or intellectual motion engaged in when we philosophize or listen to music.[21] One could be moved by those experiences, or undergo them as one would painful work. Insofar as this view lacks a place for the notion that happiness is rest and peacefulness, it strikes me as at the very least incomplete.

But neither of the two basic alternative views of happiness—the Aristotelian and the Stoic—is alone adequate. In spite of my endorsement of the association of happiness with tranquillity, however, one cannot accept that association without qualification. There are two main reasons for this.

First, it would be easy to infer that felt tranquillity is real tranquillity. But I take it that our account must preserve the possibility of self-deception or failure of self-knowledge; and therefore that, as already indicated, our account of happiness requires something like an objectivist view of the sort Aristotle articulates.

Second, the tranquillity view of happiness tends to be associated with *apatheia*, with passionlessness, detachment, or indifference. Yet to live a life of tranquillity so understood rightly strikes us as barren, dry, uninspired. To eliminate psychic motion altogether, and then to call the resulting tranquillity "happiness" seems to purchase happiness at the price of human fulfillment, serenity at the price of our humanity. Why should we accept a notion of happiness that demands so high a price? Epictetus tells us: "Never say about anything, 'I have lost it,' but only 'I have given it back.' Is your child dead? It has been given back. Is your wife dead? She has been given back."[22] Or again, Epictetus recommends that we react to the death of our child or wife just as we would to another man's loss of his child or wife.[23] Happiness is to be $\dot{\alpha}\pi\alpha\theta\hat{\eta}$, $\dot{\alpha}\tau\acute{\alpha}\rho\alpha\chi o\nu$, to have one's own affairs under one's control.[24] How shall I free myself from disturbance, asks Epictetus' interlocutor: "Have you not heard over and over again that you ought to eradicate desire utterly, direct your aversion towards the things that lie within the sphere of choice, and these things only, that you ought to give up everything, your body, your property, your reputation, your books, turmoil, office, freedom from office?"[25] To be passionate is to be moved, sometimes by things that are not under our control; at one level, then, passion is the price of *ataraxia*, precisely as Epictetus argues. In the final analysis, this view of tranquillity is so extreme as to provoke a Nietzschean question about its pathology; what sickness of soul, we are moved to ask, would lead us to sacrifice so much for happiness so understood?[26] I do not wish to answer this question, so much as to register my agreement with the reason that prompts it.

We are therefore faced with a difficult problem. If neither of the two fundamental views of happiness stands on its own, how are we to synthesize them? I have claimed that we must begin with seeing a close connection between happiness and tranquillity, but I am also claiming that happiness is to be connected, in some sense, to activity, to the passions, and to assessment. How are restfulness and spiritual motion, or detachment and attachment, or inner peace and incompleteness, to be combined?

I have suggested that two senses of anxiety should be distinguished, the first an everyday anxiety about this or that thing (missing my plane, etc.), the second a general anxiety that things are out of kilter, formless, disintegrating. I also suggested a distinction between contentment and tranquillity, to be fleshed out later. Let us link up these distinctions as follows: the antidote to the first sort of anxiety is contentment. I make my plane, get the job I wanted, have a good meal; my anxiety about these things ends and I am satisfied for now. The antidote to the second sort of anxiety is tranquillity; at heart, I know who I am, how I fit into the whole scheme, and indeed that there is a whole scheme into which I fit.

Happiness provides a sense of reflective integration over time.[27] Happiness as tranquillity in this long-lasting, structural sense is compatible with anxiety and lack of contentment in the everyday sense. It is not reducible to what Hobbes calls "felicity," because it is not so much equanimity as it is equipoise, balance, and coherence in one's basic stance. By contrast, the anxious person in the second sense of the term is fundamentally disturbed, off-balance, never settled in the conviction that this is fundamentally the right way to spend one's life. The fittingness of one's basic stance is evident through reflection and, affectively, by the feeling that basically one would change nothing in one's life. One has lived and will live in this way; at that structural level, one is at rest, and tranquillity is correspondingly a sort of rest, of peacefulness, as I suggested at the start of this discussion.

One can and indeed must have all sorts of passions, attachments, commitments. These may well be turbulent at times; they certainly put one's happiness, in the sense of mood, at risk, for to some degree they put one's happiness in the hands of others. One's life may have moments of ecstasy or transcending bliss, and moments of anxiety in our first, ordinary sense of the term. Fortune will affect the course of things at this level. At the second-order level, however, one can be tranquil in the midst of first-order level perturbance, though not every perturbance. One can be peaceful but engaged. Take Epictetus' example of losing a wife or child. My child suddenly dies; on Epictetus' account, tranquillity seems to require no, or virtually no, emotional response (see also Plato *Republic* 603e ff.). On my account it would and ought naturally lead to tremendous grief, as is proportionate to the loss. I have not therefore lost my tranquillity; for I will still say that it was right and good that I had this child. I'm not sure I would take this to the absolute extreme, and say that a person enduring the tortures of a concentration camp could still be tranquil in my sense. But a person enduring the fate of a Socrates or Boethius might well be.[28]

Epictetus thought Socrates' tranquillity on his death bed explicable on the basis that Socrates was, in effect, a Stoic. While I see why one might make that argument, I do not believe that it is faithful either to what Socrates means when he says, in the *Phaedo*, that philosophy is a preparation for death, or to Socrates' praise of eros in other dialogues. My view of the relation between tranquillity and the tumult of ordinary life allows that Socrates would both experience great tranquillity in his lifelong commitment to philosophy, and also experience everything from pain caused by the shackles to sorrow at the prospect of death. Tranquillity does not require *apatheia*. My account allows us to understand both how philosophy might provide Socrates his tranquillity, and at the same time be the sort of painful dialectical struggle for truth depicted in Plato's dialogues and reenacted in so many philosophical conversations.

Epicurus is said to have claimed that the wise man could be happy (retain *ataraxia*) even on the rack.[29] My view does not make that extreme claim. There is no mathematically precise way to describe just how resistant tranquillity is to the misfortunes of life. I am claiming both that it is not absolutely resistant, and that the example of Socrates reminds us that tranquillity is within our grasp even in the context of great misfortune, if only we have developed a reflective stance to which our lives testify.

Happiness is, I have insisted, a feeling as well as a reflective stance. But it is not this or that feeling.[30] One might say, awkwardly, that it is a sort of second-order feeling. The feelings it attends will include those of satisfaction, joy, contentment, delight, perhaps bliss; and it will itself settle over them all as does the evening's light over the mountains. There will be shadows too—feelings of, say, frustration, incompleteness in this or that regard, regrets, and so forth. These are not incompatible with the judgment that as a whole one's life has been rightly oriented. The feeling of happiness signals a recognition that one is basically satisfied with who one is, and with reason; one does not want to be somebody else.

I have been sketching a way of reconciling two fundamental notions of happiness. I have attempted, among other things, to articulate that paradoxical mix of activity and passivity, of self-directedness and of feeling as though one is being carried by events in the direction one would wish for, that characterizes the experience of happiness. But first it is important to reflect on the distinction between happiness and contentment.

II. HAPPINESS AND CONTENTMENT

> For who is content is happy. But as soon as any new uneasiness comes in, this Happiness is disturb'd, and we are set afresh on work in the pursuit of Happiness.
> —John Locke[31]

Tranquillity and contentment resemble one another, especially when one focuses on the feelings involved. The contented person has what she wants, and enough of the things one ordinarily desires, and is satisfied with that.[32] But one could be content on and off, as when we speak of being content while on vacation, that is, until we submerge again in "the real world," as we mistakenly call it; and contentment can disappear rather quickly, as when one is content until one has to go to the dentist for a root canal. Then, as Locke says in the passage quoted immediately above, a "new uneasiness" has set in. I could be content with my job interview in the sense that it went well, but be very unhappy generally, including with the whole path of life on which this job interview, indeed this job, are steps. One can be contented, even contented repeatedly, without being happy.

And even if one possessed what Hobbes calls "felicity," there is a more important way in which it is distinguished from happiness as I have characterized it; and that is the tendency of contentment to reduce itself to a state of mind severed from an appraisal of the truth of the matter. Contentment and unreflectiveness are natural allies. At the extreme, the content are, so to speak, tranquillized. I have in mind the figure of the contented slave, or the contented sinner; someone resigned to the limitations of life, someone for whom the link between the subjective feeling and an assessment of the worthiness of his life is broken.[33] It is for this reason that Nietzsche heaps such scorn on happiness understood as contentment, and Heidegger portrays daily existence as "inauthentic" and as mired unreflectively in the "everyday."[34] Contentment is the road to mediocrity. It is often compared to the life of the beasts, not without reason; my dog, for example, can certainly be happy in the sense of content. When you doze after a fine meal, you are not happy, however peaceful you may be. You are semiconscious, and contented.

One could reply that we sometimes use the word "contentment" to refer precisely to the sort of reflective tranquillity I have sketched above, and "happiness" in reference to, say, one's dog. I grant the objection, but it is merely a verbal point. We also use the words in the sense I am now isolating, and we recognize the distinction between the phenomena in question.

The confusion between happiness and contentment is, nevertheless, widespread. The often belated recognition that the two are distinct is perhaps not as widespread, but it is the stuff of which the wisdom of the elders is made. The confusion is so systematic that it has been used quite persuasively by Adam Smith to explain why it is that people strive so mightily for goods that will not, in fact, bring them happiness. Taking his cue from Hobbes, Smith sees us as naturally bent on what he calls "bettering our condition." We better our condition by accumulating the "goods of fortune"—external goods, as well as wealth, reputation, and power. We do so not in order to satisfy our bodily desires, Smith argues, but in order to find ourselves the objects of approbation; for therein, we imagine, lies happiness (TMS 1.3.2.1). Smith refers to this as a "prejudice" of the imagination, and as a "deception." Smith remarks that a man who imagines himself in the condition of the rich "thinks if he had attained all these [good things], he would sit still contentedly, and be quiet, enjoying himself in the thought of the happiness and tranquillity of his situation. He is enchanted with the distant idea of this felicity" (TMS 4.1.8, p. 181).

And to attain that superior station, he labors day and night, achieving moments of contentment, but always anxious to progress a bit further, to earn that much more admiration from society. At what point does he see that he has sacrificed "a real tranquillity that is at all times in his power"? It is in old age, once he has attained wealth and power, as he lies "in the last dregs of life, his body wasted with toil and diseases, his mind galled and ruffled by the memory of a thousand injuries and disappointments which he imagines he has met with from the injustice of his enemies, or from the perfidy and ingratitude of his friends, that he begins at last to find that wealth and greatness are mere trinkets of frivolous utility, no more adapted for procuring ease of body or tranquillity of mind than the tweezer-cases of the lover of toys" (TMS 4.1.8, p. 181). Then he sees the difference between contentment and real tranquillity.

In Smith's vignette, the unhappy social climber gains self-knowledge in recognizing that happiness is tranquillity. With that recognition, he regrets how he spent his life. He knows, somewhere in his soul, that he does not deserve to be happy, and so is not happy. He is not what he says he is. A sense of guilt, and an anxiety about being found out, bubble underneath the surface of his life. This is not an uncommon experience; it buttresses the case I am making for a distinction between happiness and contentment. In this way I grant Kant's distinction between happiness and the worthiness to be happy; except that the former I view as contentment, and the latter as happiness.[35]

Smith's compelling picture of what others would call the life of the bourgeois shows that, on an individual level, that life is vulnerable. This sort of "happiness" is vulnerable, for example, to political or social upheavals.[36] And there is never enough of "the good things" to constitute happiness. The pursuit of happiness, so understood, can never rest. The notion of happiness I have sketched above, by contrast, allows for the desired stability and security.

I have argued, however, that there are objective criteria for happiness. Let me offer four rather extreme examples by way of illustrating this point. First: suppose that a drug were invented and were dripped into one's veins, painlessly and continuously.[37] Let us pretend that the technical name of this drug is "Ataraxy." Suppose further that Ataraxy made one unaware that one was taking it. As a result one would experience contentment over the long haul, even though one's life alternated between prolonged periods as a couch potato watching soap operas, and indulgence in violent "drive-by" murders. We would want to deny that such a person is happy, however complete the feeling of tranquillity may be. For the person on Ataraxy to say of himself that he is happy (as always, in our long-range sense) is at a minimum to say that his tranquillity reflects his life's activities in a satisfying way. This in turn assumes that the person is fully aware of what those activities are. If Ataraxy prevents this awareness, then he is not happy. If Ataraxy allows this awareness, then he might be happy, but only if he has made no mistake about these activities and their capacity to satisfy. He must believe that it is "all right" to do what he does; but if he is wrong in this belief then he is not happy. Happiness is linked to beliefs about the world, and these can be true or false.

Suppose, to take another example, someone thinks herself very happy because she thinks she has discovered that Elvis lives. Impartial spectators investigate, and find that a very clever impostor has tricked her. She experienced contentment, even delight, in her belief. But since her belief was false, was she truly happy? I do not think so; for her life is not such as she would wish it to be on reflection, in the light of an accurate assessment of the situation. Or if she is truly happy, then why would she not be truly happy when on Ataraxy?

A third example: Say a homeless man woke up one day in his habitual spot, a heating vent on the sidewalk, fantasizing that he is rich. Suppose the fantasy takes hold; he believes himself to be Mr. Onassis at his winter château in Gstaad. The homeless man is very happy. Or is he? He is living in a dream world and is delighted with life, but surely he is not happy. It is not true that ignorance is bliss; he is vulnerable in his ignorance (for example, to hunger). This is not a formula for long-term tranquillity, for the sense of happiness under investigation here. It may be counted as a formula for short-term contentment at best.

Further, "happiness" by self-deluded fantasy seems truncated. As the man lies on the heating vent, he pictures the adoration bestowed on the wealthy and powerful and imagines himself its object; but he does not know their lives, their conversations, their failures, their triumphs. The image he conjures up in his dream life is a cartoon, and so at best a truncated partaking, and does not measure up to its own object.

Consider a fourth example. Suppose a woman habitually drinks too much and then regrets it the next morning. Suppose she goes on like that for years. While high, she is content; in the cold light of sobriety, as she contemplates her blood-shot eyes and pudgy face in the morning's mirror, she realizes that she is terribly unhappy, and that the contentment she finds in the bottle is a flight from the underlying deficiency of her life. This sort of experience is common, and reveals several important truths, one of which is that one cannot be happy if one harbors a well-grounded standing dissatisfaction with oneself, with how one really is.[38] And that suggests that to be happy one must have the sort of desires a reflective person would want. This helps explain why we place such a premium on long-term happiness; we see that such happiness is connected to a well-ordered life, one that is worth having.

Examples such as these suggest that while happiness is inseparable from a state of mind, it is distinguished from contentment because it is also inseparable from a reflective arrangement of one's life, and more deeply because any such arrangement of one's life must be evaluatively linked to a notion of what sort of life is worth living. Happiness is not to be understood simply as a state of mind.

The erroneous notions of happiness implied in the above examples suffer from three defects. First, that "happiness" is unstable. Because it is unstable, it is vulnerable. What one does not know *can* hurt one. Consider an example from *Othello*. Thinking Desdemona unfaithful, Othello cries: "I had been happy, if the general camp, / Pioneers and all, had tasted her sweet body, / So I had nothing known. O, now for ever / Farewell the tranquil mind! farewell content!" (Shakespeare *Othello* 3.3.1.347–50). Othello is unhappy in a false belief; he says he would rather be ignorant and happy, but in fact the dramatic irony of the scene shows us the opposite. He would in fact be happy if he had known the truth, as the tragic ending of the play underlines. This is not simply because the truth is what he wants to hear. I would hold that he would likely have been happier even if Desdemona had been unfaithful.

Happiness based on self-delusion is also susceptible to the power of the question, as when the alcoholic is made to confront head-on the question "Why are you drinking?" I do not mean that a confrontation with the question will of itself change behavior; I mean that conceits about the "happiness" supposedly provided by the alcohol are vulnerable to severe deflation. They do not stand up to (self-) questioning. I have said, however, that I am investigating "happiness" in the long-range sense, one that requires a stability of self.

Second, even if the deluded state of mind were stable in the sense of temporally long-lasting, we cannot say of it that it is "happiness" without entering into an evaluative reflection about the sorts of things or activities that provide this happiness. But this is what is missing from that state of mind.

Third, if one's experience is that of a fantasy rather than of the real thing, whatever "happiness" one derives is not a product of one's being, or doing, the real thing. If when high on booze an alcoholic imagines herself happy because beloved by a family to which she is devoted, whereas in fact her family is in tatters precisely because of her drinking; is her "happiness" of the same quality or depth as that which stems from really being loved by a family to which one really is devoted? I am suggesting that we are faithful to experience in distinguishing similarly between the "happiness" a drunkard imagines and the happiness she would possess if it were a product of reality and not fantasy.

I have been arguing that happiness is linked to a reflective affirmation of one's life. Contentment may be thought of as the satisfaction of desire(s); happiness, as the justified satisfaction that one is desiring the right things in the right way. There is therefore a connection between happiness and our conception of happiness; one needs a right understanding of it in order to have it. Since a conception of happiness must be acquired with effort, and since patterning one's life on that conception also takes effort, it follows from my account that happiness cannot simply happen to a person. Happiness requires effort. This parallels Aristotle's account of the connection between happiness and both virtues and *phronesis*. Virtues and *phronesis* do not come, in their full sense, automatically; they require sustained exertion and exercise.

III. PHILOSOPHY AND HAPPINESS

> They do not understand how that which differs with itself
> is in agreement: harmony consists of opposing tension, like
> that of the bow and the lyre.
>
>   —Heraclitus[39]

Let us say that I am tranquil in the sense described thus far. For good reasons I am satisfied with my basic stance; I am committed to the right sorts of things, in the right way, and I act accordingly. I have no significant standing dissatisfactions with myself; I have the sort of wants I would wish to have on reflection; I am reasonably well ordered; basically I am complete. Let us also say, so as to simplify, that I am neither in agony nor in despair in a day-to-day sense. Tranquillity requires assessment, evaluation of my stance; otherwise it would be difficult to distinguish between contentment and tranquillity. The question "am I happy?" develops, on my account, into the question "am I, on the whole, the sort of person I ought to be?" The assessment required by the latter question is a philosophical one. From Socrates on down through the tradition, the questions "who am I?" and "what sort of person ought I be?" are fundamental to the philosophical enterprise. The term *philosophical*, however, is said in many ways, two of which interest me here. One sense of the term is used by the Stoics especially. There it denotes something like dialogue that leads not to the investigation of epistemological or metaphysical theses, but to clarification of principles that will permit a tranquil life. That is, "philosophy" is something like the art of living; its orientation is practical rather than theoretical. Insofar as Epictetus' *Discourses* resist a turn towards speculative theory, and are intended simply to explain and defend a few basic principles as well as what is required to live in accordance with them, these dialogues are remarkably unSocratic, especially if Plato's portrait of Socrates is taken as the standard.[40] There is no upward, erotic ascent in Epictetus' dialectic; nothing of the Socratic passion for knowledge or sense of *aporia*.

Correspondingly, as in so many "philosophies of life," there is a great deal that philosophy, in a more Socratic/Platonic sense, would find question-begging. *Philosophy* in this second sense—the sense I shall use—would surely attack the connection between happiness, tranquillity, and control. But my task here is to argue that the sort of bothersome questions Plato's Socrates pursues are necessarily connected with the rational assessment of self I have made necessary to happiness.[41] I do not mean that the answers one ends up with are those of Socrates; I mean that the kind of dialogical reflection in which one engages is like that of Socrates. It is full of *aporiai*, yielding of further questions, never straightforwardly self-justifying, always lacking and incomplete.

Philosophy so understood is a passionate activity, and usually a painful dialectical labor as well. But that in itself does not establish any tension between it and happiness as I have described it, since I have argued that meta-level tranquillity and object-level perturbation are compatible. One need not agree with Aristotle that "the pleasures of gaining knowledge involve no pain" (*Nicomachean Ethics* 10.3.1173b16–17), or that the life of contemplation and philosophy contains pleasures of wondrous purity (*Nicomachean Ethics* 10.6.1177a 25–27), in order to maintain the link between tranquillity and philosophy. Aristotle's picture in the *Ethics* of the theoretical life is idealized and abstracts from philosophizing as it is in actuality.

The perpetual incompleteness and self-overcoming of this particular sort of activity, however, does suggest an underlying incompatibility with happiness. The philosopher will, on the one hand, naturally ascend from questions about human phenomena to second-order questions about whether this or that is the right stance to take towards the world, eventually settling on the philosophical stance, precisely as Socrates does over and over again in Plato's dialogues. When Socrates declares that the "unexamined life is not worth living for a human being" (Plato *Apology* 38a5–6) he is declaring his allegiance to that stance. And yet, on the other hand, one of the consistent themes in the Platonic dialogues concerns the nature and defensibility of the philosophical life. But this is just to say that the stability of a general stance towards the world, that framework which permitted tranquillity in the midst of turbulence, is undermined and itself thrown into motion. One becomes just as Socrates describes eros in the *Symposium*; in-between, lacking, desiring to overcome, perpetually in motion between poles of ignorance and wisdom, but also with resourcefulness. This is why Socrates never says that philosophizing is happiness or a happy activity (*Phr.* 256a7–b3 notwithstanding), though Crito thinks Socrates always of happy temperament and remarks on his amazing calmness as he awaits execution. In Plato's portrayal, only on the day of his death does Socrates smile.

Wisdom, by contrast, is portrayed by Socrates as supreme happiness (*Phr.* 247d; *Symposium* 212a; *Republic* 516c). For the wise, motion and rest are harmonized; this is captured rather beautifully by the image of the circular rotation of νοῦς, i.e., of the activity of mind that is contemplation by the wise (*Phr.* 247b6–e6). Happiness is this activity of simultaneous rest and repose. But, Socrates also tells us, wisdom is impossible in this life. Consequently, it would seem that happiness is impossible in this life. Thus happiness is impossible without philosophy and impossible with it.

Or is it? Consider the following. Both the practice of philosophizing and reflections about finitude and our desire to overcome it
leave us with this picture: human beings are perpetually incomplete,
and when they reflect dialectically about that incompleteness, they are
engaged in philosophy. From this bird's-eye perspective, one sees that
the stance represented by the philosophical life is superior relative to
its competitors; one sees that the philosophical life is not absolutely defensible so much as it is relatively defensible against all comers to date.
One sees that by means of it, false alternatives have been isolated; the
features of the real alternatives have been discerned and brought into
question. A metaphysics takes shape correspondingly; it provides a way
of contextualizing human life in an ordered cosmos. This metaphysics
will itself be held open to question, as is only appropriate given that we
are not wise but are lovers of wisdom. It will amount to what Socrates
calls "human wisdom" (*Apology* 20d8). The philosopher will ask
whether he has cooked up this metaphysics in a desperate attempt to
make himself happy (as Socrates himself wonders at *Phil.* 28c), or
whether it provides the best explanation of the phenomena. Has the
philosopher shown only that any competing view that offers a logos can
be out-argued? I would argue that in its openness to question, even
our most basic framework confirms the authority of the philosophical
life, for that life consists precisely in posing questions and seeking answers, always with an awareness of the possibility that one's answers
are open to further reasonable questions. Does this self-confirmation
amount to genuine openness, or to closure? Is it circular in a good or
bad sense? The Socratic philosopher will recognize these questions as
his or her own.

I am merely sketching the sort of answer I would give to the
problem I raised about my own view of happiness.[42] I am suggesting
that reflection on philosophy itself provides a sort of ledge on which
one can sit, not with complete safety, but still with stability. That place
is integrated with a commitment to philosophy, as well as the day-to-
day activity of philosophizing about this or that. Questioning the niche
we have attained philosophically confirms it performatively, since it is
an instance of the very activity that we call philosophy. This metaphysical position may be far from the summit, but on the other hand it is far
enough up so as to afford perspective and the long view. To that extent,
it is the basis for whatever tranquillity nature has afforded us, and it is
compatible with turbulence at both the first- and second-order levels

of reflection. Differently put, that stance which is the philosophical life may be espoused in a *measured* way; in a manner that is proportionate to our self-knowledge. In its measuredness, it is tranquil.

Let me close with a reformulation of the connection between philosophy and tranquillity I have been sketching. Happiness, understood as tranquillity, might metaphorically be understood as motion in a circle that is at rest. That circle or framework or stance provides the stability within which activity, passion, striving, philosophizing, are oriented. Since Socratic philosophers also feel compelled to question philosophy itself, that is, their own circle or framework or stance, they seem to undermine the basis for their own tranquillity. That process of self-undermining, however, is itself an instance of philosophizing, and therefore is confirming of philosophy as indispensable to reflective self-knowledge. The recognition that this is so as well as the recognition that even this thesis cannot be held dogmatically, are themselves the circle or framework or stance that—aporetically— form the basis for tranquillity. No tranquillity of this sort can perfectly combine rest and motion. We will never be those Platonic souls who, perfected, rest while circling and feasting on the divine. They are carried around in a comprehensive vision of truth, and need only sit still and let the mind nourish itself. So as to become like them, we must originate our own motion, and rest tranquil in the recognition that our circle is philosophical.[43]

NOTES

1. Adam Smith, *The Theory of Moral Sentiments*, ed. A. L. Macfie and D. D. Raphael (Indianapolis: Liberty Classics, 1982), 3.5.7, p. 166. (Hereafter abbreviated TMS.)

2. For an excellent treatment of Hegel on happiness, see A. W. Wood, *Hegel's Ethical Thought* (Cambridge: Cambridge University Press, 1991), chap. 3.

3. I refer to Sidgwick, *The Methods of Ethics* reprint ed. (Indianapolis: Hackett, 1981), bk. 2, chaps. 5, 6, *et passim.*

4. Bertrand Russell, *The Conquest of Happiness* (New York: H. Liveright, 1930).

5. See J. Annas, *The Morality of Happiness* (Oxford: Oxford University Press, 1993); E. Telfer, *Happiness* (New York: St. Martin's Press, 1980); S. Strasser, "The Experience of Happiness: A Phenomenological Typology,"

in *Readings in Existential Phenomenology*, ed. N. Lawrence and D. O'Connor (Englewood Cliffs, N.J.: Prentice-Hall, 1967), pp. 286–302. For a review and bibliography of other literature see D. Den Uyl and T. R. Machan, "Recent Work on the Concept of Happiness," *American Philosophical Quarterly* 20 (1983): 115–34.

6. Kant provides one explanation in Immanuel Kant, *Fundamental Principles of the Metaphysics of Ethics*, trans. T. K. Abbott (Indianapolis: Hackett, 1949), pp. 35–36. See also Immanuel Kant, *Critique of Practical Reason*, trans. L. W. Beck, 3rd ed. (New York: Macmillan, 1993), pp. 20, 25. My argument about happiness is incompatible with that presented by Kant in the text just cited.

7. Aristotle grants that people have different things in mind when they speak of happiness, but sees them as competing specifications of the same generally shared understanding of happiness as "the good life" (τὸ εὐ ζῆν) or "doing well" (τὸ εὐ πράττειν). That happiness so understood is that good at which politics aims is, he also says, the opinion of nearly everyone (*Nicomachean Ethics* 1.4.1095a14–21). These assertions are facilitated to some extent by the word he is using for "happiness" (*eudaimonia*), and they pave the way for his understanding of "doing well" as "activity of soul in accordance with excellence." They are thus crucial to the progress of his argument; both may, however, be disputed. For example, Kant did reject them.

8. This "empirical question" is, I admit, notoriously difficult to substantiate. For an attempt at an empirical determination of what people say about their own happiness, see T. Scitovsky, *The Joyless Economy: The Psychology of Human Satisfaction*, rev. ed. (New York: Oxford University Press, 1992), esp. chap. 7 ("Income and Happiness"). Perhaps it is instructive to listen to the testimony of those who have succeeded in accumulating wealth: Ross Perot declared in his Commencement address at Boston University on May 22, 1994, that he knows personally almost all of the very rich people in the world and that virtually none of them is happy.

9. Annas remarks: "The development of the debate about virtue and happiness from Aristotle through the Stoics to Antiochus rests on this point of method: how much of the content of our initial intuitions about happiness is it important to retain?" The debate concerned in part the "choice of candidate for giving us the content of happiness—pleasure, tranquillity, virtue and so on" (Annas, *The Morality of Happiness*, p. 233).

10. Aristotle *Nicomachean Ethics* 1.7.1098a18–20 (trans. M. Ostwald, pp. 17–18). Unless otherwise noted, all reference to the *Nicomachean Ethics* advert to this translation.

11. Smith, TMS 3.3.30, p. 149.

12. Compare Rousseau's remarks about happiness in the fifth Promenade (Jean-Jacques Rousseau, *The Reveries of the Solitary Walker*,

trans. C. Butterworth [New York: New York University Press, 1979], pp. 68–69).

13. In this paragraph I draw upon L. Edmunds, *Cleon, Knights, and Aristophanes' Politics* (Lanham, Va.: University Press of America, 1987), chap. 2.

14. Epictetus *Discourses* 4.4.34–38, 6.34; 4.7.27–33; *Encheiridion* 29.7.

15. Thomas Hobbes, *Leviathan*, ed. C. B. MacPherson (Baltimore: Penguin Books, 1972), pp. 129–30.

16. Ibid., pp. 160–61. For a similar contrast between "uneasiness" and "happiness" see John Locke *Essay* 2.21.42–46.

17. My distinction between the two kinds of anxiety parallels (though it may not be the same as) Heidegger's distinction between fear and *angst* in *Being and Time* 1.6 sec. 40. Heidegger there says that in the latter one feels "uncanny" (or "unfamiliar," "not at home"; *unheimlich*), which would naturally seem to be an anxious feeling. By 2.3, however, Heidegger speaks briefly of this *angst* as bringing "joy" along with it.

18. This point is also made by Rémi Brague in *Aristote et la question du monde* (Paris: Presses Universitaires de France, 1988), p. 477: "He [Aristotle] aims above all to establish the superiority of the contemplative life. In doing so, he thematizes only the *content* of happiness. The act of being happy *qua* act, in its realization, remains implicit. Aristotle has not described the experience of happiness. Yet he knows perfectly well that the act contains an internal actuality, as one might put it" (my translation).

19. He also notes at *Nicomachean Ethics* 2.3.1104b24–25 that some thinkers say that the virtues are states of "ἀπαθείας" and "ἠρεμίας," i.e., of lack of passion and rest or quietness. He rejects that view on the grounds that it omits to add "in the right manner" and "at the right time"; but he does not reject the notion completely.

20. Aristotle asks, "Why should we not call happy the man who exercises his abilities according to the highest standards of virtue and excellence in a context which affords him sufficient resources and not merely for a brief moment but throughout his life?" (*Nicomachean Ethics* 1.10.110a14–16 [trans. J. Lear in *Aristotle: The Desire to Understand* (Cambridge: Cambridge University Press, 1988), p. 155]). A person objecting along the lines I have indicated might respond: "Why should we?"

21. See Aristotle *Nicomachean Ethics* 10.4.1175a13–15: "Life is an activity (ἐνέργειά), and each man actively exercises (ἐνεργεῖ) his favorite faculties upon the objects he loves most. A man who is musical, for example, exercises his hearing upon tunes, an intellectual (Φιλομαθὴς) his thinking upon the subjects of his study (τὰ θεωρήματα), and so forth."

22. Epictetus *Encheiridion* 11.

23. Ibid., 26.

24. Epictetus *Discourses* 4.4.36–37.

25. Ibid., 4.4.33. (I have slightly emended the translation.)

26. See, for example, Nietzsche, *Beyond Good and Evil* 1.9.

27. For some helpful reflections on the temporal dimension of this integration, see Brague, *Aristote*, pp. 479–81.

28. For a moving testimony to the power of Epictetus' philosophy to save one's integrity and happiness in a situation that is close to that of a concentration camp, see J. B. Stockdale, "Courage under Fire: Testing Epictetus' Doctrines in a Laboratory of Human Behavior" (Stanford: Hoover Institution Essays, Stanford University, 1993). The "laboratory" is a North Vietnamese prison camp, in which Admiral Stockdale spent eight years, and in which he was repeatedly tortured.

29. See Diogenes Laertius *Lives* 10.118.

30. Here I am in agreement with R. Barrow, *Happiness and Schooling* (New York: St. Martin's Press, 1980), pp. 66–67.

31. John Locke, *An Essay Concerning Human Understanding*, ed. P. H. Nidditch (Oxford: Clarendon, 1990), 2.21.59 (p. 273).

32. For a useful description of "contentment," see Strasser, "The Experience of Happiness," pp. 286–88. On p. 287 Strasser remarks: "The contented person has all that he wants, because he wants nothing that he cannot have; and thus he succeeds also in being happy."

33. One could adduce the example of the happy tyrant (if there is such a thing) to the same effect. This is a notion discussed by Socrates and Polus in the *Gorgias* 469a ff., and in Xenophon's *Hiero*.

34. I have in mind Friedrich Nietzsche, *Thus Spoke Zarathustra*, Part III, "On Virtue that Makes Small"; and Heidegger *Being and Time* 1.4–5 *et passim*. By contrast, consider the distinction between happiness and contentment in Rousseau's ninth Promenade: "Happiness is a permanent condition which does not seem to be made for man here below. Everything on earth is in constant flux, which permits nothing to take on a constant form. Everything around us changes. . . . Let us take advantage of mental contentment when it comes. . . . I have seldom seen happy men, perhaps not at all. But I have often seen contented hearts; and of all the objects which have struck me, that is the one which has made me most content" (Rousseau, *Reveries of the Solitary Walker*, p. 122).

35. For Kant's distinction see the *Critique of Practical Reason*, p. 136: "morals is not really the doctrine of how to make ourselves happy but of how we are to be *worthy* of happiness."

36. As Strasser nicely puts it: the contented person "can feel at peace only so long as he knows his position is secure. This characteristic also points up the fragility of the happiness of contentment. It is not able to flourish on volcanic soil, in epochs which are shaken by spiritual fever and crises" ("The

Experience of Happiness," p. 288). The person who seeks "happiness" *qua* contentment is naturally and literally "conservative," precisely as Smith indicates in the TMS.

37. A thought experiment of this sort is elaborated by Robert Nozick in the chapter on happiness in *The Examined Life* (New York: Simon and Schuster, 1989), pp. 104–5. Recent discussion about the drug "Prozac" touches on the issues I am about to raise by means of the fictitious drug "Ataraxy."

38. My formulation is close to but less subjective than that of R. Montague in his "Happiness," *Proceedings of the Aristotelian Society* N.S. 67 (1967), p. 87: "One logically necessary condition of happiness seems then to be that the happy person should have no standing dissatisfactions which are serious from his point of view."

39. Diels, *Ancilla to the Pre-Socratic Philosophers*, trans. Kathleen Freeman (Cambridge: Harvard University Press, 1983), p. 28.

40. For example, see the discussion in Heraclitus *Discourses* 4.4.14–18, on reading philosophy books, and on what philosophy has to teach us; 2.12. on "the art of argumentation [dialectic]"; and the wonderful dialogue at 1.29.22–29.35, about the practical utility of a philosophy course.

41. There is an alternative way of understanding the sought-for assessment, however, viz., one that unfolds within the context of religious faith. Given the complexities involved in meeting the counterexample provided by revealed religion especially, I must postpone the response for another occasion. The (Socratic) approach I would take would, of course, include questioning the basic principles held in faith by the reflective religious person.

42. For a full discussion of philosophy so understood I refer the reader to my "Plato's Metaphilosophy: Why Plato Wrote Dialogues," in *Platonic Writings, Platonic Readings*, ed. Charles Griswold (New York: Routledge, Chapman, and Hall, 1988), pp. 143–67.

43. I am indebted to Rémi Brague, Ronna Burger, Bob Cohen, Ed Delattre, Doug Den Uyl, Steven Griswold, Drew Hyland, Knud Haakonssen, Erazim Kohak, Mitch Miller, Christopher Ricks, David Roochnik, Lee Rouner, Jim Schmidt, Roger Scruton, Roger Shattuck, and Fred Tauber, for their comments on earlier drafts of this paper. This essay was presented on Feb. 23, 1994, as part of Boston University's Institute for Philosophy and Religion series "In Pursuit of Happiness." Subsequent drafts were presented at the annual meetings of the American Philosophical Association (December 1994) and at Vassar College (January 1995).

Subject Index

243

Author Index